4405

ENCYCLOPEDIA OF THE PAPACY

ENCYCLOPEDIA

OF THE

PAPACY

By

HANS KÜHNER, Ph.D.

PETER OWEN LIMITED

LONDON

PETER OWEN LIMITED
50 Old Brompton Road
London SW7

Translated from the original German

LEXIKON DER PAEPSTE

by Kenneth J. Northcott

ENCYCLOPEDIA OF THE PAPACY

The College of Cardinals and the Papal Election

The present number of the College of Cardinals, or Holy College, from whose midst the Pope is elected, was finally settled at seventy —after the example of the seventy elders of Moses—by Sixtus V on December 3, 1586. However, the characteristic features of the College of Cardinals were foreshadowed as early as the eleventh century.

The college, which is seldom complete, consists of three categories of cardinals; cardinal bishops of whom there are six, cardinal priests to the number of fifty, and fourteen cardinal deacons. Of these categories the first two are consecrated as bishops whilst the cardinal deacons are consecrated priests, though right up to the nineteenth century they were sometimes the recipients of a lower grade of consecration. The cardinal bishops are the incumbents of the seven suburbicarian sees which lie round Rome: Ostia, Albano, Frascati, Palestrina, Porto and Santa Rufina, Sabina and Poggio Mirteto and Velletri: the dean of the college is always the incumbent of the sees of Ostia and Porto and Santa Rufina. It would devolve upon him to consecrate an elected Pope who was not already a bishop. The remaining five cardinal bishops, besides serving in many congregations, act as vice-dean of the college, as Vicar-General of Rome (the Pope's representative in his capacity as Bishop of Rome), as secretary of the Holy Office, as archpriest of the Lateran basilica and prefect of the sacramental congregation, as secretary of the consistorial congregation and archpriest of St. Peter's and as datary. The number of cardinal priests may, in certain circumstances, exceed fifty. Most of them are resident patriarchs, archbishops and bishops in all countries and continents; the remainder reside as curial cardinals in Rome.

1

The cardinals are appointed by the Pope in secret consistory, after which, in a semipublic consistory, they receive the biretta, and in an audience immediately afterwards the red cap, the callotta. Finally in a ceremonial public consistory in St. Peter's they receive the red hat, and on this occasion they appear for the first time in the Cappa Magna, the robe with the long train. The red hat, which can be seen on the cardinal's coat of arms, used previously either to be worn or allowed to hang down the back. Today it makes its appearance only on the day of the public consistory, in the course of which the Pope places it on the new cardinal's head for an instant, and again on the catafalque of the dead cardinal during the exequies. After the public consistory the second secret consistory takes place and consists of the old ritual of opening and closing the cardinal's mouth, the presentation of the ring and the naming of the title church or deaconry in Rome, one of which is occupied by each cardinal after he has taken possession of it in a ceremonial act. From this moment on, the cardinal's coat of arms must be displayed on the main portal of the church, together with that of the Pope. The cardinals received the title "Your Eminence" from Urban VIII in 1630.

It remains reserved to the Pope to select a cardinal at a consistory without mentioning his name. He is registered as *riservato in pectore* and gains precedence. At a later consistory such a cardinal is given the first place on the publication list. After ten years a cardinal deacon can be chosen for promotion to the rank of cardinal priest, if a place is vacant; on the other hand, only the oldest cardinal priest can be chosen for promotion among the bishops. The cardinal's hat always goes to the archbishops of Turin, Milan, Venice, Florence, Naples, Palermo, Paris, Westminster, Toledo, Lisbon, Munich, Cologne, Esztergom, and New York.

Pius XII was the first Pope to make the college of cardinals truly international, when, in 1946, he created a Chinese, an African, an Australian and the Armenian-Caucasian patriarch cardinals, in addition to the Patriarch of Antioch, whom Pius XI had already invested with the red hat.

The special offices outside the Roman congregations with which the curial cardinals are entrusted are those of grand penitentiary (combined today with that of Grand Prior of the Order of St. John of Jerusalem and Grand Master of the Knights of the Holy Sepulchre), secretary of state, librarian and archivist of the Roman Church, chancellor of the Roman Church, and cardinal camerlengo of the Roman Church. The last-named office only assumes importance after the death of a Pope, when during the *sedes vacans,* it becomes the most important office in the curia, while at the same time the offices of secretary of state and datary automatically terminate. The camerlengo becomes the interim head of the college of cardinals, takes the white veil from the face of the dead Pope, and, speaking his baptismal name, touches his forehead three times with a little silver mallet, saying "The Pope is truly dead." After this the fisherman's ring is broken into pieces, theoretically into seventy, as a sign that the ruling power has now been transferred to the college of cardinals until after the new election.

The new Pope is elected in the conclave by cardinals, who assemble from all corners of the world. The period of time which should elapse between the death of a Pope and the new election was fixed by Pius XI at three weeks. The first real "enclosure" took place in 1241 before the election of Celestinus IV, but the conclave has undergone many changes since that most brutal proceeding. The last veto spoken by a temporal power against the election of a Pope was after the death of Leo XIII, when Austria pronounced the "exclusion" against the election of Cardinal Rampolla. Pius XII fixed the valid electoral majority at two-thirds plus one vote. Since the end of the sixteenth century the conclave has taken place in the Sistine Chapel, in which the cardinals are completely shut off from the outside world. Round the walls of the chapel, seats, tables and canopies are placed for all the cardinals. The maestro di camera acts as governor of the conclave and also issues the Vatican postage stamps during the *sedes vacans,* while the marshal of the conclave is generally the head of the princely house of Chigi Albano della Rovere—until recently the same person as the Grand Master of the Knights of St. John. The most recent electoral law is Pius XII's *Vacantis Apostolicae sedis* published on December 5, 1945. On the morning after the enclosure the cardinal dean celebrates the Mass of the Holy Spirit. Normal

3

votes are cast on prescribed votingpapers, called scrutinies. If, as a result, no clear majority is attained the crowd, waiting on the Piazza S. Petro are informed by a gray column of smoke, for in this case the voting papers have to be burned with a little straw in the stove, whose chimney pipe leads from the Sistine Chapel to the Piazza S. Petro. If however, the elections is successful, the voting papers are burned alone and the column of smoke is white. The Cardinal-Dean asks the chosen one if he accepts the election. Meanwhile all the cardinals, except the one who has been elected, lower their canopies. The successful one is asked by the dean whether he will accept the result of the election and which name he wishes to assume. While the new Pope is being attired in his papal vestments, the senior cardinal deacon appears on the loggia of St. Peter's and pronounces the old Latin sentence: *"Annuncio vobis gaudium magnum, habemus papam. . . ."*—"I pronounce a great joy unto you, we have a Pope." Whereupon the new Pope is led out onto the loggia and gives his first blessing *Urbi et Orbi.* There then follow two ceremonies: the papal coronation by the senior cardinal deacon, before which a bundle of burning tow is help up to the Pope with the famous words: *"Sancte Pater, sic transit gloria mundi,"* and the taking possession of the Lateran as the Pope's episcopal church. The title borne by the Pope, who has no higher grade of consecration than that of bishop, is "Bishop of Rome, Governor of Jesus Christ, Successor of the Apostolic Prince, Pontifex Maximus of the Catholic Church, Patriarch of the Occident, Primate of Italy, Archbishop and Metropolitan of the Province of Rome, Ruler of the Pontifical State." He is addressed as "Your Holiness" or "Holy Father."

PETER

33 to 67

"Thou art Peter and on this rock will I build my church, and the gates of Hell shall not prevail against it. And I will give unto thee the keys of the Kingdom of Heaven." This command given to Peter by Christ and recorded by St. Matthew in Chapter 16, verse 18 of his gospel marks the birth of the papacy and the inception of the prince of the apostles as the first pope. Nowadays few doubts are raised, even by non-Catholics, about the validity of this command, the less so as there is definite evidence for the institution of the Primacy exactly as it is manifested in the Roman papacy, in a number of places in the New Testament. After Christ's death Peter lived first in Antioch and then moved to Rome. As leader of the Christian community in Rome, he combined the offices of Bishop of Rome and of Pope. There are no grounds for the doubts expressed about his sojourn in Rome, nor was his activity confined to that city. He was martyred in the course of Nero's persecution of the Christians between 64 and 67, though there is no evidence for the legend that he was crucified upside down, nor for the idea that he died on the same day as St. Paul. Michelangelo painted the picture of his martyrdom in the Pauline Chapel of the Vatican. Only two of the Petrine epistles have been proven genuine. In the course of excavations which were begun in 1940 in St. Peter's, remains, which are most probably the skeleton of the apostle, were found under the Confessional, in the place where, as is now definitely established, St. Peter was buried.

LINUS
67? to 76?

The dates of his pontificate, and of those of his successors for the next two centuries are not reliably recorded. There are no authentic accounts of his activities.

ANACLETUS
76? to 88?

Anacletus is also known as Cletus or Anencletus: records which speak of Cletus and Anencletus as two different popes are incorrect. The earliest incontestable list of popes, compiled by St. Irenaeus towards the end of the 2nd century only records the name Cletus.

CLEMENT I
88? to 97?

Clement was the author of an important epistle to the Corinthians dealing with obedience and the essential form of the hierarchy, which is one of the earliest documents of the Roman Primacy and is the counterpart of a letter of St. Ignatius of Antioch in which he describes the church in Rome under its leader as the leading force in early Christianity. From St. Ignatius also derives the term "Catholic Church." Many of the leading figures of the Roman nobility were converted during Clement's pontificate and he is thought to have worked with St. Paul. There is no evidence to show that the apostle John was martyred in Rome at this time, although Tertullian records that he was.

EVARISTUS
97? to 105?

The only thing known about Evaristus, apart from the fact that he was a Greek born in Bethlehem, is his name.

ALEXANDER I
105? to 115?

Nothing authentic is known about Alexander.

SIXTUS I
115? to 125?

Sixtus is also known as Xystus: nothing more is known of him.

TELESPHORUS
125? to 136?

Telesphorus was a Greek hermit: there is no record of his pontificate.

HYGINUS
136? to 140?

Hyginus was the son of an Athenian philosopher: there are no authentic records of his pontificate.

PIUS I
140? to 155?

Pius who was leader of the church during Hadrian's persecutions of the Christians is supposed to have built Santa Pudenciana, which, according to the records, is the oldest church in Rome.

ANICETUS
155? to 166?

During the pontificate of this Syrian pope, Polycarp, the Bishop of Smyrna, came to Rome for discussions on the celebration of Easter. Anicetus was brought into opposition with the false doctrine of the Montanists and their concept of a spiritual church.

SOTER
166? to 175?

Soter reigned during Marcus Aurelius's persecutions of the Christians.

ELEUTHERUS
175? to 189

This Greek pope is the last to be mentioned in the first list of popes to be compiled by St. Irenaeus, who was the most important exegetist of the papacy in Asia and in Gaul. Eleutherus, too, was called upon to combat Montanism.

VICTOR I
189 to 199

The name of this African pope is closely linked with the dispute over the celebration of Easter, which arose during Anicetus's pontificate. In the course of the dispute Victor excommunicated, in the first authoritarian measure ever to be adopted by the papacy, the communities of Asia Minor, because of their refusal to adhere to Roman practice. While St. Irenaeus in no way denied Victor's right to act in this way, he rejected the excommunication on the grounds that it arose from a liturgical and not a dogmatic dispute. Victor gave way and so avoided the danger of schism. During his pontificate the false doctrine of monarchianism arose, which saw in Christ merely a human being and not a divine one.

ZEPHYRINUS
199 to 217

Zephyrinus was pope during the persecutions under Alexander Severus.

CALLISTUS I
217 to 222

Callistus opposed Sabellius's false doctrine of modalistic monarchianism, which regarded Christ not as a member of the Trinity, but solely as a manifestation of God the Father. After Callistus's death, 'Hippolytus,' the founder of ditheism, a zealotic doctrine of atonement, was proclaimed the first anti-pope, thus starting a schism which lasted until 235. The catacombs of Callistus in Rome are named after this Callistus. In contrast to all his predecessors and contrary to legend he appears to have died a natural death and not to have been martyred.

URBAN I
222 to 230

Nothing of note occurred during Urban's pontificate.

PONTIANUS
21st, December 230 to 28th, September 235

New persecutions under Maximinus Thrax led to the banishment of both Pontianus and the anti-pope to Sardinia, where they both died, after Pontianus had renounced the Holy See in 235. St. Cecilia was martyred in Rome on 22nd, November 232 during Pontianus's pontificate.

ANTERUS
21st, November 235 to 3rd, January 236

Anterus's pontificate lasted for only a few weeks.

FABIAN
10th, January 236 to 20th, January 250

Fabian was in contact with Origen, the great authority of the Eastern Church on questions of creed. According to records Anterus divided Rome into seven deaconries with seven deacons and forty-six priests, which are the original foundations of the titular churches of the cardinals as they exist to-day. Fabian was martyred under Decius and in 1915 his sarcophagus was discovered in the catacombs of Callistus in Rome.

CORNELIUS

March 251 to June 253

It was not possible to hold the papal elections for eighteen months because of Decius's persecutions, during which time 'Novatian,' the head of the Cathari had risen to be anti-pope. Cornelius who was responsible for establishing the church hierarchy was exiled under Gallus to Civitavecchia, where he died. His portrait can be seen on a wall-painting in the catacombs of Callistus.

LUCIUS I

25th, June 253 to 5th, March 254

Lucius, too, was exiled, but he was subsequently allowed to return, and finally died a natural death.

STEPHEN I

12th, May 254 to 2nd, August 257

The dispute with Bishop Cyprian as to whether baptism performed by heretics was valid or invalid arose during Stephen's pontificate. Stephen rejected the idea of the re-baptism of believers who wished to accede or return to the Roman church.

SIXTUS II

30th, August 257 to 6th, August 258

Sixtus restored peace after the dispute over heretics. Although he was martyred under Valerian and enjoyed the greatest respect

11

of all the early martyr popes, the archdeacon Laurentius who was martyred after him has made a greater impression on the Christian consciousness. The lives and works of both of these men have received the highest artistic expression in the fresco cycle by Fra Angelico in the Niccolo V chapel in the Vatican. Sixtus was also immortalised by Raphael in his painting of the Sistine Madonna.

DIONYSIUS
22nd, July 260 to 26th, December 268

A decree of Gallienus, the son of Valerian, spared Dionysius persecutions during his pontificate, which was, however, marked by the dispute with the doctrine of subordination, the direct opposite of the monarchianistic doctrine opposed by Callistus I. The exponent of this new doctrine was Dionysius of Alexandria, who, within the framework of the Trinity, regarded God the Son as being subordinate to God the Father, because of his origin as a creation of God.

FELIX I
5th, January 269 to 30th, December 274

There are no records of his pontificate. Persecutions ceased for a generation.

EUTYCHIANUS
4th, January 275 to 7th, December 283

No details are known about this pope. His tombstone was discovered in the catacombs of Callistus.

CAIUS
17th, December 283 to 22nd, April 296

Caius was a relative of Diocletian. The details of his pontificate are obscure.

MARCELLINUS
30th, June 296 to 25th, October 304

Marcellinus was the first pope of the house of Colonna. The great persecutions of the Christians by Diocletian began during his pontificate, in which much is still obscure, it is for instance alleged that he handed over the Bible to the persecutors and made sacrifices to the Gods. Many lists of the popes make no mention of him, even though it is possible that he died a martyr. In spite of this his tomb in the catacombs of Priscilla has been respected.

MARCELLUS I
27th, May or 26th, June 308 to 16th, January 309

Because of Diocletian's persecutions Marcellus could only be elected after a *sedes vacans* of four years, the longest in the history of the papacy. He dealt very severely with those who had seceded during the persecutions—a course of action which caused con. siderable confusion. He died in exile.

EUSEBIUS
18th, April 309/10 to 17th, August 309/10

The confusion caused by the measures taken by Marcellus continued during the pontificate of this Greek pope, who died in exile in Sicily.

MILTIADES
2nd, July 311 to 11th, January 314

Also known as Melchiades, Miltiades, an African, was elected after a *sedes vacans* of two years. The battle of Ponte Milvio which ended in the victory of Constantine over Maxentius, and so introduced a decisive epoch for the papacy, took place during his pontificate. The giant fresco which depicts this battle was painted by Giulio Romano and is in the Sala di Constantino. In 313 Augustus Licinus became emperor of the Eastern empire, while Constantine remained sole ruler of the West. In this same year the Edict of Milan elevated the church to the status of world church. During Miltiades's pontificate the donatist movement began, a movement which was to last for a hundred years and was concerned with the question of the validity of the sacraments irrespective of the moral reputation of the administrator.

SYLVESTER I
31st, January 314 to 31st, December 335

Although Sylvester's pontificate coincides more or less with the reign of Constantine the Great, the pope recedes into the background behind the all-embracing activity of the emperor. The legends which surround Sylvester have made him into something which he never was at any time of his life. After the fall of Licinus in 324 Constantine became the sole ruler of the Eastern and the Western empires. Besides the rights which he relinquished to the church he decreed Sunday as a state holiday, built the two main basilicas in Rome, the Lateran and St. Peter's, in which the tomb of St. Peter was erected and also built St. Croce in Jerusalem and, although he was responsible for freeing the church and the papacy, he did, at the same time, lay the foundation of that rivalry between Church and State which later was so often to have fatal conse-

14

quences. In the Eastern empire the dispute which Arius started with his denial of the divinity of God the Son and which involved the Arians and the Athanasians arose at this time. Arius's doctrine was rejected and the Nicaean creed proclaimed, which defines the identity of being of God the Father with God the Son, the *homoiousios*: here for the first time the Council displayed the dogmatic authority of the pope. Shortly afterwards Constantine turned to Arianism, banished Athanasius and was baptised an Arian before his death. Constantine who never seems to have recognized the primacy of the pope and Bishop of Rome, dedicated Constantinople, his capital, as New Rome, in 330. Scenes from the legend of Sylvester are preserved on the thirteenth century fresco in the church of the Quattro Coronati in Rome.

MARCUS
18th, January 336 to 7th, October 336

Marcus's short pontificate of ten months' duration passed without incident. The presentation of the pallium which is worn by the pope and the archbishops, to the Bishop of Ostia, with whose office that of the cardinal dean is associated, is ascribed to Marcus. His portrait is one of the few early works to be rescued from the fire in the basilica of the St. Paul in 1823.

JULIUS I
6th, February 337 to 12th, April 352

Julius was responsible for a new definition of the primacy of Rome and of the papacy, for the East as well as the West. After the synod of Sardica/Sofia in 341 he tried to make peace between the Arians and the Athanasians after their long dispute, but his efforts came to nothing. The Arians left Sardica, whilst the remaining adherents of Nicaea recognized the authority of Rome.

15

LIBERIUS
17th, May 352 to 24th, September 366

Liberius became pope when the dispute between Arius and Athanasius was at its height. Constans of West Rome, the son of Constantine the Great, was murdered in 350. His brother Constantius persecuted the church, summoned the synod of Arles in 353, at which he condemned Athanasius and the Council of Nicaea; the papal legates who were present, subscribed to this condemnation without the knowledge of Liberius. In the same year the Pope summoned the synod of Milan, to which he was forcibly brought from Rome, at the emperor's command, so that he could be forced to agree to the condemnation of Athanasius. When, however, Liberius refused to agree he was banished to Beroa in Thrace, and the emperor elected 'Felix II' as anti-pope. Liberius was allowed to return in 358 and 'Felix II' had to flee. The Pope had not borne himself unequivocally while he was in exile, for, spiritually shattered as he was, he had accepted, for the sake of peace, a formula for *homoiousios*, the equality of God the Father and God the Son, which as far as the Nicaean creed was concerned was a compromise, taking up a position between Athanasius and Arius. Meanwhile, however, the disturbances which occurred on the succession of Julian the Apostate marked the beginning of the decay of Arianism. Liberius once more took up a position which was violently hostile to the doctrine, particularly after the division of the empire in 364, when Valentinian I received West Rome and his brother Valens, East Rome and Byzantium. In 352 Liberius laid the foundations of the arch-basilica of Santa Maria Maggiore, which, as the Basilica Liberiana, became the central church of the Virgin Mary of the Western Church. According to legend Liberius was commanded by the Virgin Mary in a dream to build a basilica on the spot where he would find snow on August 5th; because of this the basilica was also known as Santa Maria ad Nives. The most famous picture of this story is by Grünewald and hangs in Freiburg im Breisgau.

DAMASUS I
1st, October 366 to 11th, December 384

The Arians put up 'Ursinus' for a while as anti-pope against Damasus, who was a Spaniard. The Pope succeeded in bringing about the final eclipse of Arianism by peaceful means and he was supported in this by the temporal power of the Emperor Theodosius and the spiritual power of Gregory of Nyassa, Basilius the Great and Gregory of Nazianus. The doctrine of the Trinity was finally affirmed under Damasus, whilst the heretical Arian doctrine preached by Macedonius and Marathonius that the Holy Ghost was a creature of Christ, was finally condemned at the second General Council held in Constantinople in 381. The creed which had be defined by the Council of 325 now received its present form as the Nicaean-Constantinopolitan creed, but it was not embodied in the Roman Mass until the time of Benedict VIII. St. Ambrose was elevated to the See of Milan and St. John of Chrysostom was at work during Damasus's pontificate. St. Jerome was the papal secretary and he was commissioned to write the authentic Latin text of the Bible, after the canon of the Holy Writ had been laid down at the synod of Rome in 382. Damasus, who was one of the leading popes in the fourth century laid the foundation of the church's right to make laws and secured the position of the primacy in Rome. He was an excellent writer and archaeologist, who had the catacombs, which had been closed by Diocletian, reopened and restored, thus performing an inestimable service for later research workers. He composed Latin inscriptions of impeccable metrical form for the tombs of the martyrs. The representation court of the Vatican, the Cortile di San Damaso, is named after Damasus.

SIRICIUS
15th, 22nd, or 29th, December 384 to 26th, November 399

Siricius continued his predecessor's work. The first papal decretal, or papal order, not the half-private letter, sent out as a request, which had been common up to that point, was introduced by Siricius and treated church discipline. He distinguished himself by his sternness and justice, yet he demanded a mild treatment for the Priscillians, who were the supporters of a gnostic-manichaeistic heresy. During his pontificate, in 391, St. Augustine was appointed Bishop of Hippo, his *Confessiones* were published and the arch-basilica San Paolo fuori le mura was built. The mosaics in Santa Pudenciana, which were completed by Innocent I were also begun during his pontificate.

ANASTASIUS I
27th, November 399 to 19th, December 401

Anastasius was a member of the House of Massimi, the members of which later became princes. During his short pontificate, which received the praise of St. Jerome, the teachings of Origen were refuted and condemned.

INNOCENT I
22nd, December 401 to 12th, March 417

Innocent, who took a very lively interest in the affairs of the Eastern church, especially after the expulsion of St. Chrysostom from his metropolitan see in Constantinople, underpinned papal authority and, for the first time in history, defined papal doctrinal decisions in question of the faith. He was supported by St. Augustine in his fight against the heretical doctrines of Donatism, Pelagianism and others which had sprung up in North Africa. His political astuteness is demonstrated by his attempt in 410 to effect an understanding between the emperor Honorius and Alaric, King of the Goths, who plundered Rome on 24th, August. The accusations which the heathens leveled against Christianity after this catastrophe spurred Augustine on to write his *De Civitate Dei*. By negotiating with Alaric Innocent contrived to save the most important churches, and, in marked contrast to the secular power, managed to give the populace real succour.

ZOSIMUS
18th, March 417 to 26th, December 418

This Greek pope managed, during his short pontificate, to strengthen the papal primacy, though he was primarily concerned with proving objectively whether Pelagius was really a heretic. He did not condemn his doctrine until later. His lack of sympathy with the psychological processes of foreigners led Zosimus to commit a number of blunders within the church which were to cause his successors considerable embarrassment.

BONIFACE I
28th or 29th, December 418 to 4th, September 422

Simultaneously with Boniface's election, "Eulalius" put himself up as anti-pope, at first with the support of the emperor Honorius who, however, recognized the illegality of his claim after a year and deserted him. The edict which Honorius issued as a result—the first political papal electoral law—according to which, if there was no clear-cut result in the election, both contestants were to withdraw and a new election was to be held, never had any real significance.

CELESTINE I
10th, September 422 to 27th, July 432

During Celestine's pontificate the internal ecclesiastical discussions in North Africa continued under the guidance of St. Augustine, who had long been recognized as the leading apologist in the church and of whom the Pope said: "My predecessors, too, thought him one of the best teachers." In Constantinople, the Patriarch Nestor started a dispute over the concept of the Virgin Mary as the Mother of God and disputed, too, the divine nature of Jesus Christ: Nestor was condemned at the third General Council. Celestine is believed to have introduced the Introit into the Mass.

SIXTUS III
31st, July 432 to 19th, August 440

Sixtus was the second Pope to come from the Colonna family; he successfully concluded the efforts to make peace over questions of dogma and inaugurated a vigorous building program in Rome, during which the arch-basilica of San Lorenzo fuori la mura was built. Sixtus completed the baptistry in the Lateran, and, to commemorate the Council of Ephesus he put marble mosaics into the arch-basilica of Santa Maria Maggiore, which had been rebuilt by him.

LEO I ("THE GREAT")
29th, September 440 to 10th, November 461

Leo, who regarded the maintenance of incorruptibility in dogma and in the primacy as his most urgent task, had already proved his worth as a deacon during the pontificate of Celestine I. As part of this task he felt obliged to fight the Manichaeans and those sects which had found favor in East Rome and in the eyes of the Emperor Theodosius II and which were concentrated at the anti-Roman Synod of Ephesus (the "Robber Council of Ephesus"), at which

Eutyches defended the doctrine of monophysitism, a doctrine which denied the humanity of Christ. The two emperors who ascended the throne in 450, Marcian and Pulcherian, were both friendly towards Rome and in 451 summoned the fourth General Council, which was also acknowledged by the members of the "Robber Council" to Chalcedon. Leo's over-brusque rejection of the aspirations of the East Roman metropolitans and his appointment of an apocrisiar, by which he became the founder of the nunciature, were the results of an administrative blunder made in good faith, but they may well have laid the foundations of the later schism and break with Rome. Though he resisted any interference by the state in the affairs of the church, yet in an emergency he offered his services unconditionally to the state; thus when Attila overran Upper Italy in the spring of 452 the weak emperor, Valentinian III, who was already prepared for flight, asked Leo to negotiate with Attila. Thus the spiritual and intellectual power of the papacy, without any armed support, met the Barbarian, in person, at Mantua, persuaded him to withdraw at this turning point of history and so became the savior of the Western world. The encounter has been painted by Raphael in a work which hangs in the *stanza d'eliodoro* in the Vatican. It was not long afterwards, however, in 455 that Leo was once more called upon to meet the barbarians at the gates of Rome, this time Geiserich the King of the Vandals, and though he was unable to prevent the looting of Rome he did prevent Geiserich's sacking the city and destroying the population. Leo has been styled "The Great" not only by the church but by history as well, for he was both a statesman and a pope, who considered his duty to consist of service to the whole community. His epistles, writings and sermons, are distinguished by their classical style, their great perfection of form, their beauty and their moving expressions. Benedict XIV in 1754 elevated Leo, who is buried in St. Peter's beneath the altar which is dedicated to him, to the status of Church father. Leo is responsible for the saying which has achieved such importance for the papacy: *"Petri dignitas etiam in indigno herede non deficit"*—"the dignity of St. Peter is not lacking even in an unworthy heir." A fresco, which depicts Leo, is preserved in Santa Maria Antiqua.

HILARY
19th, November 461 to 29th, February 468

Hilary, who was a native of Sardinia, had been Leo the Great's legate at the Robber Council of Ephesus, where his life had been in jeopardy. He continued the policy of his predecessor and opposed Arianism, which was again making its appearance. Few of the early Popes furnished the Roman churches so generously with works of art as Hilary, who also built the two oratories of John the Baptist and of the Apostle John in the Lateran.

SIMPLICIUS
3rd, March 468 to 10th, March 483

Simplicius was involved in the struggle against the East Roman measures in favor of monophysitism. During his pontificate the West Roman empire, whose last emperor, Romulus Augustus, was deposed on 4th, September 476, finally collapsed after Odoacer had become king of the Germanic peoples in Italy—with his throne in Ravenna—on August 26th of the same year. In 482, the Emperor Zeno of Constantinople issued the Henotikon, which indirectly condemned the decrees of Chalcedon, and thereby caused the rupture with Rome. This first schism is also known as the Acacius-schism after the patriarch of Constantinople.

FELIX III
13th, March 483 to 1st, March 492

Felix, who is styled "III," although "Felix II" was an anti-pope, was elected under Odoacer, who, though himself an Arian, protected the Catholics. Felix was married before taking orders and he is thought to be the great-grandfather of Gregory the Great. He succeeded in bringing to an end the cruel persecution of the Catholics which was taking place in Africa under Hunnerich, the son of Geiserich and the Arian King of the Vandals.

GELASIUS I
1st, March 492 to 21st, November 496

Shortly after the election of this outstanding and intelligent African Pope, the Ostrogoth King, Theodoric the Great, succeeded in establishing in 493 sole dominion over Italy in succession to Odoacer. Theodoric, who, like the predecessor, resided in Ravenna was like him an Arian but a protector of the Catholics. Gelasius represented the East Roman emperor, Anastasius I, in making important formulations with regard to the relationship of the state to the Roman primateship. The celebrated Gelasian book-decree, which is a catalogue of books of the Holy Writ, patristic as well as heretic, dates from the 6th century and not from his pontificate. Gelasius abolished the last heathen festival—the lupercalia—whose place was probably taken by Candlemas.

ANASTASIUS II
24th, November 496 to 19th, November 498

The most important event in Anastasius's pontificate was the conversion of Chlodwig (Clovis), King of the Franks. In his attempts to achieve a reconciliation with East Rome Anastasius sometimes showed an excess of zeal, so much so that after his death an anti-pope was set up.

SYMACCHUS

22nd, November 498 to 19th, July 514

The ultra-Byzantine supporters of Pope Anastasius put up "Laurentius" as anti-pope, who succeeded in maintaining his position until 506 in spite of the fact that Theodoric gave his support to Symacchus who had received the majority vote. The synod of Rome in 499 issued the first papal electoral decree, which was directed at the prevention of schisms within the church, and which was even signed by the anti-pope. Symacchus did not succeed in settling the conflicts with East Rome nor in suppressing monophysitism. He ordered the singing of the *Gloria* in the Mass on Sundays and on the feasts of the martyrs.

HORMISDAS

20th, July 514 to 6th, August 523

It was not until 518, on the accession of Justinus, who sought reconciliation with Rome, to the imperial throne of Byzantium that the schism of 482 could be ended. Although Theodoric was in agreement with this course of action he feared that the safety of his empire would be endangered by this rapprochement between East and West Rome and as a result he began to oppose the pope. The greatest sacrifice of this new and dangerous situation was Boethius who was condemned to death by Theodoric in 524, and whose *De Consolatione Philosophiae*, written while he was in prison, belongs to the great literature of the world.

JOHN I

13th, August 523 to 18th, May 526

Theodoric compelled John to go to Constantinople in 525–thus making him the first Pope to visit that city—in order to force Justinus, whom he crowned at this time, to rescind the measures which had been taken against the Arians. Although Justinus went far to meet Theodoric's demands, the latter was not satisfied and threw the Pope into prison a few days after his return home; John perished a few days later. The Pope was a friend of Boethius whom Theodoric had condemned to death and some of Boethius's works were dedicated to him.

FELIX IV
12th, July 526 to 22nd, September 530

Felix is styled the fourth pope of this name, although "Felix II" was an anti-pope. His election was held under the influence of Theodoric, who died, however, in August 526. Theodoric's daughter, who was the Regent Amalaswintha set about the task of ironing out the differences which had arisen between Theodoric and Felix's predecessors and for a short time she had some success. The greatest event of Felix's pontificate was the foundation in 528 of Monte Cassino by St. Benedict of Nursia and since this time no fewer than twenty-four popes have been members of the Benedictine order. Felix founded the church of Santi Cosma e Damiano in the forum, which contains some important mosaics.

BONIFACE II
22nd, September 530 to 17th, October 532

Although Felix IV took the unusual step of delivering up the pallium of the Archdeacon Boniface before his death in order to ensure that Boniface should be his successor, an anti-pope "Dioskurus" of Alexandria, a man who had done much to repair the schism, was set up, but died soon afterwards. Boniface, who was a Roman-born Goth and the first "Northern" Pope only achieved true recognition later. In the course of his uneventful pontificate in

527 Justinian ascended the throne of Byzantium and set about the task of trying to achieve imperial unity in faith and in law.

JOHN II
2nd, January 533 to 8th, May 535

John's real name was Mercurius and he thus became the first Pope to adopt a different name on his election. During his pontificate a far-reaching rapprochement with Justinian was achieved.

AGAPETUS I
13th, May 535 to 22nd, April 536

Agapetus was sent to Constantinople for the purpose of preventing Justinian's war against the Ostrogoths by Theodahad, who had become king after Amalaswintha's son Athalrich had died at an early age. Agapetus, who died in Constantinople, did not succeed in his mission, but he did manage to depose the monophysitic patriarch of Constantinople. In collaboration with Cassiodorus, the great statesman, historian and monk, he furthered the study of the Bible, but a plan which they had conceived for the establishment of a theological university in Rome could not be carried out because of the wars against the Goths.

SILVERIUS
1st or 8th, June 536 to 11th, November 537

Silverius was the son of Pope Hormisdas and was elected under the auspices of King Theodahad. On 9th, December 536 Belisarius

ALEXANDER VII   CHISIVS SENEN
PONTIFEX   MAXIMVS·
CREATVS DIE VII   APRILIS MDCLV·

M. Morčai. Pinx. Iefeph Teflana Genuē delin. et Scul. Io. Iacobi de Rubeis Formis Romæ ad Templi Pacis cum Priuil. S. Pontif.

PLATE 1. Alexander VII

ALEXANDER VIII OTTHOBONVS
VENETVS PONTI- FEX MAXIMVS
Creatus die VI Octobris et *Coronatus XVI 8.ᵉ MDCLXXXIX.*

PLATE 2. Alexander VIII

PLATE 3. Benedictus XIII

PLATE 4. Benedictus XV

PLATE 5. Clemens XIV

PLATE 6. Eleutherus

EVGENIVS . IIII . PAPA . VENETVS .

PLATE 7. Eugenius IV

GREGORIVS · XII · PAPA · VENE TVS ·

PLATE 8. Gregorius XII

occupied Rome and Byzantine occupation began. By welcoming the approach of the Byzantine army Silverius succeeded in avoiding bloodshed, but in spite of this he was court-martialled by the occupation forces on charges of high treason and sympathizing with the Goths. The court which was influenced by Belisarius and his wife Antonia first exiled Silverius to Syria and then, through the decree of his successor, Vigilius, to the island of Palmaria, where Silverius, now a broken man, resigned in favor of Vigilius for the sake of peace and finally died.

VIGILIUS
29th, March 537 to 7th, June 555

The empress Theodora believed that by installing the greedy and ambitious apocrisiar, or nuncius, Vigilius as pope in place of Silverius, who had been enthroned by the Goths, she had found someone who would do her will in supporting the doctrine of monophysitism, to which she herself subscribed. However, Vigilius who was appointed by Belisarius in 537 changed his position, which had up till then been an ambiguous one, in favor of orthodoxy. He was not legally recognized until after Silverius's death. Neo-Origenistic dogmatic disorders which had been artificially enflamed led Justinian, who thought in this way to win over the Manichaeists, to issue a series of decrees in condemnation of doctrines which were no longer in existence, and in order to achieve the recognition of his measures in the West he had Vigilius brought to Constantinople by force in 544. The Pope signed the decrees while stressing the earlier decisions of the council, but he met with widespread indignation, since the originators of these heresies had long since died after making their peace with the church. Vigilius who was a weak and vacillating character was unable to reach a position which was not equivocal and fled in 551 to Chalcedon after being the victim of ill-treatment on the way there. In 553 Justinian summoned the fifth General Council in Constantinople, which Vigilius at first refused

27

to attend and then took up a vacillating attitude towards, for fear that an anti-pope might be nominated. The council managed to achieve relative unity and Vigilius's return home was made possible. He died in Syracuse. Meanwhile the Ostrogoths under their last king, Teja, had been defeated by Narses in 533; simultaneously with this the confirmation of the Codex Justinianus reaffirmed the rule of Roman Law and assured its continuance for the next fifteen hundred years. During the pontificate of this equivocal Pope, who was the first since St. Peter not to be canonized, St. Benedict, "The Father of the Occident" died.

PELAGIUS I
16th, April 556 to 4th, March 561

Pelagius who had been Vigilius's representative and apocrisiar in Constantinople and who owed his election to Justinian, had given outstanding service to the city and people of Rome in 545 during the siege by Totila, the last Gothic king but one, though in 551 during his stay in Constantinople he had proved himself as undecided as Vigilius. In consequence, after the election, he met with widespread mistrust which he only managed to dispel gradually. His chief concern during his pontificate was the alleviation of suffering in Italy after the Gothic wars and the counteraction of simony, which was assuming critical proportions.

JOHN III
17th, July 561 to 13th, July 574

The main event of John's pontificate was the invasion of Italy by the Langobards in 568.

BENEDICT I
2nd, June 575 to 30th, July 579

He, too, had to be confirmed in his appointment by Justinus II, Justinian's successor. When in 579 the Langobards reached the outskirts of Rome, Benedict who was powerless to do anything tried to the best of his ability to alleviate the sufferings of his country.

PELAGIUS II
26th, November 579 to 7th, February 590

Pelagius was a Roman-born Goth and succeeded, by means of bribery, in persuading the Langobards to withdraw from Rome. It is a fact of great historical significance, that Pelagius following the advice of the Byzantine emperor, who was unable to give him any aid, turned to the Franks for assistance, though another two hundred years were to pass before the Franks made their appearance as the third Germanic power in Italy. Pelagius died of the plague: his most important creative act was the rebuilding of the arch-basilica of San Lorenzo fuori le mura.

GREGORY I ("THE GREAT")
3rd, September 590 to 12th, March 604

Gregory who was apparently born in Rome about the year 540 as the son of a distinguished family, became a civil-servant and at the age of thirty was praetor or chief magistrate of Rome, an office in which he proved himself a distinguished lawyer, only to give it up after a short while in order to found a Benedictine monastery in his palace. Here he lived as a simple monk and proceeded to

dispose of his estates, which extended as far as Sicily, partly for
the foundation of six monasteries, and partly for charitable purposes. Benedict had entrusted him with pastoral cares and Pelagius
made him apocrisiar-nuncius in Constantinople in 579, where he
achieved an international political reputation as a brilliant diplomat,
yet he never forsook his monastic way of life. He returned to Rome
—as an abbot?—in 585. He was loth to accept his election as pope,
even going so far as to ask the Emperor Mauritius to reject him
and, when that failed, attempting to escape. As Pope he at first
devoted himself exclusively and personally to charitable works,
proving his excellence as an administrator by forming out of the
patrimonium Petri, the extensive gifts of land which had been con-
veyed to the church for centuries, and the forerunner of the pontifical state, the first social state in the world, based entirely upon
Christian principles and using measures which were far in advance
of their time. Even people still officially recognized as slaves were
included in it as Christians. The Jews, too, found in Gregory a protector and their rights were guaranteed them, at least as far as
the popes were concerned, for several centuries to come. Gregory,
whom the Emperor Mauritius called a "simpleton" succeeded in
593 in making peace with the Langobards in spite of the intrigues
of the exarch governor of Byzantium, only to be treated officially as
a traitor for his efforts. He declined to accept the praise which was
due to him. Gregory represented the rights of small nations against
the Great Powers and it was only a new preventive war, which was
waged by the exarch that led to new devastations. What is difficult
to understand, even for the ecclesiastical historian, is the letter
which Gregory wrote to Phocas, the murderer of the Emperor
Mauritius and his family, and the perpetrator of the most frightful
atrocity to take place under the rulers of Byzantium, when he ascended the throne in 602. Gregory was responsible for the conversion of the Langobards and the Anglo-Saxons, the latter under St.
Augustine of Canterbury. It was in this field that Gregory's influence within the church had its crowning success, for here was ample
demonstration of his wise moderation and of the sagacity of his
great-heartedness in the evaluation of national characteristics and
heathen ideas. His numerous writings on all subjects form a just

basis for his elevation to the rank of fourth among the great teachers of the Western church, taking his place after Ambrose, Augustine and Jerome, but the genius of Augustine did not have its counterpart in Gregory. The essential features of his activity were his charity and the reform of the Roman schola cantorum and the Mass, though the Gregorian chant is not in fact named after Gregory with complete certainty, since it cannot be proved that Gregory actually composed any Gregorian melodies. The rule of St. Gregory has, for the secular priesthood, the same significance as the rule of St. Benedict for the monastic. The tomb of St. Gregory, who has been called the "last Roman" before the Middle Ages depicts the great saint as God's consul.

SABINIANUS

13th, September 604 to 22nd, February 606

Sabinianus tried to blacken the name of his predecessor and is remembered chiefly for selling corn out of the church's stocks, to the hungry populace of Rome, who had always been the object of Gregory's charity, at extortionate prices. The people were so enraged, that on his death they tried to seize his corpse.

BONIFACE III

19th, February 607 to 12th, November 607

A year had to elapse while imperial confirmation was awaited from Byzantium before Boniface could be consecrated. He issued a decree which forbade canvassing for votes during the lifetime of a pope, and forbade the holding of a new election until three days had elapsed after the pope's death.

BONIFACE IV
25th, August 608 to 8th, May 615

Boniface, who was considered in his time a saintly pope, was a Benedictine: during his pontificate he converted the Pantheon in Rome into the Christian church of Santa Maria the Martyr. Boniface had obtained the temple from Phocas, the East Roman emperor, to whom was erected in 608 the last imperial column in history, probably with the Pope's approval.

DEUSDEDIT
19th, October 615 to 8th, November 618

Deusdedit who was also known as Adeodatus enjoyed a great reputation as a holy pope. There is no record of any notable happening during his pontificate.

BONIFACE V
23rd, December 619 to 25th, October 625

Boniface's chief work was the despatch of missionaries to England. During his pontificate, the exarch of Ravenna made his first attempt to break away from Byzantium.

HONORIUS I
27th, October 625 to 12th, October 638

Honorius who was a pupil of Gregory the Great and also devoted himself successfully to missionary work in England took an important part in political affairs in Italy, developed a wide building program and, because of his administrative ability, gained the title *dux plebis*. The controversy which arose during his pontificate over the doctrine, accepted in Byzantium, of monotheletism or monergism, exercised theologians, as the "Honorius question," until well into the nineteenth century. This doctrine taught that there was in Christ only one will and arose from the doctrine of monophysitism, the heresy which taught that Christ has only one nature. Honorius in his desire to find a compromise solution declared the doctrine non-heretical in his edict *Esthesis*. Mohammed died in 632 during Honorius' pontificate, and the year marks the beginning of Muslim plans for world conquest.

SEVERINUS
28th, May 640 to 2nd, August 640

Severinus was elected after a *sedes vacans* of one year and seven months. During his short pontificate the exarch of Ravenna invaded Rome and plundered the churches there.

JOHN IV
24th, December 640 to 12th, October 642

The pontificate of this Dalmatian pope was filled with arguments which arose from the controversy over monotheletism which had begun under Honorius.

THEODORE I
24th, November 642 to 13th, May 649

Theodore, a Greek born in Jerusalem, was also involved in the arguments over monotheletism, until the Emperor Constant II issued his decree *Typos* which proscribed the dispute.

MARTIN I

July 649 to 16th, December 655

Martin, who like many of his predecessors had been apocrisiar-nuntius in Constantinople roused the Emperor Constant II against him by allowing himself to be consecrated before receiving imperial sanction from Byzantium, an act which was contrary to the practice of all the popes from the time of Gregory the Great. Martin summoned a synod to the Lateran, which rejected monotheletism,— Honorius I's *Esthesis* and Constant II's *Typos* publicly on dogmatic grounds and not half-privately as his predecessors had done, thus making the synod a demonstration against the imperio-papistry of Byzantium and the self-decreed theological competence of East Rome. It has been said that the exarch of Ravenna planned to have the Pope murdered for taking this course. A new exarch arrested Martin who was by this time a sick man, while he was at the altar of the Lateran basilica, giving as his reason Martin's allegedly illegal assumption of the papal office. Martin was taken first to the Isle of Naxos, then exposed to the most frightful tortures and thrown into prison in Constantinople, where, after a shameful trial, he was put into chains. The sentence of death which was passed on him was, however, not carried out. The Pope, by now mortally ill, was deported to Cherson, where he lived for a further year with insufficient food and subject to the most inhuman treatment. Martin was the greatest sacrifice made by Rome to imperio-papacy and his trial and martyrdom remained unequalled. He was later canonized and is also a saint of the Greek church.

EUGENE I

16th, September 655 to 2nd, June 657

Eugene was put up as an anti-pope, on the Emperor's command, on 10th, August 654, but he did not consider himself legally pope until after the death of Martin I. He showed strong opposition to Byzantium and died as he, too, was about to be deported.

VITALIAN

30th, July 657 to 27th, January 672

In 663 this complaisant pope who was spared dogmatic conflict with Byzantium ceremonially received the Emperor Constant II in Rome. The tyrant expressed his thanks for this act by systematically plundering the works of art in the city, including the bronze tiles of the Pantheon, and by autocratically bringing about a schism between the exarchy of Ravenna and Rome. In spite of this, after the murder of Constant II in 668 Vitalian supported the succession of his son Constantine IV against the claims of the usurper Mesecius. The new emperor who, by virtue of the Arab advance, had lost large areas of his empire where the monophysitic and monotheletic cults reigned, had no further interest in continuing the dispute with Rome and made efforts to bring about a reconciliation with the West.

ADEODATUS II

11th April 672 to 16th, June 676

Adeodatus is styled "the Second" as Pope Deusdedit is also known as Adeodatus. His pontificate passed without event. The understanding with Byzantium which had been initiated had not yet reached formal completion. Adeodatus conferred upon Venice the right to elect doges.

DONUS

2nd, November 676 to 11th, April 678

The letter which the emperor had written and which was to have brought the long dogmatic dispute to a close never reached Donus, whose short pontificate passed peacefully.

AGATHO

27th, June 678 to 10th, January 681

Agatho took up the positive suggestions of the Emperor Constantine IV and confirmed the dogma of the two forms of the will and operation of Christ which had been defined by Martin I at the synod of 649 as a rejection of monotheletism. The sixth General Council which was held in Constantinople in 680 and 681 set aside the long dogmatic dispute and so represented a logical continuation of the five general councils already held. Pope Honorius I was declared a guilty party to the dispute.

LEO II

December 681 to 3rd, July 683

Since Byzantium was deliberately withholding its sanction, Leo, who was a highly educated and saintly man, could not be consecrated until 17th, August 682. Leo was the first of a line of popes, who resorted to a procedure, strange in the papacy, of condemning their predecessor, Honorius I, because he had been declared a guilty party to monotheletism. The Pope succeeded in bringing to an end the schism with Ravenna, which had been artificially inspired by Constant II. In Rome he built the church of San Giorgo in Velabro for the Greeks.

BENEDICT II

26th, June 684 to 8th May 685

Benedict, who was a member of the House of Savelli, was the first pope for whose consecration the emperor of Byzantium renounced his right of confirmation and delegated his right to the exarch of Ravenna, a move which concealed new dangers of intervention.

JOHN V

23rd July, 685 to 2nd, August, 686

John was the first of a series of nine Popes of Eastern extraction, Greeks, and Syrians, which included all the popes except Gregory II, until Pope Zacharias: a fact very significant for the understanding of the tension between the Eastern and Western churches.

KONON

21st October, 686 to 21st September, 687

Konon was considered a distinguished and learned man, but his pontificate is not marked by any event of importance.

SERGIUS I

15th December, 687 to 8th September, 701

The exarch of Ravenna had been bribed by the archdeacon 'Pastoralis' to propose him as anti-pope, but Pastoralis did not pay the promised sum, so the exarch recognized the legal Pope and extorted money from him, a rather special form of simony. The archpriest 'Theodore' was also set up as anti-pope, but his reign was short-lived. The emperor Justinian II again sought to harass Rome and called the Council *in Trullo* in 692, which, though it brought about no new dogmatic conflict, did undermine the authority of Rome and the Western church in matters of discipline. Sergius rejected all the articles of the Council including the one that opposed celibacy. The emperor wished to banish the Pope, but Sergius was protected by force of arms. Sergius introduced the *Agnus Dei* into the Mass, improved relations with the Franks and made Willibrodus, the apostle of peace, a bishop.

JOHN VI

30th, October 701 to 11th, January 705

The pontificate of this Greek pope was taken up with new wars against the Langobards, whom he finally managed to dissuade from further depradations by buying them off. The exarch of Ravenna also renewed his threats against the Pope.

JOHN VII

Ist, March 705 to 18th, October 707

John, too, was a Greek and he succeeded in making peace with the Langobards; his attitude towards Byzantium, on the other hand, was cowardly and he refused to reject the disciplinary resolutions of the Council *in Trullo* of 692. This highly cultured Pope began an extensive building program in Rome, where he was particularly interested in the art of mosaics. Remains of his former chapel of the Virgin in St. Peter's may be found to-day in Santa Maria of Cosmedin; the mosaic portrait of the Pope can be seen in the grottoes of the Vatican. John rebuilt the monastery of Subiaco, the first hermitage of St. Benedict, which was destroyed in 601.

SISINNIUS

15th, January to 4th, February 708

A pontificate without any importance. Sisinnius was a Syrian.

CONSTANTINE

25th, March 708 to 9th, April 715

Constantine, who was a Syrian, is sometimes known as Constantine I, though 'Constantine II' was an anti-pope. He was the third and last pope to go to Constantinople, where he achieved a peaceful settlement of the Synod *in Trullo* of 692. Three months later Justinian II, the last Heraclid, a tyrant like Phocas before him, was assassinated and his head was brought to Rome, where the Pope had to witness the fearful procession in which the howling mob bore the head round the city—the bloody symbol of the irresistible breach with the Eastern church. The usurper Philippikos Bardanes tried for a short time, to restore monotheletism by force. Constantine's refusal to recognize the usurper completed the political rupture with Byzantium.

GREGORY II

19th, May 715 to 11th, February 731

At the beginning of his pontificate, Gregory, the second pope of the house of Savelli, began, in historical continuance of the policy of Pope Constantine, to turn the attention of the papacy to the Frankish kingdom. Meanwhile in East Rome the accession of Leo III to the throne in 717 marked the beginning of the Isaurian dynasty. In 718 Winfrid the English Benedictine monk, who was later to be known as St. Boniface, came to Rome and received the Pope's command to proceed with the conversion of Germany, for in all matters which concerned missionary activity Gregory continued the policy of his predecessor and namesake, Gregory the Great. Winfrid's mission to Germany marks the beginning of that cross fertilization of Roman and Germanic cultures which has lasted to the present day. Byzantium exacerbated the differences between the East and the West, partly by making illegal tax demands, and partly by the iconoclast edicts of 726 and 730; besides this the emperor Leo III did, in fact, wish to have Gregory assassinated and an anti-pope set up in his place, but at this juncture the Langobards declared themselves the protectors of the papacy. The whole of Italy rose, in what was the first revolution in the country, on the side of the Pope and drove out the Byzantine governors. Leo threatened Gregory with the same fate as Martin I, but several letters of great historical significance which passed between Gregory and Leo bear witness to the true fact of the situation. The exarch of Ravenna occupied Rome, and new campaigns by the Langobards made the Pope's position one of great delicacy, since he wished at all costs to avoid a break: finally in 722 he allied himself with Charles Martel the Frankish ruler.

GREGORY III
18th, March 731 to 29th, November 741

The pope's political influence increased as the Langobards grew more and more powerful in Italy and in 733 he called upon Charles Martel for help against the pillaging expeditions being waged by Leo III. His request was refused by Charles, who did, however, at the same time support the missionary activity in Germany of St. Boniface, who had by now been made an archbishop. Gregory was the last pope, who in the interests of good understanding, sought and obtained the sanction of Byzantium upon his election, in spite of the continuance of iconoclasm there. In the East the Pope was supported by St. John of Damascus Chrysorrhoas ("river of gold") who was the greatest theologian of the century, the author of several speeches against the iconoclasts and who was named a church father by Pope Leo XIII. The battle of Poitiers and Tours, in which Charles Martel saved the West from the encroachment of the Islamic empire, took place, in 732, during Gregory's pontificate.

ZACHARIAS
3rd, December 741 to 22nd, March 752

Zacharias, the last of the nine Eastern popes, was a benevolent and astute man who strengthened relations with the Franconian empire, where the last Merovingian, Childerich III, was put into a monastery and Pippin, after his brother Karlman had renounced the throne and gone himself as a monk to Monte Cassino in 751, was anointed King by St. Boniface. He was the first king in history to be anointed by a papal plenipotentiary, and he was anointed again by the Pope some years later. Zacharias made peace with the Langobards. In Byzantium the iconoclasm which had prevailed under Constantine V continued to rage under his son Leo III. A fresco, painted in 741, on which the pope is represented, is preserved in the church of Santa Maria Antiqua in Rome.

STEPHEN II
25th, March 752 to 26th, April 757

Immediately after the death of Zacharias, a Stephen was elected pope, who died three days later, before he could be enthroned; he is, therefore, not included among the popes. Stephen II was the first pope of the House of Orsini. The Langobards once more broke their peace treaty with Rome and in 753 Stephen became the first Pope to cross the Alps when he went to visit Pippin. According to the Franconian annals Stephen begged Pippin, in sackcloth and ashes, to give him aid against the Langobards and placed himself under Pippin's protection, whom he regarded as the protector of the Apostle Peter. He thus raised the agreement which had its roots in international law to the status of a religious dedication, which received its liturgical expression when the Franconian church took over the Roman liturgy in place of the Gaulish. The whole question of responsibility for the protection of the Holy See remained alive until the time of Napoleon and the dissolution of the Pontifical State. The agreement came into force in 754 at Quierzy-Laon, though the document which was known as the "Donation of Pippin" has been lost and many a decisive question of medieval history has been left unanswered. The areas which were included in the defense treaty were listed a few years later by the biographer of Hadrian I in what is generally regarded as an accurate account; however, the other question of which areas were to go to the Franconian kingdom and which to the Patrimonium Petri after the defeat of the Langobards has still not been settled. In the same year, 754, the Pope anointed

Pippin and his two sons Charles and Carloman in St. Denis and at the same time bestowed upon the King the title *Patricius Romanorum*; another sign of the breach with Byzantium, since until this time this title had been borne by the exarch of Ravenna, and had been bestowed by the emperor of Byzantium—but Stephen still showed no wish to make a formal break with East Rome. It was not until 756 that Pippin defeated the Langobards. A new document of donation drawn up between Stephen and Pippin and embracing large areas of land served as the foundation of the pontifical state—allegiance to Byzantium had become a pure fiction. It has been proved that the notorious forgery of the "donation of Constantine" derives from Stephen's time and not from the ninth century, its purpose being to presuppose the demands of the Patrimonium Petri. Its effect was fatal, the more so since it was included in the pseudo-Isidorian decretals, though it was later supported even after the decretal had been shown to be spurious by Cardinal Nicholas of Cusa and Lorenzo Valla.

PAUL I

29th, May 757 to 28th, June 767

Paul was his predecessor's brother, and thus the second pope of the House of Orsini. He tried unsuccessfully to continue his brother's policy, but Pippin reacted coolly to his suggestion that he should attack the Langobards who were once more rising up under Desiderius. In Byzantium inconoclasm reached its zenith and developed into a regular crusade against the monkhood. At the same time the emperor tried unsuccessfuly to win Pippin over to his side.

STEPHEN III

1st, August 767 to 24th, January 772

After the death of Paul I, the first attempt in the history of the papacy at forcible intervention in the papal election was made by the Duke Toto of Nepi, who set up his brother 'Constantine II' a layman, as anti-pope. The King of the Langobards also put up an anti-pope, 'Philip,' who soon withdrew, whilst 'Constantine' was overthrown after thirteen months. It then became possible to hold a new, legal election, which was, however, dominated by Christophorus, a brutal deacon: the anti-pope 'Constantine' was blinded and his party subjected to bloody persecutions, while Stephen who proved himself a weakling was powerless to intervene. All these happenings, signalled the beginning of the great factional battles which were to rage in the ensuing centuries around the papal dignity and the papacy itself. Stephen was recognized by Charles and Carloman, the sons of Pippin, and summoned a synod in 769 which again condemned the wretched, blinded and ill-treated anti-pope, a course of action for which Christophorus was responsible. The synod resolved that in future only cardinals or cardinal deacons should be elected pope, that the election of laymen should be banned and that, contrary to the established custom, laymen should be disenfranchised and only the clergy allowed to vote at papal elections. These resolutions received little or no recognition for some time. The remainder of the pontificate of this twilight figure was taken up with disputes with Charles, Carloman and Desiderius, whom he first of all reviled and then praised. Carloman died shortly after Stephen and Charles, who was later called "The Great" remained the sole ruler of the Franconian kingdom.

HADRIAN I

1st, February 772 to 25th, December 795

Hadrian was the third pope of the House of Colonna. After the final attacks of the Langobards under Desiderius, who still held large tracts of the Patrimonium Petri, Charles the Great liquidated the Langobardic kingdom which had been in existence for two centuries by the capture of Pavia. In Rome at Easter of the same year the Pope for the first time met Charlemagne, who placed the documents which confirmed the donation agreement signed between

Stephen II and Pippin in the Quierzy agreement on the altar and tomb of St. Peter in the church of St. Peter's. Modern research gives little credence to the doubts which have been expressed about the truth of this meeting. The new power constellations under Charlemagne, the King of the Franks and the Langobards, inevitably led to his establishing a certain supremacy over the pope and the Pontifical State. Up to 781, when Charles made a second journey to Rome nothing had been done to implement the donation agreement. Hadrian anointed Charles's son Pippin, King of Italy, but it was not until 787 that Charles showed any willingness to make any significant concessions. Even then Hadrian still did not attain to sovereignty while Charlemagne remained *Patricius Romanorum*. The dating of papal documents according to the number of years of the pontificate and not according to the number of years which the emperor of Byzantium had been reigning began in 781. In 787 the Empress Irene who was regent for her son, Constantine VI, summoned the seventh General Council to Nicaea, where iconoclasm was condemned. Charlemagne who was not invited to Nicaea retaliated by making his own somewhat milder decrees against the worship of idols and summoned a rival synod to Frankfurt, to which even Hadrian sent envoys, thus elevating it to the status of a General Council, although it is not included in the list of councils. Hadrian's greatest merit lay in his building program which included the construction of the great Roman water systems, and the furnishing of a number of churches. As a political figure he is still the object of controversy even to-day, especially for the scrupulous and importunate way in which he made his demands for the return of territories—he even went so far as to threaten the emperor of Byzantium with excommunication—and for his complaisance, which so often appeared in the wrong place. He could not match Charlemagne's powerful personality. In spite of all this and of the difficulty of the times in which he lived, he managed to rescue much and to increase his possessions. To the ever-needy population he was a great helper, and in the vestibule of St. Peter's the marble tablet can still be seen, upon which Alcuin by command of Charlemagne and in spite of all the disputes between them praised Hadrian as a pope and as a friend.

LEO III
26th, December 795 to 12th, June 816

Immediately after his election, Leo, who had up to that time been the cardinal presbyter of Santa Susanna sent the key of St. Peter's tomb and the banner of Rome to Charlemagne as an official recognition of his supremacy. He also commissioned the magnificent mosaic which depicts St. Peter standing between Charlemagne and the Pope, and which was restored in 1743, for the Triclinium of Leo III in the Lateran. Supporters of his predecessor attempted to blind and assassinate him in 799, and after being severely ill-treated he fled to Charlemagne in Paderborn, where the strictures which were raised against his way of life were only partly answered. He returned to Rome and Charlemagne arrived there in November 800 to institute an enquiry, after which, on 23rd, December 800 Leo, in the presence of Charlemagne and the populace of Rome swore the oath of purification which had been prescribed under Roman Law. The event is commemorated in the fresco by Giovanni Francesco Penni in the Stanza dell'Incendio in the Vatican. The 25th, December 800 became a red-letter day in the history of the World for on this day the Pope, without Charlemagne's previous knowledge, carried out his coronation as emperor, before himself kneeling at his feet. His motives and the background to this action, which was entirely the Pope's doing, will never be entirely explained, although there are many suppositions with a smack of truth in them, which are based on Charlemagne's first act as emperor and successor of the Byzantine emperor, which was to punish Leo's would-be assassins, whose death sentence was mitigated at the Pope's request to that of exile. The Western idea of the empire did not develop until later, but it had been set in motion, however unwittingly, by Leo. On the great coronation fresco in the Stanza dell'Incendio, which is presumably also by Penni, the Pope has the features of Leo X and the emperor those of Francis I of France. Leo visited the emperor once more in 804 at Aix-la-Chapelle and in France. His building program affected nearly all the churches of Rome, which he either restored or furnished with endowments of works of art.

STEPHEN IV
22nd, June 816 to 24th, January 817

Stephen, who was the fourth Pope of the House of Colonna, went to Reims to crown and anoint Louis the Pious, Charlemagne's son—the first time that such a rite had taken place, and by virtue of this the papacy claimed the right to consecrate the emperor.

PASCHAL I
25th January, 817 to 11th February, 824

Paschal was the abbot of Santo Stefano and the second pope to come from the House of Massicini. The *Pactum Ludovicanum* which was concluded between him and Louis the Pious, and of which only eleventh-century copies are extant, has been the object of considerable controversy. Among other things it confirmed the pope's sovereignty over the pontifical state. At the same time a demand was made for complete incorruptibility in the papal election without any suspicion of simony. In 823 Paschal crowned Louis's son Lothair. Paschal, an energetic and hard-driving Pope who roused considerable dissatisfaction, built three of the most important of the early Roman churches, in each of which a portrait of him can be seen: they are Santa Prassede, Santa Maria in Domnica and, most important of all, Santa Cecilia in Trastevere, in which there is a very precious mosaic in the apse, which has been preserved in its original condition and in which the Pope is standing on the extreme left.

EUGENE II
6th, June 824 to 27th, August 827

Eugene was presbyter of Santa Sabina. Critical disturbances forced the emperor Lothair, the joint-emperor with Louis, to come to Rome and proclaim strict legal measures, the *constitutio Lothari,* which represented the peak of imperial power over the pope and partly rescinded the *Pactum Ludovicanum.*

VALENTINE

August 827 to September 827

Valentine's pontificate lasted for two uneventful weeks.

GREGORY IV

October 827 to 25th, January 844

Gregory's pontificate lasted during the struggle within the Carolingian empire between the four sons of Louis the Pious and their father, and among each other, which finally ended in the fall of the Carolingian empire. The resistance of the Franconian bishops to the Pope also took place during this pontificate, and Gregory tried to mediate personally on the "Field of Lies" at Colmar, but he was not a strong personality and was quite incapable of orderly and reasonable intervention. In 843 the final division of the empire was completed by the Treaty of Verdun, according to which Lothair was to remain emperor and retain his sovereignty over Italy, Charles the Bald was to become King of France and Louis the German was to retain the Eastern territories. In the Pontifical State Gregory saw himself threatened by the Saracen advance and he fortified Ostia. In 843 Byzantine iconoclasm came to an end after one hundred and fifty years; the Orthodox church celebrates the day as the Feast of Orthodoxy.

SERGIUS II

January 844 to 27th, January 847

Sergius was the fifth pope of the House of Colonna. Simultaneously with his election 'John' tried to make himself pope. Sergius

47

power, denying the right of the state to interfere in the affairs of the church or of the church to interfere in affairs of state, a stand which gives, in some ways, a philosophical basis to the primacy of St. Peter. Nicholas condemned the use of war unless it were purely defensive. The distinction which he drew between *verus rex* and *tyrannus* is especially significant for us in view of the recent past and shows Nicholas to have been the first great man to defend human rights against the state. He also taught that the use of torture upon thieves and robbers is a crime against humanity. His vision of eternity often lent him the power to see beyond chains of events which were conditioned by their time. As an intellectual personality and as a pope, Nicholas represents the central pillar of the bridge which spans the pontificates of Gregory the Great and the zenith of the Middle Ages. Ranke says of him that he belonged "to those men who can be looked upon as the incarnation of a system." Nicholas was a man of integrity, filled with a sense of calling who was always ready to listen to the needs of his people and who remained inflexible in the face of the great men of his day, but he was above all else a priest filled with a high sense of responsibility. His high intellectual gifts found little following in the years immediately succeeding his death. Anastasius Bibliothecarius, the antipope who been set up against Benedict III was his secretary.

HADRIAN II
14th, December 867 to 14th, December 872

Hadrian was the sixth pope to come from the family of the Colonnas. He was a pleasant, kindly but weak man, who had been married before taking orders, and now saw the abductor of his wife and daughters become their murderer. A brief reconciliation with the Eastern church was effected during his reign at the eighth General Council in Constantinople—the last to be held in East. This council which had been initiated by the emperor Basil I, the founder of the Macedonian Dynasty, condemned the schism which Photius had effected. Hadrian who had grown old and who had lacked any sort of purpose tried in vain to interfere in the dispute over the Carolingian succession which had arisen during his pontificate. Cyril and Methodius, the two Slav apostles, came to Rome during Hadrian's pontificate and he recognized the Slavonic liturgy.

JOHN VIII

14th, December 872 to 16th, December 882

John crowned Charles II emperor in 875. The occupation of Rome by Italian princes meant that he was imprisoned for weeks before being able to make his escape to France, where he crowned Louis the Stammerer, the son of Charles the Bald, King in 878. After his return to Rome he crowned Charles III ("The Fat"), the son of Louis the German, emperor. The struggle against the princes and new attacks by the Saracens brought him no help from the Carolingians, so that the Pope found himself, after renewed rebuffs from Photius, forced to pay humiliating tribute to the Saracens. Finally, a number of his relatives conspired against the old man and killed him with a hammer, after they had found poison too slow. He was the first pope to be assassinated. John, whose whole efforts were directed toward peace and justice was compelled by the conditions of his time to function in an almost exclusively political role. His murder was the first sign of that decay in the papacy which led Cardinal Baronius, the ecclesiastical historian to characterize the tenth century as a *saeculum obscurum*.

MARINUS I

16th, December 882 to 5th, May 884

The two popes named Marinus are included in the lists of popes under Martin. For the first time a bishop was elected to the Holy See. The pontificate of this pious and gifted man passed uneventfully.

HADRIAN III

17, May 884 to September 885

Hadrian was the seventh pope of the House of Colonna. He reigned for little over a year and died while on his way to visit Charles the Fat, who was in the neighborhood of Modena. In 1891 official recognition was granted to the cult which had treated him as a saint.

STEPHEN V

September 885 to 14th, September 891

Under his pontificate the deposition of the Emperor Charles the Fat, the last of the Carolingians, took place in the year 887. He was succeeded by Arnulf of Carinthia. By a peculiar form of nepotism, Stephen adopted the most powerful Italian prince, Duke Wido of Spoleto, as his son. In the mounting confusion, with no real leadership anywhere, not even from Byzantium, this prince was regarded as a source of aid. Wido's enemy, the Margrave Berengar of Friuli, had himself crowned King of Italy, while the Pope, who had solicited help from Arnulf of Carinthia, crowned Wido as Emperor in 891, although he was not recognized as such anywhere outside of his own domain.

FORMOSUS

6th, October 891 to 4th, April 896

While Bishop of Porto, Formosus had achieved fame for his missionary work in Bulgaria, but thanks to the imprudent refusal of Nicholas I to keep him there as archbishop, Bulgaria was lost to the Western church and became orthodox. Formosus later joined the conspiracy against John VIII and was suspended as a bishop, though he was sent as a legate to the emperor, Louis II. He was reappointed Bishop of Porto by Marinus I. As pope he was forced to continue Stephen V's policies and in Ravenna in 892 he crowned Wido's son emperor as well. Their increasing power caused the Pope to call upon Arnulf for help. After Wido's death his widow Ageltrude reigned in Rome, and when Arnulf appeared in Rome for the second time Formosus was powerless to resist him and he was crowned emperor. Arnulf, however, was forced to retire from Italy a sick man. Formosus who died soon afterwards was an irreproachable, though perhaps ambitious pope; he restored St. Peter's and furnished many other churches.

BONIFACE VI

April 896

A man completely lacking in dignity who had been dismissed from office on several occasions, Boniface reigned for only two weeks. In spite of a decision of the Council of Ravenna to erase his name from the list of popes, he is counted as one.

STEPHEN VI

May 896 to August 897

Stephen was one of the most macabre figures ever to attain to a position of power. The story of a most atrocious and infamous action has been passed down about him. He is said, out of friendship for the House of Spoleto, which had returned to power, to have exhumed the body of Formosus which had been buried for nine months, and to have placed it on a throne clad in its papal garments, so that he could sit in judgment upon the dead man. Although Stephen had been Bishop of Anagni before his election, a post which he held thanks to Formosus, he accused the body, among other things, of translation from Porto to Rome. This sadistic psychopath had the fingers with which Formosus bestowed his blessings cut off the corpse's right hand, and then cast him first into the burial ground of strangers and later into the Tiber, amidst the complaints of the population. This frightful atrocity has gone down in history as "the synod of the corpse". The people of Rome were now mad with anger and Formosus's supporters threw Stephen into prison and strangled him a few months later.

ROMANUS
August 897 to November 897

Romanus who was the brother of Pope Marinus reigned for only four months. He declared all the acts of his predecessor invalid.

THEODORE II
December 897

The pontificate of this peace-loving and honorable pope lasted for only three weeks. He had the body of Formosus, which had been recovered, buried with the highest honors. He annulled once more all the measures taken at the synod of the corpse and reinstated those who had been deposed or declared invalidly consecrated by Stephen VI. Stephen's supporters for a short time set up the unscrupulous count of Tusculum as an anti-pope, 'Sergius', who was at first unable to sustain his claim to the papacy, but later became Sergius III.

JOHN IX
January 898 to 6th, April 900

John was a protégé of the emperor, Lambert, who having made peace with Berengar of Friuli was now residing in Ravenna and reigned over almost the whole of Italy. This weak, though dignified and intelligent pope went to Ravenna under Lambert's protection and held a synod of reparation which completed the work begun by Theodore II.

Peace seemed on the point of being re-established when Lambert suffered a fatal accident. As Lambert died without heirs, Berengar of Friuli took over the command and encountered no opposition, since the sole heir of the emperor Arnulf, who was mortally ill, was the child Louis III.

BENEDICT IV

May/June 900 to July 903

Benedict continued the policies started by John IX, but there was an alarming increase in factional strife. The coronation of Louis of Provence had no effect and Berengar continued to rule over Italy. Benedict fought unsuccessfully against corruption.

LEO V

5th, August 903

This holy and frugal Pope, after only one month in office, was thrown into prison by the presbyter Christophorus and tortured to death. An old Breton legend identifies him with the saintly Tugdual, a Benedictine monk who was said to have come to Rome and there to have become Leo, the Breton Pope.

CHRISTOPHORUS

September 903 to January 904

This papal usurper really only deserves to be counted as an anti-pope. After a few weeks he himself was thrown into prison and was strangled, together with his predecessor, by the former anti-pope "Sergius," the count of Tusculum, who had returned from exile to become pope.

SERGIUS III
29th, January 904 to 15th, April 911

Sergius was a sinister figure, the murderer of his two predecessors, the friend of the ghoul Stephen VI and the opponent of Formosus. He treated all those who had been consecrated by Formosus and all whom they in their turn had consecrated in the basest possible way. At this time a noble family consisting of Theophylactus, his wife Theodora and his daughters Theodora the Younger and Marozia rose to a position of omnipotence in Rome. This family together with a line of inferior or weak popes carried on the rule of pornocracy in Rome until 935, and the cardinal and historian, Cesare Baronius, writing about 1600 called this the dark age of the papacy. Marozia whose first marriage was the Margrave Alberich of Spoleto was also Sergius III's mistress. Even if all that Luitprand of Cremona, the author of the most important chronicle of the day, writes is not true—and he is given to exaggerations—it does little to alter the shameful position which the papapcy occupied vis-à-vis Christianity at this time. From this time on Theophylactus assumed the title of Duke, Consul and Senator of Rome, the elder Theodora and Marozia also took the title of Senator. Sergius rebuilt the basilica of the Lateran which had collapsed during an earthquake at the time of the "synod of the corpse"; this was the one act of service in the whole of his pontificate.

ANASTASIUS III
April 911 to June 913

The pontificate of this pope passed uneventfully.

LANDO

July 913 to February 914

Nothing is known about Lando except that he was dependent upon Theodora the Elder whose protégé he made archbishop of Ravenna until he was succeeded by him.

JOHN X

March 914 to May 928

John who was an energetic though morally dubious pope was elected through the influence of Theodora the Elder; he had been a former archbishop of Ravenna and succeeded in building up a Grand Alliance against the Saracens, who were besieged in 915 on the Garigliano by the Pope and Theophylactus and defeated in August of that year. The Pope is supposed to have taken a personal and courageous part in the battle. At the close of year John crowned Berengar of Friuli emperor. After Berengar's assassination after Hungarian invasions and bloody battles in Upper Italy, Rudolf II of Upper Burgundy was elected in Berengar's place, but he was ejected by Hugo of Provence, who had been summoned by Wido of Tusculum, Marozia's second husband and who enjoyed the Pope's support. Hugo was elected King of Italy in 926. In such circumstances all talk of the universal significance of the papacy was vain. Things sank to such a point that John made a five-year-old child archbishop of Reims. Marozia had become the sole ruler of Rome, and when John, who towards the end of his life seems to have taken an interest in the affairs of the church dared to oppose her, she had him imprisoned and murdered.

LEO VI

5th, June 928 to 5th, February 929

Leo was an insignificant creature of Marozia's with no will of his own.

STEPHEN VII

929 to February 931

He too was one of Marozia's creatures and was most probably assassinated like his predecessor.

JOHN XI

March 931 to December 935

John was the son of Marozia and, almost undoubtedly, Sergius III and was imprisoned by his mother. After Wido's death Marozia married a third time, this time Hugo of Provence, to whom she hoped to give the imperial crown. However, Alberich II of Tuscia, Marozia's highly-gifted son by her first marriage, won the honor and threw his mother and the Pope, his half-brother, into prison, where they were both murdered one after another: this was the end of the pornocracy. Alberich reigned undisputed for twenty-three years as "Prince and Senator of the Romans" and his main efforts like those of Odo, the abbot of Cluny, were directed towards bringing order into the affairs of the church. The papacy was completely subject to his positive influence.

LEO VII

9th, January 936 to 13th, July 939

Leo and his three successors were popes against whom no criticism can be levelled; they were all active in the powerful secular reform movement which started in Cluny, and they were all powerfully supported by Alberich. Leo began his pontificate in the year that Otto I came to power in Germany. Odo, the abbot of Cluny, visited Leo in Rome during his pontificate and discussed the revival of religious life with him.

PLATE 9. Gregorius XVI

IVLIVS . II . PAPA . SAVONENSIS . LIGVR .

PLATE 10. Julius II

PLATE 11. Leo X

NICOLAVS . V . PAPA . SERGIANENSIS .

PLATE 12. Nicolaus V

PLATE 13. Paul III

VRBANVS . VI . PAPA . NEAPOLITANVS .

PLATE 14. Pius II

PLATE 15. Pius VI

PIVS . II . PAPA . SENENSIS .

PLATE 16. Urbanus VI

STEPHEN VIII
14th, July 939 to October 942

Stephen was probably a relative of Otto I. The historian Martin of Poland reports that the Pope's nose was mutilated as a result of a conspiracy. During Stephen's pontificate King Hugo managed to recapture Rome, but he was driven back again by Alberich.

MARINUS II
30th, October 942 to May 946

Marinus is also known as Martin III, as both of the popes who bore this name were later included under the name Martin. Nothing is known of the pontificate of this pope. In 947 Hugo retired from Italy after being driven out by Berengar of Ivrea, the grandson of Berengar of Friuli.

AGAPETUS II
10th, May 946 to December 955

In 950 Berengar of Ivrea had his son Adalbert crowned King. He imprisoned Adalheid (the daughter-in-law of Hugo of Provence and the widow of his son Lothair) who was later to become the great empress: eventually she called upon Otto I for his help. He set her free and then married her in 951. As her father had been King of Italy for a short time she laid claim to the inheritance. After overthrowing Berengar, Otto resided until 952 as King of the Franks and Lombards, in Pavia. Agapetus and Alberich II rejected Otto's claim to the imperial crown. Alberich died in 954 after forcing Agapetus and the Roman nobility to swear to elect his son Octavian, Count of Tusculum, pope on Agapetus's death and combine the secular and spiritual offices in one person.

JOHN XII

16th, December 955 to 4th, December 963

John's father had destined him at an early age for the priesthood and he became Pope at twenty. He was one of the basest and most miserable figures ever to occupy the Holy See. Under him the Lateran degenerated into little more than a brothel, as historians of all faiths readily admit. He was completely uneducated in every way, was only able to speak Italian and loved to play the role of secular tyrant and cynic. When Berengar of Ivrea and his son, Adalbert, advanced southwards in 960 John recalled Otto I to Italy and it is one of the ironies of history that Otto who had done so much to restore imperial dignity and Adalheid, the greatest of all the medieval empresses, should have been crowned by the libertine, John on 2nd, February 962. A short time after, John began to set up a European coalition against Otto the Great in conjunction with the defeated Adalbert of Ivrea. As a consequence of this, at a synod in St. Peter's in November 963, the Emperor, who had just come to Rome, placed Adalbert under indictment for his many temporal and ecclesiastical crimes and declared John deposed. Leo VIII was chosen as the new Pope. He was a distinguished layman who was given consecration, which was canonically impossible. When the Emperor had left Rome, John came back and Leo fled. Before the Emperor's return, John, who had taken savage revenge on his enemies, died on May 14, 946. He lived only eight days after having been severely beaten by the husband of a woman with whom he had committed adultery.

LEO VIII

4th, December 963 to 1st, March 965

Although some authorities regard Leo as an anti-pope he was in fact the legal successor to John XII, and he was supported by the emperor when the Romans tried to set up Benedict V. The remainder of Leo's pontificate passed without incident. Documents which bear his name and which purport to renounce the donations of Pippin have been proved to be forgeries and to date from the time of the emperor Henry IV.

BENEDICT V
22nd, May 964 to 23rd, June 964

Like Leo VIII, Benedict is also included in the list of popes. He was a priest of the highest integrity and a well-known scholar with the name Grammaticus, who tried during his short pontificate and as far as lay within his power to eradicate the shame of the past years. Otto the Great and Leo VIII, however, deposed him and he was exiled to Hamburg, where he died as a deacon on 4th, July 966.

JOHN XIII
1st, October 965 to 6th, September 972

John was Bishop of Narni and was probably the son of Theodora the Younger, Marozia's sister. As a follower of Otto the Great he ruled so autocratically that there was a rising in Rome in 965, in the course of which John was imprisoned, but he succeeded in escaping a few months later and in fleeing to the emperor, who restored him about a year later and attempted to exile those who had been responsible for the rising. Otto restored the Pontifical State and returned important areas to the Patrimonium Petri. John crowned Otto emperor at Christmas 967. Lengthy discussions with Byzantium finally terminated in a peaceful agreement, which was sealed in 972 by the marriage of Otto II with Theophano, the daughter of the emperor John Tzimiskes.

BENEDICT VI

19th, January 973 to June 974

The Crescenti set themselves up as the emperor's chief opponents under Crescentius, the son of Theodora the Younger, and so presumably a brother of John XIII. Otto the Great died on 7th, May 973. Crescentius threw the Pope into prison and set up "Boniface VII" as an anti-pope, who then proceeded to strangle the Pope who had been deposed, only to have to flee to Byzantium in the face of new attacks by the emperor. "Donus II" who is included in some lists of popes between Boniface VI and Boniface VII never existed.

BENEDICT VII

October 974 to 10th, July 983

Benedict, a Count of Tusculum and Bishop of Sutri, was a pope of great dignity and spent his pontificate working intensively along the lines of the Cluniac reform. He aimed his sharpest attack at simony, which was condemned at a special synod.

JOHN XIV

10th, December 983 to 20th, August 984

Peter of Pavia, Otto II's arch-chancellor in Italy was elected to the papacy as a result of the emperor's zeal for reform. After Otto's death on 7th, December 983 the anti-pope 'Boniface VII' reappeared in Rome, threw John into prison and left him there to starve. Otto is the only German emperor to be buried in Rome; his sarcophagus is in the grottoes of St. Peter's.

BONIFACE VII
April(?) 984 to March(?) 985

This cruel usurper was barely in office a year before he was assassinated and his body was dragged in pieces through the streets of Rome.

JOHN XV
August 985 to March 996

John probably owed his election to Crescentius Nomentanus, the son of the first Crescentius, who styled himself Patricius Romanorum. He made himself detested by his nepotism, which was of the worst form and by his greed for money. In 989 the empress-regent, Theophano, came to Rome, but she was unable to shake Crescentius' powerful position. Quarrels arose in the city and John fled to Tuscany and from here he summoned Otto III to come to Italy to aid him and to be crowned emperor. The accession of Hugo Capet in 987 set the Capet dynasty upon the throne of France. The first papal canonisation took place in 993 when Ulrich of Augsburg was made a saint.

GREGORY V
3rd, May 996 to 18th, February 999

Otto who was the great-nephew of Otto II and son of the Duke of Carinthia was a very well educated and stern man and the first German to succeed to the Holy See during the Middle Ages. On 21st, May 996 the Pope, then twenty-four years old, crowned the sixteen-year old Otto III emperor, but when the latter had left Rome, Crescentius Nomentanus rose up once more and drove out the Pope, who had always treated the antagonism of the Roman people with great mildness. Crescentius set up a Greek as the anti-pope "John XVI" and it was not until 998 that Gregory was able to return to Italy. The anti-pope who had fled was taken prisoner and, without the emperor's knowledge, maltreated, led through Rome on a donkey and finally sent to a monastery where he lived another fifteen years. Even the intercession of the hermit St. Nilus of Rossano, who had warned the anti-pope on his accession, could not alter his fate. Crescentius was beheaded in the Castel S. Angelo. Gregory approached the task of reform, which he regarded as being of the first importance, with prudence and firmness. He died at the age of thirty of malaria and not, as some authorities say, of gout.

SYLVESTER II
2nd, April 999 to 12th, May 1003

The first German pope was succeeded by the first French one, when Gerbert of Aurillac received the tiara. Gerbert was the friend and teacher of Otto III. His short pontificate was first and foremost concerned with the missions to Poland and Hungary, to whose first king, Stephen, he sent the crown. In the latter part of his life Sylvester, who was always a confirmed enemy of simony turned his attention more and more to church reform. He worked in close collaboration with Otto III who resided in Rome until an uprising led by the Count of Tusculum drove both the Pope and the Emperor out of Rome. Otto III died on 24th, January 1002 in Paterno on Mount Soracte; his successor was Henry II. Sylvester was able to return to Rome, where John, the son of Crescentius Nomentanus, who had been executed during the preceding pontificate, was now in power. The Pope who was one of the greatest scholars of all time, mathematician, astronomer, philosopher, scientist and writer had studied at the feet of Arabian teachers in Seville and Cordova. His uncanny knowledge soon passed into the realm of legend and he was long considered to have been a sorcerer, and was later regarded as the prototype of Dr. Faustus. The sound of bones rattling behind his tomb in the Lateran is supposed to presage the death of the Pope. Sylvester left a host of writings. The events of the pontificates of Gregory V and Sylvester II have been described by Strindberg in his *Historical Miniatures.*

JOHN XVII
16th, May 1003 to 6th, November 1003

John is styled XVII although the sixteenth pope to bear this name was actually an anti-pope. Nothing is recorded about his pontificate.

JOHN XVIII
25th, December 1003 to July 1009

John's chief concern was the church in Germany. Henry II's life ambition, the founding of the See of Bamberg, was realized during John's pontificate.

SERGIUS IV
31st, July 1009 to 12th, May 1012

Sergius was a peaceful and charitable pope, the first to call—unsuccessfully—for a crusade.

BENEDICT VIII
8th, May 1012 to 9th, April 1024

After the death of John Crescentius, the counts of Tusculum once more came to power, while the Crescenti for a short time set up the anti-pope "Gregor." The Tusculi countered by forcing through the election of Count Theophylactus, the cardinal of Porto, whose brother Alberich was given the title *consul et dux.* The anti-pope

65

went to Henry II's court, but Henry rejected him in favor of Benedict and he and his wife, Kunigunde, were crowned in Rome on
14th, February 1014. The Pope visited Henry in Bamberg in 1020.
Benedict cast himself loose from all dynastic politics and ensured
his authority in the Pontifical State, but more in the capacity of a
secular ruler than as one who showed interest in ecclesiastical
reform. He was an excellent general and defeated the Saracens,
Pisa and Genoa. He supported the national uprising against Byzantium which, in 1019, had triumphed in Lower Italy against the
Normans, who had first appeared at the Battle of Cannae, but new
reverses came in 1022 when the Byzantine army withstood the
Pope and Henry II. The emperor was compelled to banish Benedict
and carry through ecclesiastical reform according to the Cluniac
pattern. The Pope followed suit at a great synod held in Pavia in
the same year, at which for the first time the marriage of priests—
still a widely practised custom—was officially forbidden, on pain
of loss of office. The practical results of the synod were however
negligible, since both the Pope and the emperor died shortly afterwards. Henry I persuaded the Pope finally to accept the *Credo* of
the Council of 381 into the Mass.

JOHN XIX
April/May 1024 to January(?) 1033

John was a brother of Benedict, his predecessor, and as Romanus,
Count of Tusculum he had also held the title *consul et dux* of Rome;
he secured his election by bribery and was consecrated on the first
day of his pontificate. He now began a shameful trade in simony
and it was only with the utmost difficulty that this avaricious man
could be prevented from selling the primatial rights, which till then
had been jealously guarded from the Patriarch of Byzantium, to
the Patriarch himself. In view of the fact that Byzantium closed its
list of popes at this time, the schism with the Eastern church can
be considered complete. At Easter 1027 Conrad II, the first of the
Salic emperors and his wife were crowned in Rome.

66

BENEDICT IX

January(?) 1033 to 1st, May 1045

Benedict who was also a Count Theophylactus of Tusculum and a nephew of both of his predecessors contrived to become Pope at the age of fifteen, thanks to the bribery of his father, Alberich III of Tusculum and the support of the emperor, Conrad. He was a complete tool of the emperor and had no mind of his own; perhaps he may best be compared to John XII for baseness and shamelessness. In 1044 a rising led by the Crescenti forced Benedict to leave Rome, whereupon a certain Bishop John bought the papal tiara and called himself Silvester III, but he was soon deposed and Benedict returned, only to sell the papal office for a large sum of money on 1st, May 1045. Benedict was formally declared deposed by Henry III at a synod in Rome held at the end of 1046, yet he re-appeared as anti-pope and did not die until 1055. Since the pontificate of Benedict the popes have borne coats-of-arms.

SYLVESTER III

20th, January 1045 to 10th, February 1045

Although the canon law position of many of the popes during this period of rampant simony is somewhat obscure, Sylvester, who succeeded in asserting himself against Benedict for a short time, is included in the list of popes.

GREGORY VI

John Gratianus Pierleoni

5th, May 1045 to 20th, December 1046

Gregory, an arch-presbyter, was the godfather of Benedict IX and came of the wealthy Jewish House of the Pierleoni. It was a curious paradox that this pope, whose personal life was quite blameless, who was pious, zealous in reform and highly thought of by his contemporaries, should have come to power by a shameless act of simony. It is more or less credibly asserted that he allowed this to happen so that he could rescue the church from the moral slough into which it had fallen. He purchased the papal office from Benedict IX. Gregory was welcomed most enthusiastically by Petrus Damianus and the Cluniac reformers, who were unaware, however, of the simoniacal practice which had brought him to the Holy See. The intervention of the emperor Henry III was most earnestly sought on two occasions, once by a letter, which probably emanated from Odilo of Cluny and once by a summons addressed to him by the Hermit Gunther, a man who enjoyed the highest respect, in which he said: "Come down in judgement, Henry, as the representative of almighty God. . . . a pope worthy of the name must be chosen and he will be worth more than a thousand of this sort." Henry finally intervened out of his desire to reform the church and in 1046 received Gregory in Piacenza, where he learned for the first time the true facts about Gregory's election. He summoned the famous synod of Sutri in December of that year and both Sylvester III and Gregory VI were deposed, though many sources maintain that Gregory resigned. The pope was banished to Cologne, where he died.

CLEMENT II
Suitger, Count of Morsleben
24th, December 1046 to 9th, October 1047

Clement was Bishop of Bamberg and is the first of four popes who owe their election to Henry III. The political and ecclesiastical situation which arose from this contained the seeds of future conflicts at a time when the empire was beginning to tower over the papacy, which it had raised up from the depths. Clement collaborated with Cluny mainly in order to combat simony. It is possible that he was poisoned by Benedict IX.

DAMASUS II
Count Poppo
17th, July 1048 to 9th, August 1048

Even before the Bishop of Brixen, who had been selected by Henry III as pope, could be enthroned, 'Benedict IX' appeared on the scene once more and asserted himself—this time as anti-pope —until July 1048. On the approach of the emperor and Damasus, however, 'Benedict' fled and died soon afterwards; actually very soon after the death of Damasus, whose pontificate only lasted for twenty-three days; but long enough for him to gain considerable respect. It has also been rumored that he, too, was poisoned.

LEO IX
Bruno, Count of Egisheim-Dagsburg
12th, February 1049 to 19th, April 1054

Bishop Bruno of Toul is one of the most holy figures in the whole history of the papacy, indeed in the whole of world history. Börries von Münchhausen has narrated the legend of his election in his ballad *Graf Egisheim*. Leo was a cousin of Henry III and was elected at the imperial diet of Worms in 1048: he entered Rome barefoot and among those who accompanied him was Hildebrand, a former secretary to the exiled Gregory VI, who was later to become Gregory VII. Leo refused to accept his election until he had been recognized by Rome as well, thus presenting a picture of a pope steeped in the highest traditions of legal ethics at a time when all else was out of control. He gathered a number of celebrated advisers around him, among whom was Hildebrand, the first real secretary of state and a very conscientious finance minister, and St. Petrus Damianus. Both of these men incorporated the highest ideals of the Cluniac reform, which was now to come to full fruition. The college of cardinals was internationalised by the addition of gentleness, saintliness and kindness. He was ready to attack abuses in the priesthood, especially simony and the marriage of priests, sharply and forcefully: this he did at a number of synods. No other pope has ever travelled so widely through the length and breadth of Europe and everywhere he saw to it that his orders and reforms were carried out, seeking in this way contact with the common people, to whom he preached and who, in their turn, loved him dearly. Politically Leo did not have great good fortune. The city of Benevento which was besieged by the Normans sought his aid and the emperor appointed him its governor; he was taken prisoner by the Normans at the Battle of Civita del Mare in 1055. Petrus Damianus criticised him for his behaviour for, instead of living as their liege-lord, he remained their prisoner throughout the winter. The Norman victory can be regarded as the real foundation of the Norman state, of which the Pope was liege-lord and which was to have profound significance in the politics of the ensuing centuries. The final, formal breach with East Rome took place at this time: the actual date is fixed as 16th, July 1054. Leo relied upon the pseudo-Isidorian decretals, not then known to be forgeries, to determine the legal definition of the Patrimonium Petri and the donations of Constantine, but nothing practical resulted. King Macbeth of Scotland was among the pilgrims who visited Rome during Leo's pontificate. Leo, who was canonised shortly after his death embodied in its purest form, for his own and succeeding generations, the idea and the form, the greatness and the driving force of the papacy in all its universality.

VICTOR II
Gebhard, Count of Hirschberg
13th, April 1055 to 28th, July 1057

The *sedes vacans* which arose after Leo was partly the fault of the Bishop of Eichberg who refused to accept his election. The emperor Henry III once more insisted that a German should be elected pope, and in so doing was closely following the advice of Hildebrand. Victor's pontificate continued along the lines laid down by his predecessor. He was considered a just and generous pope and had Hildebrand as his adviser: he died in Arezzo while on the return journey from his visit to Henry III on his deathbed.

STEPHEN IX
Frederick of Lorraine
3rd, August 1057 to 29th, March 1058

Stephen, who was the son of a duke and the abbot of Monte Cassino, created St. Petrus Damianus a cardinal with special responsibility for ecclesiastical reform and greatly extended his sphere of activity. The saint then turned his attention to lay investiture, one of the most fateful ecclesiastical evils of the time and was so successful generally in winning the people over to his ideals of reform that a popular movement started in Upper Italy against the simoniacal clergy; the movement was mockingly referred to by the nobility as the *Pataria* a word derived from the Italian word *pattari* which means 'a secondhand dealer'. The Pope was finally forced to intervene to prevent further acts of violence. Hildebrand, who had become Stephen's right hand man and was quite indispensable to him, made several journeys through France and Germany in the service of reform.

BENEDICT X
John, Count of Tusculum
5th, April 1058 to 18th, December 1058

Once more the disastrous House of the Tusculi succeeded in contriving the election of a pope, who lasted until Hildebrand and St. Petrus Damianus at the head of the reformed clergy succeeded in deposing him and holding a new election. Benedict died after 1072 and Hildebrand had him buried with full papal honors.

NICHOLAS II
Gerhard of Burgundy
18th, December 1058 to 27, July 1061

The Bishop of Florence was the candidate of the reforming faction and was enthroned on 24th, January 1059. The Easter synod held in the Lateran in 1059 issued the papal election decree, which stated that the cardinals alone were allowed to elect a pope to the Holy See, an action probably taken at the instance of the energetic Hildebrand. In addition to this, pre-requisites for celibacy were imposed and the acceptance of ecclesiastical office from laymen was forbidden. Simultaneously with this the power of the German court was limited. In July of this year the synod of Malfi was summoned, again at the instigation of Hildebrand: at this synod the Norman Robert Guiscard was created a Duke, and entered into an alliance with the papacy.

ALEXANDER II
Anselmo da Baggio
1st, October 1061 to 21st, April 1073

The Crescenti and Tusculi, who had already brought so much evil upon the Papacy, stood to the last against church reform and had an anti-pope, "Honorius II," designated in Basel. He was Peter Cadalus, the former chancellor of Henry III. In accord with the papal decretals, the Council of Mantua, under the leadership of Hildebrand, elected the Bishop of Lucca as the legitimate Pope. With the support of the Empress Agnes, who was regent for her son Henry IV, the anti-pope had his own court in northern Italy until 1064. Alexander was a clever diplomat and a pious priest, who soon found recognition in Germany where Archbishop Hanno of Cologne, the administrator for Henry IV, held sway. Behind Alexander's consistent work for reform, the influence of Hildebrand can be seen. It was unavoidable that the Papacy and the

Empire, in which reform and its enemies were sharply separated, should be near to a collision.

GREGORY VII
Hildebrand of Soana
22nd, April 1073 to 25th, May 1085

Gregory first appears in history as the companion of Gregory VI during his exile in Cologne. It is not certain whether he was in fact the son of a carpenter or a member of the Aldobrancheschi family. He was educated in Rome and then went to Cluny becoming a driving force behind the reform movement and gaining great influence over all the popes from Leo IX onwards, who entrusted him with the most important tasks. He repeatedly opposed election to the papacy and accepted in the end in the face of unprecedented unanimity and the absence of any suggestion of simony. Even Henry IV confirmed the canonic election. The simoniac circles in Rome were Gregory's bitterest enemies and during the Christmas Eve Mass of 1075, in what Gregorovius has described as one of the most frightful episodes in the history of the Middle Ages, they tore him away from the altar by his hair, maltreated him, hurled insults at him and finally threw him into prison: he was eventually rescued by the infuriated populace on Christmas Day and borne back by them to Santa Maria Maggiore where he continued the singing of the Mass where he had been interrupted. He forgave his enemies. The orders which had been issued forbidding simony and enjoining celibacy at the synod of 1074 were repeated in a Lenten synod in 1075. At this synod Gregory excommunicated a number of German and Italian bishops and issued the decree forbidding the bestowal of ecclesiastical offices by laymen, including the filling of bishoprics by the King: it was inevitable that his course should lead to a conflict between the state and the papacy. Gregory wished to establish the complete independence of the church in all spheres. Henry IV answered the decree by "deposing" Gregory at the imperial synod held in Worms in 1076, when a demand for the election of a new pope was sent to Rome. Gregory in turn replied by excommunicating the King; an action without precedent, the immediate result of which was to cause the majority of the bishops to desert Henry and invite Gregory to an Imperial Diet at Augsburg to settle the whole affair. It was a mark of Gregory's political astuteness that he did not wish to have Henry deposed. Gregory was on his way to Augsburg when Henry—no less astute and far-sighted than the Pope—appeared in Italy in the winter of 1077, when Gregory was at the castle of the celebrated countess Mathilde of Tuscany in Canossa. The King arrived at Canossa and spent three days in the village—not, as the Pope's enemies maintain, barefoot in the snow in the castle courtyard—before appearing as a penitent barefoot before the castle and begging release from his excommunication. The countess and his godfather Hugo, abbot of Cluny, interceded for him. Ever since Bismarck used the term in connection with the *Kulturkampf* the word Canossa has been used in proverbial contexts which bear no relationship to the secular and spiritual conditions of the Middle Ages. From the political point of view Henry was the victor, but the power of the papacy was re-asserted when the statesman was subjected to the priest. When Henry, having declared war on Rudolf of Hapsburg, demanded his deposition and excommunication and threatened to set up an anti-pope if Gregory did not acquiesce, while at the same time retaining the right of investiture, Gregory excommunicated him for a second time and renewed the ban on lay investiture, but this time his action had far less effect. Henry proceeded to set up Wibart, his chancellor in Rome, as the anti-pope 'Clement III', captured Rome with his aid and had himself crowned emperor in 1084. 'Clement III' enjoyed considerable support and Gregory was held prisoner in the Castel S. Angelo for several weeks until he was freed by Duke Robert Guiscard, who then plundered Rome. Gregory moved south with the Normans and died a year later in Salerno: to the end he was convinced of the justice of his cause. His last words have been engraved on the memory of history: "I loved justice and hated injustice, that is why I die in exile." Friend and foe alike agree that Gregory was one of the greatest figures of the Middle Ages, and though his political decisions still arouse controversy there was something of the old Roman in him; St. Petrus Damianus called him the "Holy Satan." He incorporated the highest expression of the theocratic element of the papacy combined with a certain harshness and he was determined at all costs to realize Augustine's *civitas dei.* Gregory's outstanding traits were his forcefulness, his sure understanding, the inflexibility and strength of his will and his indubitable sense of responsibility. He was canonised by Paul V in 1606 and his feast day was ordained by Benedict XIII. The great wealth of his writings which have been preserved in their entirety offers a very decisive key to his personality.

VICTOR III
Desiderius, Prince of Benevento
24th, May 1086 to 16th, September 1087

Although the anti-pope 'Clement III' continued to assert himself in Rome the majority of the cardinals elected the abbot Desiderius of Monte Cassino and cardinal of St. Cecilia in Trastevere, but he at first retired to his monastery and would not be consecrated until May 1086 after a *sedes vacans* of a year. He continued the ban on lay-investiture, did not rescind the excommunication of Henry IV and began a campaign against the Saracens in North Africa where he gained a victory.

URBAN II
Odo of Chatillon
12th, March 1088 to 29th, July 1099

Urban who was a former prior of Cluny and a cardinal bishop still had to brook the opposition of 'Clement III', who was, however, finally compelled to leave Rome, though he did not die until the beginning of the next pontificate. Urban continued the policy of Gregory VII in all matters. In 1092 Henry IV's son, Conrad, went

75

over to the Pope. Urban's name is linked with the first crusade which was planned at the synod of Piacenza and Clermont and announced on 27th, November 1095. Urban also demanded the expulsion of the Moors from Spain—it was the time of the Reconquista and the Cid Campeador. Sicily was won back to the church. Urban was especially concerned with the spiritual culture of his time and appointed St. Anselm of Canterbury, the father of scholasticism, as archbishop of the metropolis of England. In 1098 Robert of Molesme founded the Cistercian order. Urban, who was canonised in 1881, died two weeks after the capture of Jerusalem by the crusading army under Geoffrey of Bouillon.

PASCHAL II
Ranieri da Bieda
14th, August 1099 to 21st, January 1118

Paschal was a Cluniac monk and the cardinal of San Clemente. "Clement III" who died in 1100 was succeeded by another anti-pope "Theodoric" and, after his capture, by "Albert," who was, however, only destined to last for a few weeks. In 1105 the emperor's supporters set up yet another anti-pope who styled himself "Sylvester IV," while Henry IV continued his anti-papal policy. After Henry's deposition his son, Henry V, also turned on Rome and in spite of a number of suggestions for the attainment of peace, which the Pope made, he insisted on retaining the right of investiture. In 1110 he came to Rome, took Paschal prisoner and released him only after he had promised Henry the right of investiture without simony: a promise which quite rightly laid the Pope open to reproach. Paschal crowned Henry on 13th, April 1111 and soon withdrew his promise, after which he was forced to flee to Benevento to escape from Henry and he died shortly after he had returned to Rome again. One of Paschal's most estimable decrees was that which forbade trial by ordeal, against which Nicholas I had already taken a stand. During his pontificate St. Bernard founded Clairvaux.

GELASIUS II
Giovanni Coniuolo
24th, January 1118 to 28th, January 1119

Gregorovius described Gelasius as "one of the most touching figures in the whole history of the papacy": he was an aged monk of Monte Cassino, the cardinal of Santa Maria in Cosmedin and tried in vain to resist his election; his pontificate was nothing but a chain of sorrows. His election which was held according to the strict principles of canon law was secret in order to avoid interference from Henry V; however, the emperor's supporter, Cencius Frangipani, a member of another savage Roman family which was in power at the time, broke the conclave, dragged Gelasius off in chains to his tower to torture him and refused to surrender him to the people, who had risen up in his support, until the next day. Gelasius forgave his tormentor, but the Frangipani denounced him to the emperor, who hastened to Rome from the river Po. Gelasius succeeded in making a hairbreadth escape to Gaeta, whereupon Henry V, whose demands Gelasius had refused, set up an anti-pope, "Gregory VIII," who gained great support and ruled in Rome. Gelasius returned to Rome as a poor pilgrim, but he found little succour there and was forced to flee again when the Frangipani were once more on the point of attacking him while he was celebrating mass. The tortured man was found by some women sitting alone in a field. He managed to continue his flight to France by way of Pisa where he was feted and honored and where he consecrated the cathedral. He was accompanied everywhere by his loyal cardinals. He died in Cluny clad in his monk's habit and lying on the floor. "It is not possible for any sympathetic person to look upon his last sacrifice to the investiture quarrel without feeling pity for him," writes Gregorovius.

CALLISTUS II
Guido, Count of Burgundy
2nd, February 1119 to 13th, December 1124

Callistus was related to the Salians and the Capets; he was elected in Cluny and confirmed in Rome. In 1119 at the Imperial Diet of

Tibur, the Pope and the emperor concluded the "Imperial Peace," which was, however, very short-lived. Callistus excommunicated the emperor at a synod in Reims and returned to Rome; the anti-pope "Gregory VIII" fled, was taken prisoner by the Normans and sent by the Pope to a monastery. Eventually the investiture quarrel was settled by the Concordat of Worms signed on 23rd, September 1122, by which Henry V renounced the right to elect bishops, while the Pope, for his part, admitted the right of the emperor to be present at the election of imperial bishops and abbots and to invest them with the sceptre and regalia; it was hoped that this would result in the abandonment of force and of simony. In 1123 the ninth General Council was summoned to the Lateran—it was the first General Council to be held in the West–to sanction the decrees of the Concordat of Worms. Callistus erected the papal altar, which was in use for four hundred and seventy years and which is underneath the present papal altar in St. Peter's.

HONORIUS II
Lamberto dei Fagnani
15th, December 1124 to 13th, February 1130

In place of the Houses of Tusculum and Crescentius which had previously exercised so great an influence on the papal election the power of the wealthy Jewish House of Pierleoni and of the notorious Frangipani began to make itself felt. "Celestinus II," who was legally elected by the cardinals, at once laid down his office and was afterwards elected anti-pope. Honorius's election was contrived by the Frangipani. A few months later the Salian Imperial House came to an end with the death of Henry V and, with Honorius's agreement, Lothar III ascended the throne. Honorius quarrelled with the Normans.

INNOCENT II
Gregorio Papareschi
14th, February 1130 to 24th, September 1143

Honorius had made efforts to secure the free election of his successor, but in spite of this only a few hours after the Cardinal of Sant' Angelo had been legally elected, the majority of the cardinals elected "Anacletus II" Pierleoni, who with the support of King Roger of Sicily managed to maintain himself in Rome until his death in 1138. Pierleoni drove Innocent out of Rome and he fled to France where he found support from Bernard of Clairvaux. Several synods in five different countries declared their support for Innocent, who returned to Rome with Lothair III, whom he crowned. The Pope had to take flight again after the emperor's departure, even though St. Bernard of Clairvaux was now gaining support for him on all sides; even after the Pope's return to Rome another anti-pope, "Victor IV" was set up, but he yielded to the Pope after a short while. In 1135 Conrad, the first Hohenstaufen, succeeded to the throne of Germany and the great struggles between the Guelphs and the Hohenstaufens or Ghibellines began: the former identified themselves with the papacy, the latter with the empire. In 1139 Innocent summoned the tenth General Council to the Lateran; in the course of the council the schism of "Anacletus II" was condemned, the laws against simony were newly defined and Arnold of Brescia, a pupil of Abelard, who had fomented a rising against the Pope in 1143, was condemned. The disorders which arose at this time were to last for twenty-four years.

CELESTINUS II
Guido di Castello
26th, September 1143 to 8th, March 1144

Celestinus's short pontificate was devoted to the vain attempt to settle the disorders which had risen under his predecessor. During his pontificate Héloise's unhappy lover Abelard, whose pupil Celestinus had most probably been, died in the Cluniac monastery of St. Marcel in Chalons.

LUCIUS II
Gherardo Caccianemici
12th, March 1144 to 15th, February 1145

Lucius, too, was incapable of mastering the situation in Rome, where Giordani Pierleoni, the brother of "Anacletus II" had declared himself Patricius and Head of the Republic. Lucius received no aid whatsoever and personally took charge of the siege of the capital, in the course of which he was fatally wounded.

EUGENIUS III
Bernardo Paganelli
15th, February 1145 to 8th, July 1153

Bernard of Clairvaux, under whom Eugene had studied, dedicated his work *De Consideratione* to this pious monk. Eugenius's pontificate was largely taken up with continuous struggles and he spent but a short while in Rome; the disturbances started by Arnold of Brescia reached such a pitch in 1143 that savage looting broke out in the city and the republic was proclaimed. Eugenius resided first in Viterbo, moved to France in 1147 and later to Trier. At his command St. Bernard sent out the call for a new crusade, but it remained unanswered. Eugenius was unable to return to Rome, even for a short period, until 1149. Conrad III died on 1152 and was succeeded by Frederick Barbarossa. Even as Pope, Eugenius, who was beatified in 1872, retained the monastic humility which he had learned in Clairvaux.

ANASTASIUS IV
Corrado della Subarra
12th, July 1153 to 5th, December 1154

The pontificate of the aged Anastasius, who was famed for his gentleness passed without incident.

HADRIAN IV
Nicholas Breakspeare
4th, December 1154 to 1st, September 1159

Hadrian is the only Englishman who has, so far, become Pope. He went to France as a poverty-stricken priest, was taken to Rome by Eugenius III, who made him cardinal of Albano and sent him as his legate to Norway where he established the church. Hadrian exerted all his energies in trying to restore order in Rome after the disturbances caused by Arnold of Brescia and even went so far as to impose the interdict upon the city. He crowned Frederick Barbarossa emperor on 18th, July 1155, but because Frederick had entered the city as a conqueror, the people rose against him and he left the city taking Hadrian and the cardinals with him. He probably ordered Arnold's execution shortly afterwards. When the emperor had departed Hadrian turned his attention unsuccessfully to William of Sicily, the son of Roger II, who was busy laying waste the Southern provinces and was threatening the Pontifical State. Hadrian also made enemies again with the emperor, who at the Imperial diet held on the Roncaglian fields at Piacenza in 1158 was, with the support of the University of Bologna, trying to extend his authority in the interests of imperialistic absolutism and to the detriment of the papacy and in so doing was interfering with the legal rights of the papacy. Hadrian died in Anagni—a strong, awe-inspiring figure very reminiscent of Gregory VII, whose ideas he shared.

ALEXANDER III
Orlando Bandinelli
7th, September 1159 to 30th, August 1181

The pontificate of this famous scholar was disturbed by a schism which involved no fewer than four anti-popes: the first of these was supported by Barbarossa and is known as "Victor IV" although there had already been an anti-pope with that title in 1138. The Pontifical State was threatened and Alexander who had been "exiled" by the anti-pope was forced to flee to France, where the majority of provinces recognized him: he resided in Sens. The anti-pope died in 1164 and was succeeded by "Paschal III" who was forced by Barbarossa to canonize Charlemagne and to crown Barbarossa emperor, for the second time, in Rome on 1st, August 1167. Alexander's return to Rome, for a short while, had been made possible by an uprising against Barbarossa in Northern Italy in 1165. In 1168 the emperor nominated the third anti-pope, "Calixtus III." Alexander now placed himself at the head of the Confederacy of Lombardy, which defeated the emperor at Legnano in 1176: Verdi perpetuated the glory of this fight for freedom in his opera, *La Battaglia di Legnano,* composed in 1849. Barbarossa entered into negotiations with Alexander and in 1177 the Peace of Venice was concluded, followed in 1183 by the Peace of Constance, which he concluded with the Lombards; he recognized Alexander and withdrew his support from "Calixtus III." The great scene at which the emperor knelt before Alexander and received the kiss of peace from him is one of the most moving in history: Vasari painted it in a fresco in the sala regia of the Vatican. Alexander summoned the eleventh General Council in the Lateran in 1179, and among other business that was contracted was the confirmation of the peace, the promulgation of new measures for papal elections, by which a clear two-thirds majority was necessary, the condemnation of the heresies of the Waldenses, the Catharia and the Albigenses and the reservation of the right of canonization to the Holy See. For a short time the Roman nobility set up "Innocent III" as the fourth and last anti-pope of this pontificate. Unrest once more drove Alexander from Rome and he died in Civita Castellana. During his pontificate in 1170, Thomas à Becket, the great primate of England was murdered by knights of Henry II: Alexander canonized the martyr Becket in 1174 and Bernard of Clairvaux one year later. This Pope, who was distinguished above all else by his moderation was one of the truly great figures of his age. Pisanello's decorative fresco depicting the history of Alexander III in the Doge's palace in Venice has been destroyed.

LUCIUS III
Ubaldo Allucingoli
1st, September 1181 to 25th, November 1185

Allucingoli was cardinal bishop of Ostia and Velletri and was only able to stay in Rome for a few months. In 1184 a settlement was reached, in Verona, of disputes, dating from the time of Gregory VII, which had arisen with Barbarossa over the estates of the Countess Mathilde, who had bequeathed them first to the Holy See and then to the emperor. The heresies condemned under Alexander were again condemned in Verona and the inquisition was inaugurated. The betrothal of Barbarossa's son Henry to Constance of Sicily, Roger II's daughter, which brought about the union of the two empires, was an event which was to have an effect until the middle of the thirteenth century. Lucius died in Verona.

URBAN III
Uberto Crivelli

25th, November 1185 to 20th, October 1187

Urban's short pontificate was filled with renewed disputes with Barbarossa. Before his election in Verona Crivelli had been archbishop of Milan: he never entered Rome as Pope. King Henry, Barbarossa's son, whose marriage with Constance took place on 27th, January 1186 in Milan, invaded the Pontifical State. Urban died in Ferrara: shortly before his death the Sultan Saladin had captured Jerusalem which had been captured by Geoffrey of Bouillon in 1099 during the first crusade.

GREGORY VIII
Alberto del Morra

21st, October 1187 to 18th, December 1187

Gregory spent the two months of his pontificate in trying to settle the dispute with Barbarossa and in supporting the idea of a crusade. He died in Pisa and he, too never set foot in Rome.

CLEMENT III
Paolo Scholari
19th, December 1187 to 30th, March 1191

Clement had been cardinal bishop of Palestrina and was at last able to return to Rome where he officially recognized the Senate, which had been in existence for twenty-four years. The Pontifical State which King Henry had seized was also restored. Clement's pontificate was overshadowed by the third crusade, during which Barbarossa was drowned near Seleucia. The use of bells during the celebration of the Mass was begun during Clement's pontificate.

CELESTINUS III
Giacinto Boboni-Orsini
30th, March 1191 to 8th, January 1198

For the third time a member of the House of Orsini was elected Pope. The first official act of this eighty-five year old Pope was the coronation of Henry VI, who was on his way to Sicily, where, by virtue of his marriage to Constance, he intended to seize the Norman inheritance: he was not successful in this until 1194. On Christmas Day 1194 he was crowned King of Sicily in Palermo, and on the following day his son and successor, Frederick, was born, who was destined to be one of the greatest rulers of the Middle Ages. Henry, who was one of the most cruel Kings in the Middle Ages, tyrannized Sicily and, as Gregorovius says: "dreamed of the enslavement of Italy and the destruction of the Gregorian papacy." He threatened the Pontifical State for the second time and broke with the Pope, whom he pre-deceased by three months.

INNOCENT III
Lothario, Count of Segni
8th, January 1198 to 16th, July 1216

When Innocent, who was the nephew of Clement III and cardinal of San Sergio, was elected at the age of thirty-seven, Walther von der Vogelweide made his famous complaint about his too great youth. Innocent was a trained lawyer and theologian, a man of great intellectual gifts, whose whole efforts were bent to achieving the complete secular independence of the church; he soon succeeded in shaping Rome and the Pontifical State in accordance with his views and in doing so went a long way to meet Italian nationalist sentiment. Shortly before his death Henry VI reconciled himself with the Pope, and his widow, who recognized Innocent's feudal authority over Sicily, named him, on her death in 1198, the guardian of her son, Frederick II. In Germany, Philip of Swabia, the brother of Henry VI, was elected, but the Guelphs put up Otto, a son of Henry of Lion in opposition to him: after Philip's assassination, Otto was generally recognized and the Pope crowned him on 9th, October 1209. The next year, however, saw a breach between Rome and Otto, when the latter decided on the conquest of Sicily, the heritage of Innocent's ward, Frederick, and was excommunicated. The German princes withdrew their support from Otto and pledged themselves to Frederick as the future emperor: he was crowned in Mainz in 1212 and Otto was finally defeated in 1214 at the Battle of Bouvines. Soon after the election, Innocent began preparations for a new crusade, which took place in 1203, but the Doge Enrico Dandolo, who was in charge of the expedition ignored Innocent's protests and directed the attack against Constantinople, which the army proceeded to sack on two separate occasions before setting up a Latin empire which, though it endured for seventy-five years, never succeeded in establishing itself. The crusaders' infamous actions were partly responsible for exacerbating the schismatic situation which existed between East and West Rome. Innocent was involved in an action with England in 1206, when King John, who was short of land, attempted to occupy the estates of the Primacy of Canterbury by a wilful and illegal election. Innocent excommunicated John and laid the interdict upon England. John finally yielded to Innocent in 1213. In 1215 Innocent summoned the twelfth General Council to the Lateran, where its chief concern was the measures to be adopted against the Albigenses and the condemnation of a publication by Joachim of Fiore. A new crusade was arranged for 1217. Innocent died the year after the Council; the inscription on his tomb reads: "Misericordia superexaltatur

judico"; his skeleton was taken into the Lateran by Leo XIII.
Innocent did much to further the newly-formed and expanding
orders of the Franciscans and the Dominicans, and Thomas Aquinas
tells Dante of this in the eleventh canto of the *Paradiso* in the *Divine
Comedy*. In Assisi there is a painting by Giotto of a vision of
Innocent seeing in a dream Francis of Assisi, whom he first met
in 1210, support the basilica of the Lateran as it is on the point of
collapsing; a second fresco depicts the Pope's granting the saint
the right to preach and confirming the first rule of St. Francis, an
act which was painted for a second time by Giotto in Santa Croce
in Florence and by Ghirlandaio in Santa Trinita in the same city.
An important fresco by an anonymous artist which shows Innocent
and St. Francis is to be found in Sacro Speco in Subiaco, and a
contemporary mosaic from the old apse of St. Peter's is in the Villa
Catena near Poli. Innocent confirmed the doctrine of transubstan-
tiation or metamorphosis of the eucharistic elements. His works
were first published in Cologne in 1551. Innocent belongs among
the great historical figures of the world; simple as he was in his
personal life, he had a complete grasp of his function as the successor to St. Peter and as Christ's representative upon earth, and
it was he who conceived the monarchistic view of the papacy with
Rome in the position of a feudal overlord above all the empires of
the world; an idea which he represented to the world with dignity
and authority, as the true Pontifex Maximus of the Middle Ages.
He anticipated in his life much of the teaching of St. Thomas Aquinas, at the same time reaching back in his concept of the papacy to
the *Ordo Melchisedech*, so that simony meant no less than treason
and lèse-majesté to him. The living example of Innocent III was
of the greatest significance for the coming era: to him is owed the
foundation of the Ospedale di Santo Spirito, which was rebuilt by
Sixtus IV.

HONORIUS III
Cencio Savelli
18th, July 1216 to 18th, May 1227

The tutor to the young Frederick II and the Cardinal of San
Giovanni e Paolo, the kind and noble Savelli, a man of great

86

strength of character, whose family had already provided two incumbents of the Holy See, was elected to the pontificate, in Perugia, when he was already an old man. He was quite unable to match the energy and genius of his predecessor. His first thought was for the fifth crusade which had been decided upon at the Lateran Council and he called upon Frederick II to fulfill his obligations, for although Frederick had made his preparations, he was delaying his departure; as a result of this and because of the inability of the leaders, the crusade was unsuccessful. Honorius crowned Frederick and his wife Constance on 22nd November, 1220 and again demanded a promise that Frederick would set out on a crusade, but Frederick's only concern at this time was the fortification of his Sicilian empire; however, the Pope did contrive to extract the promise later on in the Treaty of San Germano, with the proviso that if Frederick did not fulfill it he would be excommunicated. Honorius confirmed the Dominican order in 1216 and the Franciscan order in 1223; events mentioned by Dante in the eleventh canto of the *Paradiso*. There is a fresco by Giotto which shows St. Francis preaching before Honorius.

GREGORY IX
Ugolino, Count of Segni
19th, March 1227 to 22nd, August 1241

Ugolino, who was the cardinal bishop of Ostia and already an old man on his election, had exactly the same outlook as his relative Innocent III, yet he gives the impression of being far less well balanced. He had formerly been cardinal protector of the Franciscan order and he canonized his friend Francis on 16th July, 1228, not two years after his death. Frederick II kept his promise, set out on a crusade, but returned a few days after embarking because of ill health—whether genuine or simulated, is not known —in any case he was excommunicated according to the terms of the Treaty of San Germano which he had made with Honorius III. The excommunication which was formally justified, was nevertheless a mistake on the Pope's part for it merely gave grounds for reprisals. In 1228, in spite of his excommunication, the emperor went to Cyprus and Acre where he was received enthusiastically and soon a split developed here, too, between the supporters of the Pope on the one hand and the supporters of Frederick on the other. Frederick gained some important successes, won back the Holy Places for Christendom and fortified the kingdom of Jerusalem, where he crowned himself king. At this time Gregory invaded Sicily after the pontifical state had been attacked: Frederick returned, defeated the papal troops and reconciled himself with the Pope in 1230 by the Peace of Ceperano, which was negotiated by Hermann von Salza, the famous master of the Teutonic Order. Frederick, who returned the occupied areas of the pontifical state, accorded the church certain rights within his empire and visited Gregory in Anagni, was received back into communion with the church. This peace endured for almost ten years until Frederick still striving for absolutism and wishing to subject Lombardy and the League of Cities which had opposed the emperor since the days of Barbarossa, to his centralized power, surrounded the pontifical state and so sparked off a new rising. He was again excommunicated in 1239 and from this time on the struggle continued until the final tragic collapse of the Hohenstaufen dynasty: Gregory's declaration, which was denied by the emperor, that Frederick had described Moses, Jesus and Mahomet as the greatest deceivers in history has never been proved, but it did however, exert a significant influence upon public opinion. Frederick's answer to his excommunication was to seize one hundred prelates who were on their way to a council, which had been summoned in Rome in 1241, and which was now made impossible by Frederick's action. He was planning a march on Rome when Gregory died. A few months before Gregory's death the Mongols were finally driven out of Europe at the Battle of Liegnitz. In 1231 Gregory organized the Inquisition, which he turned over to the Dominicans. In 1234, by means of his decretals, he commanded the earliest form of the *Codex Juris Canonici* to be drawn up. A contemporary fresco in Subiaco showing Gregory in Assisi depicts St. Francis showing the sleeping Pope the stigma of the wound in his side. According to many sources Gregory was almost a hundred years old when he died. He was a harsh and inflexible Pope, but one of imposing stature.

CELESTINE IV
Goffredo Castiglione
25th, October 1241 to 10th, November 1241

Celestine's actual election is important for it was the first time that the cardinals had been enclosed at the conclave. Senator Matteo Orsini used the methods customary at this time and shut them up in most brutal fashion using armed force where necessary, so that some of the cardinals died as a result of this ill-treatment and the majority fell ill. The cardinals were split into two factions, the stronger of which wished to make peace, while the smaller desired the continuation of the war against Frederick II, who was encamped in front of the gates of Rome and was exerting pressure upon the city. The result was that Celestine was elected, only to die a few days later, after he had excommunicated Matteo Orsini for the way in which he had treated the cardinals.

INNOCENT IV
Sinisbaldo Fieschi, Count of Lavagna
25th, June 1243 to 7th, December 1254

Those cardinals who had suffered at the last conclave fled from Rome, and only three who were loyal to the emperor remained. Senator Matteo Orsini had the most important of these three, Giovanni Colonna, thrown into prison and so started the long era of hatred which had destructive effects for both these great families. Two other cardinals had been held prisoner by the emperor since 1241, and the conclave could not be held until May 1243. Innocent, Cardinal of San Lorenzo was, by birth, a friend of the emperor and Frederick II later said that he had lost a cardinal who was his friend, only to find an enemy in the Pope. At the outset no one doubted that Innocent desired peace and Frederick II who was still excommunicated was ready to make any concession which was asked of him. The whole situation was aggravated by Cardinal Rainer of Viterbo, who, possessed of an almost apocalyptic hatred of the Emperor, slaughtered the imperial troops. Attempts at mediation by Louis IX (Saint Louis) of France, one of the most brilliant figures of the century, met with only partial success: true, the peace of 1244 was concluded, but when Frederick invited the Pope to a meeting at Narni in order to clear up outstanding questions, Innocent made the fatal mistake of deciding to flee to France. Here in 1245 he summoned the thirteenth General Council to Lyons: Louis the Pious again tried to intervene and persuade the Pope to receive the Emperor back into communion, but Frederick, who had declared himself ready to take any course necessary for reconciliation gave yet another ground for the breach when he plundered Viterbo as a reprisal. Rainer immediately began to influence the Council of Lyons by a series of inflammatory pamphlets, which went beyond the bounds of sense and moderation. Innocent declared the emperor deposed and in 1247 named William of Holland as his successor. The Pope rejected all efforts to make peace: he not only decided on a sixth crusade, but also on another against the Emperor—both of which failed. King Louis was taken prisoner and tried, for the last time, to persuade Innocent to make peace with the Emperor, threatening him that if he failed he would expel him from France. The King of England, for his part, refused to shelter the Pope because of his extreme loathing for his fiscal policy. Innocent finally returned to Italy in 1250, after Frederick's death; here King Conrad IV and King Manfred were strengthening anew the power of the Hohenstaufens and the struggle with the Pope continued until Innocent's death in Naples, where he was planning the conquest of Sicily. The picture of Innocent presented by history is a discordant one unrelieved by any inner greatness. Innocent was sharply rebuked by King Louis for his continual overstepping of the bounds of his competence; he was a politician who was completely reckless of the means which he used to achieve his ends, deposing and excommunicating kings in a manner which can only be called senseless–in addition to the Emperor, he excommunicated Sancho II of Portugal and James I of Aragon. He it was who gave permission to the secular rulers to use the rack on heretics.

ALEXANDER IV
Rinaldo, Count of Segni
12th, December 1254 to 25, May 1261

Alexander IV who was the third Pope of the House of Segni, the cardinal bishop of Ostia, a nephew of Gregory IX and so a relative of Innocent III, tried as gently as possible to continue the policies of his predecessor. He enfieffed Edmund of Lancaster, the eight year old son of Henry III of England with Sicily, although he was never able to take possession of it, for in the meanwhile Manfred, the son of Frederick II was crowned in Palermo in 1258 and started to exert pressure upon the Pontifical State, so that the Pope was forced to live for some time in Naples before returning to Rome. Alexander supported William of Holland as anti-king in Germany, but after William's death he remained neutral when Richard of Cornwall and Alphonso X ("The Wise") of Castille stood for election as King, though he did oppose the election of Conradin, the last of the Hohenstaufens. In 1260 he elevated Albertus Magnus, the *doctor universalis* to the See of Regensburg. In the same year one of the most tragic phenomena of the Middle Ages, the penitent movement of the flagellants arose, as a result of the general sorrow of the time, probably appearing first in Perugia, but later extending its influence to Rome.

URBAN IV
Jacques Pantaléon
29th, August 1261 to 2nd, October 1264

The College of Cardinals which by now had only eight members left, agreed in Viterbo to elect the Patriarch of Jerusalem, a cobbler's son, who happened to be present at the time. Urban resided in Viterbo and never set foot in Rome. Germany could not reach agreement on the question of succession, and in order to protect himself from Manfred, Urban took one of the most fateful decisions in the history of the papacy: he summoned Charles of Anjou, the terrible brother of King Louis, to Italy, and handed Sicily, which was still regarded as a papal fief, over to him. Urban introduced the Feast of Corpus Christi into the church in 1264, the office for which was composed by Thomas Aquinas in 1261, while he was theological adviser at Urban's court in either Viterbo or Orvieto.

CLEMENT IV
Guy le Gros Foulques
5th, February 1265 to 29th, November 1268

Clement was the court lawyer of Louis IX, and did not take orders until after his wife's death: he subsequently became Cardinal of Santa Sabina. He was elected in Perugia after a *sedes vacans* of four months. Charles I of Anjou had, meanwhile, occupied Sicily after the death of Manfred at Benevent in 1266. In the third canto of the *Purgatorio*, Manfred laments to Dante that he had been mercilessly exhumed by Clement. The excommunicated corpse and his skeleton were "exposed on the banks of the Verde, and torn to pieces by the wind and the rain." Conradin, the last of the Hohenstaufens, a youth of fourteen, fell into Charles's hands in 1268, and was executed by him, in order to assuage his thirst for vengeance on Manfred's widow and her children. On the other hand he did nothing to prevent the action, a fact which has blackened his memory. The papacy gained nothing from Charles of Anjou, who had been appointed by Clement, since he did all in his power to undermine its reputation. Clement supported the efforts of Charles in Byzantium, where, as the heir of Baudoin II who had fled, he was attempting to revive the crumbling Latin empire which had been in existence for forty-seven years, having been founded during the crusade of 1214. The emperor Michael VIII, Palaeologos, managed to meet this danger. Clement, who died in Viterbo, was never guilty of nepotism. A few weeks after his election to the Holy

Seat, Dante was born: Dante's universal poem, the *Divine Comedy,* was to become the court of judgment on the great men of his century, among whom were numbered many of the Popes. Thomas Aquinas, too, was active in the court at Viterbo for the two years immediately preceding the Pope's death. At the time of Conradin's death he was writing his tract *On Rulers and the Reward of Kings.*

GREGORY X
Tebaldo Visconti
1st, September 1271 to 10th, January 1276

After the death of Clement IV there was a *sedes vacans* of three years, during which time the eighteen cardinals in Viterbo were unable to reach agreement on whom to elect. It was the longest interregnum since the year 307, and coincided with the "terrible" period when Germany was without an emperor after the fall of the Hohenstaufen dynasty. Gregory was not a cardinal, but an archdeacon of Liège. At the time of his election he was at Acre in the Holy Land. He entered Rome, in which neither of his predecessors had ever set foot, on the 14th March, 1272, and on the same day King Enzio, the sole surviving son of Frederick II, died in Bologna, forgotten by the whole world after having been held prisoner for twenty-two years. With decisive support from Gregory, Rudolf of Hapsburg, the founder of the archdynasty which reigned until 1918, was elected King. During the period in which there had been no Pope, the unsuccessful seventh crusade had taken place. In the course of this crusade, King Louis died of the plague, whilst his more retiring brother, King Charles I of Anjou managed to chaffer away all that had been gained in the East. The fourteenth General Council was summoned to Lyons in 1274. At this time the Pope's main thought was for the new union with the Eastern Church, which had been realized between him and the emperor Michael VIII, the founder of the Palaeologic dynasty, but which had met with little support in Byzantium. Gregory enacted new regulations for the conclave, with a view to avoiding another endless *sedes vacans.* These regulations, however, though cast in a milder form, were based on the "conclave" held before the election of Celestine IV, and consequently aroused bitter opposition among the cardinals. Gregory tried in vain to resuscitate the thought of a crusade. A few days after the end of the Council in Lyons came the death of St. Bonaventura, the cardinal bishop of Albano, the *doctor seraphicus* and the greatest saint of the Franciscan order after St. Francis. Bonaventura had not lent decisive support to Gregory's election, but he had contributed much to the union which had been reached in Lyons. Thomas Aquinas, the *doctor angelicus,* had died before him, in March of the same year, while on his way to Lyons. Rudolf's coronation, which had been planned, did not take place during Gregory's pontificate. Gregory was not a man of great intellectual gifts, but he was a noble priest whose thoughts were for nothing but peace and reconciliation. After his death, which took place in Arezzo while he was journeying home from Lyons, he was mourned by all except Charles of Anjou. He was canonized in 1713.

INNOCENT V
Pierre de Champagni
21st, January to 22nd, June 1276

Innocent V, the one-time archbishop of Lyons and later cardinal bishop of Ostia was the first Dominican to become Pope. This famous Pope, who is sometimes known as *famosissimus doctor,* was a supporter of Charles of Anjou, and could only achieve minor successes in the sphere of reconciliation during his short pontificate. He was canonized in 1898.

HADRIAN V
Ottobono Fieschi, Count of Lavagna
11th, July to 18th, August 1276

This aged man, a nephew of Innocent IV and the cardinal deacon of Sant'Adriano was elected in a conclave held under the supervision of Charles of Anjou. The severity of this conclave caused Hadrian to rescind the regulations for the conclave laid down by Gregory X. His pontificate passed without incident. Dante meets Hadrian in the *Purgatorio* among the Gluttons, and Hadrian tells him that he first recognized the "deceptions of life" as such, when he was the chief shepherd, and that the papacy was nothing but a burden to him.

JOHN XXI
Peter Rebuli-Giuliani
8th, September 1276 to 20th, May 1277

The cardinal bishop of Tusculum is the only Portuguese to have become Pope. He ought really to be designated John XX: an anti-pope 'John XX', who in fact never existed, was assumed by Gregory VI, and included in his list of Popes. As a result of this error, a false numbering of all the Popes called John came about from this time on. John made peace with Philip the Bold of France and Alphonso X of Castile, and was concerned first with the strengthening of the alliance of 1274, and secondly with a new crusade. There is no doubt that the papacy suffered a loss when John was killed by the collapse of a ceiling. He was considered a scholar of great gifts in the fields of scholasticism and medicine. At the time of the Council of Lyons he was still functioning as the physician-in-ordinary to Gregory X. His works were disseminated throughout all lands.

NICHOLAS III
Giovanni Gaetano Orsini
25th, November 1277 to 22nd, August 1280

The cardinal of San Nicola in Carcere, an inquisitor-general and son of the senator Matteo Orsini, who had organized the cruel conclave of 1241, Nicholas was the third Pope to come from the House of Orsini, which attained, through him, to its full power. Whilst possessing many of the characteristics of Innocent III, he was by no means as great a man as Innocent. As a bitter enemy of Charles I of Anjou, he reduced the latter's growing influence, and demonstrated his skill as a politician, especially vis-à-vis Rudolf of Hapsburg, from whom he received a golden Bull, guaranteeing the complete freedom and independence of the pontifical state. He also further strengthened the union with Byzantium. Nicholas was an exclusively secular ruler. Dante's verdict on him and on his boundless simoniac nepotism, is inspired as much by righteous anger as by a sacred respect for the power of the keys of St. Peter. In the nineteenth canto of the *Inferno*, Nicholas, the simoniac, confesses his great guilt to the poet in the fiery, rock-bound chasm, and reveals his one real interest: the elevation of the House of Orsini. In 1278 he built the Sancta Sanctorum, the private chapel in the Lateran. The old Vatican palace is his work.

MARTIN IV
Simon Mompitié
22nd February, 1281 to 28th March, 1285

Nicholas III died in his castle at Viterbo, the old Papal seat near Rome, and for this reason it was here that the election of Mompitié, the cardinal of Santa Cecilia, took place. Martin had been keeper of the seal under King Louis IX and Urban's Legate in the kingdom of France, where he had conducted the negotiations leading to Charles I of Anjou's taking over Sicily. As both Popes by the names of Marinus are counted as Martins, he is known as Martin IV. He was completely dominated by Anjou, who regained under Martin what he had lost under Nicholas III. The fateful policies which Martin pursued, of supporting Anjou, played their part in destroying the union which Gregory X had effected with Byzantium in 1274, since Charles was hostile to Byzantium. On the 31st March, 1282 the Sicilian Vespers, which enjoyed the support of the emperor Andronicus II of Byzantium, befell the Pope. Like the Battle of Legnano, this event has been glorified on the stage by Verdi. It brought about the end of the hereditary rule of the hated House of Anjou in Sicily, and brought to the throne King Peter III ("the Great") of Aragon, the son-in-law of Manfred and heir to the Staufens and the King of Spain. It was a major error on Martin's part to identify himself more closely with Anjou by excommunicating Peter. Large areas of Italy rose up against the French. The Pope, who had never resided in Rome, but in Orvieto, died in Perugia a few months after Charles of Anjou, whom he had once brought with him into the country. He was a steady and modest, yet feeble Pope. Dante banished him into the company of the gluttons in the twenty-fourth canto of *Purgatorio*.

HONORIUS IV
Giacomo Savelli
2nd April, 1285 to 3rd April, 1287

Honorius, the cardinal of Santa Maria in Cosmedin, a man of high reputation, old and almost completely paralysed, assumed the name Honorius in honor of his great-uncle, the first Pope of the House of Savelli. He was elected in Perugia and then returned to Rome. He exercised greater caution in dealing with the ding-dong struggles of his day, than had his predecessors. Nevertheless, he excommunicated Peter III's son, James of Aragon, who had inherited Sicily. Charles II, the son of Charles I of Anjou was a prisoner of Aragon: the kingdom of Naples, which still belonged to him, found in Honorius a protector against all kinds of tyrannical attack. The coronation of Rudolf of Hapsburg which had again been planned, still did not take place, and Rudolf was never to receive the imperial crown in Rome. The Pope did a great service by instituting chairs of oriental languages, especially Arabic, at the University of Paris in connection with his missionary plans on Islamic territory and among the Eastern schismatics. His magnificent tomb stands in Santa Maria in Aracoli.

NICHOLAS IV
Giralomo Masci
22nd February, 1288 to 4th April, 1292

The cardinal bishop of Palestrina, legate in the Orient and the patriarch of Byzantium, was elected after a *sedes vacans* of eleven months. He was the first minister-general of the Franciscan order to become Pope. A peace-loving, unselfish man, he resided chiefly outside Rome. After Charles II of Anjou was released from Spanish captivity, Nicholas crowned him King of Naples in 1288, but Sicily finally remained in the hands of Aragon. The medieval crusading idea finally collapsed with the fall of Acre on 13th May, 1291, two months before the death of Rudolf of Hapsburg. This simple, learned Pope was the founder of the universities of Montpelier and Lisbon: his portrait is in the apse of the Lateran Church, and on Torriti's mosaics in the apse of S.M. Maggiore.

CELESTINE V
Pietro Angelari da Murrone
5th July, 1294 to 13th December, 1294

The election of Celestine which took place in Perugia after a *sedes vacans* of two years was one of the most remarkable happenings in history—his tragedy, one of the most moving in the history of the papacy. After the death of Nicholas IV, the cardinals, split by the sharp division between the houses of Orsini and Colonna, formed two factions and were unable to reach agreement. The other two factors in this conflict were, on the one hand, Charles II of Anjou, who was concerned with the re-conquest of Sicily, and on the other, the Franciscan spirituals, who were distinguished from the conventuals chiefly by the fact that they rejected the papacy as a secular form of government, and recognized the prophecies of Joachim da Fiore and the ideal of absolute poverty. Charles II exercised a great influence on the papal election, which did not choose a cardinal but a hermit, who had been withdrawn from the world for fifty years. During this period, he had lived a life of contemplation as head of a thriving Benedictine congregation, on top of Mount Majella near Aquila in the Abruzzi mountains on the borders of the Kingdom of Naples and the Pontifical State. Charles II personally led the ass which bore this unhappy man to his misfortune through Aquila, where Celestine was crowned. Whilst the King saw in the election merely an opportunity for political advancement, the spirituals, and with them a large body of Christendom, saw in Celestine the angel pope of the Apocalypse, that object of so many ancient prophecies. Charles forced Celestine to reside in Naples, where he hoped to turn him into his puppet. Inside the college of cardinals, Cardinal Benedetto Caëtani had for the first time, achieved a decisive influence. One of the few governmental measures undertaken by Celestine was the revival of Gregory X's orders governing the conclave. He was so incapable of performing his office, that after five months he abdicated. There is little doubt that Cardinal Caëtani exercised a decisive influence on this action. The document of abdication which was prepared by Caëtani, constituted a most unusual step and marked the destruction of all the hopes held by the spirituals who were Caëtani's most bitter enemies. Celestine was brought to Rome by his successor; he fled, was apprehended again and incarcerated in the Fumone fortress. Whilst Jacopone da Todi, in one of his poems warned Celestine against the world, and Petrarch praised him for his humility, Dante, in the third canto of the *Inferno*, thrust this unhappy man among the cowards, because he "refused the great commission which had been laid upon him," and so in Dante's eyes, rendered impossible the expected revival from within the church itself. Celestine, who died of natural causes in prison on 19th May, 1296 is still the object of the deepest veneration in the Abruzzi mountains. He was canonized by Clement V in 1313.

BONIFACE VIII
Benedetto Caëtani
24th December, 1294 to 11th October, 1303

Boniface was born at Anagni between 1220 and 1230; he was, on his mother's side, a nephew of Alexander IV. He was one of the most sinister and violent figures ever to ascend the Papal Throne. He had distinguished himself in several difficult missions, and was, like almost all his immediate predecessors a notable lawyer. He had been created deacon of San Nicola in Carcere by Martin IV. While still a cardinal he started to lay the foundations of power of the House of Caëtani—the present-day Dukes of Caëtani—Sermoneta and Teano. He secured the support of Charles II of Anjou for election. His first action on becoming Pope was the brutal arrest of his unhappy predecessor, who had fled, and whose resignation had not been recognized by the cardinals Jacopo and Pietro Colonna nor by the spirituals. Boniface had good grounds for fearing a schism. The conflict with the Colonna cardinals and with the poet-Spiritual Jacopone da Todi, who by signing their opposition manifesto in 1297 identified himself with them, took the most severe form. Both cardinals were deposed and excommunicated, their family seat, the lovely town of Palestrina, together with its churches, was razed by Boniface in an excess of destruction, and a new town called Civitas Papalis was built in its place. The pope confiscated the property of the Colonnas, partly to enrich his own family, the Caëtani, and partly for the Orsinis, with whom he wished to ingratiate himself. As a supporter of Anjou, he denied the right of the House of Aragon to the ownership and crown of Sicily, but his efforts in this direction came to nothing. The first condition for a new crusade, which he was actively planning, was peace between Philip IV (the Fair) of France and Edward I of England. His suggestion, made in 1298, in order to clarify the situation, that the status quo before the war should be restored was ignored. The Pope's refusal to come to the help of Flanders, which had been conquered by Philip IV, made the situation more difficult. In addition, the question which had been constantly recurring ever since the eleventh General Council, held by Alexander III, of taxation of churches and clergy, which had been rejected by the popes, except in cases of emergency, led Boniface to publish his notorious bull *Clericis Laicos* in 1296 with its insulting introduction stating that "the laity is the enemy of the clergy." After a temporary armistice, the latent enmity between the king and the pope broke out again. The crowning point of these conflicts came in 1302 when

Boniface issued his Bull *Unam Sanctam*. This Bull has been the subject of discussion for centuries, for it contains the conception of papal authority over all crowned heads and peoples, of the precedence of spiritual over secular affairs in the most exaggerated and crass form and conveys the idea that all existence outside the church should be subject to the church. The Catholic Church last referred to this Bull at the eighteenth General Council in Lateran in 1517. Insofar as pretension to temporal power in concerned, Leo XIII officially dissociated himself from it in his encyclical *Immortale Dei* in 1885. Holding to the same general viewpoint is the authoritative address delivered by Pius XII before the historians of all countries in December 7, 1955. The value of it as a document can only be assessed by reference to its author. Philip IV, one of the most unscrupulous tyrants of the time took up his struggle with Boniface again and ordered one of his men, who entered into a conspiracy with the Colonna and one or two other cardinals, to attack him in Anagni, where Boniface was staying in 1303. The defenseless Pope rejected the conditions which were laid before him, among which was his abdication, with the courageous words, "here is my neck, here is my head." A few weeks after this complete humiliation in Anagni–the abduction, which had been planned, did not succeed —the eighty-six year old Boniface died in Rome, in complete solitude. He was unable to achieve anything permanent in the political sphere. He found himself forced to make an agreement with King Albert, the successor of Rudolf of Hapsburg, because he was so completely taken up with the quarrel with France. The claims which he made to power made him completely blind to the realities of history and the political situation. In 1297 Boniface canonized the crusading King Louis IX of France. In 1300 he announced, from the loggia of the Lateran, the Church's first Holy Year. The event is recalled in Giotto's small fresco portrait in the Lateran basilica. He supported the arts only so long as they served his own personal glorification. Arnolfo di Cambio built him a burial chapel which was destroyed in the rebuilding of St. Peter's: a bust of the Pope by the same artist is in the Grotte Vaticane in Rome. It has been established that during his lifetime Boniface put up statues to himself in a large number of towns. The verdict which his contemporaries and posterity afterwards passed on this man who sowed nothing but hatred and who marked the end of an era is unanimous. He has also been compared to Innocent III, but whereas Innocent was a ruler, Boniface was nothing but an uncontrolled tyrant—if Innocent showed noble moderation and a sense of power, Boniface showed an extreme of pride, an immoderate lust for power and a pathological theatricality as on the occasion when he appeared before the cardinals dressed alternately as a Pope and an emperor shouting, "ego sum Caesar, ego imperator." Dante and Jacopone da Todi sat in judgment on him. The Pope had seized Jacopone and imprisoned him for five years, until the new Pope set him free. Dante on the other hand, who valued the idea of the papacy at the turn of the fourteenth century as did few others, and who had been the Florentine ambassador to Boniface, saw in him merely the prototype of degeneracy of the man, who, as Peter says to the poet in the twenty-seventh canto of the *Paradiso*, "usurped my power on earth." Nicholas III stands ready waiting for his successor in the fiery, rocky chasm of the simoniacs. The hey-day of the medieval papacy ended in two extremes, with the humble hermit, Pope Celestine V, and with Boniface VIII who was completely divorced from all that was spiritual.

BENEDICT XI
Niccolo Boccasini
22nd October, 1303 to 7th July, 1304

Benedict, who had once been the learned master-general of the Dominican Order and the cardinal bishop of Ostia, most probably supported his predecessor, but was in everything his opposite; dignified, pious, irreproachable, and conciliatory. His chief concern during his short pontificate was the resolution of the contradictions which had arisen out of conditions under Boniface VIII. He even revoked the excommunication of Philip the Fair, Boniface's opponent, and declared all measures taken against France invalid. Only the two Colonna cardinals were not restored to their offices, though the rest of the house was treated leniently by the Pope. Unrest caused Benedict to move to Perugia where he died. Clement XII canonized him in 1736. Benedict marks the beginning of the period of transition in the papacy, which lasted throughout the exile in Avignon and the great Western schism, until the year 1417, the opening of Martin V's pontificate and the beginning of the Renaissance. His impressive tomb, of the school of Arnolfo di Cambio, stands in San Domenico in Rome.

CLEMENT V
Raymond Bertrand de Goth
5th June, 1305 to 20th April, 1314

Clement, a former archbishop of Bordeaux, was born in Billandreau in Gascony, and succeeded to the Holy See through the intrigues of the cardinal Napoleon Orsini and the French cardinals. Boniface VIII's anti-French bias was now followed by Clement's equally fateful pro-French bias. The first surprising step which the new Pope took was to call the cardinals to Lyons for his coronation. Clement did not leave France during the whole of his pontificate and there began the so-called Babylonian exile of the church, which was to last for seventy years, during which time the papacy came to be completely dependent upon the kings of France. In 1309 Clement finally moved to Avignon. Two years later, at the fifteenth General Council at Vienna, the Pope gave his moral and active support to Philip the Fair of France in his terrible action to exterminate the Templars, an act of unforgivable subjugation on the Pope's part. The action which was organized by the state was undertaken because Philip wished to take over the property of the Templars. In the course of the action Clement did not hesitate to use the rack. He died in Roquemare a month after the Grand Master of the order had been burned at the stake. Only on one occasion did Clement oppose the King—after the assassination of King Albert of the Hapsburgs in 1308, Clement supported the election of Henry VII instead of a French prince, and had Henry crowned emperor in Rome in 1312, though he was later to frustrate his plans. Clement founded the universities of Perugia and Orléans. During his pontificate we see the beginning of that luxury at the court of Avignon, which was the disgust of the Christian West, together with all its concomitant phenomena, political jobbery, corruption and nepotism. This is the reason why Dante cursed Clement with that curse which has re-echoed down through the centuries. Dante had begun his *Divine Comedy* in 1307, and was constantly concerned with the idea of the incorruptible morality of the papacy. In the nineteenth canto of the *Inferno*, Pope Nicholas III in the fiery, rocky chasm of the simoniacs announces the descent into hell of Boniface VIII and of Clement V —"for after him the West shall have a worse, an unbridled shepherd of souls." Clement's nepotism was frightening; he made no less than five of his relatives cardinals, and several others bishops. Andrea da Firenze painted him in the *Triumph of St. Thomas* in the Capella degli Spagnuoli in Florence.

JOHN XXII
Jacques Duèze
7th August, 1316 to 4th December, 1334

Duèze, the son of a cobbler from Cahors, became bishop of Avignon and a cardinal. He was elected in Carpentras after a *sedes vacans* of nearly two years, during which the election was violently impeded on a number of occasions, under the influence of cardinal Napoleon Orsini and King Robert of Naples, Charles II of Anjou's successor. No less a person than Dante himself had warned the Italian cardinals to elect an Italian Pope and so pave the way for the return of the Pope to Rome, and put an end to the subjection of the papacy to France. John was a ruler in every sense of the word, he lacked self-control and was reckless, yet he was considerate to his enemies. He had a notable intellect and was an enthusiastic supporter of learning (who founded chairs of Hebrew, Arabic and even Chaldean at the universities of Paris, Oxford, Salamanca and Bologna). He had to dispute with the ever-growing movement of the

Franciscan spirituals, the fraticelli, and intervened in the struggles surrounding the election of the emperor, in which Louis of Bavaria finally emerged as victor, in 1322, against Frederick the Fair. John refused to recognize Louis and excommunicated him. In the confusion which arose from this act, the Minorite monk, Peter of Corbara, was put forward as the "anti-pope," Nicholas V, but he yielded to John in 1330. Although he was himself a modest man, always ready to help, he increased the wealth of the Holy See by a fiscal policy which aroused great anger—he left, in modern currency, about twelve million dollars. He was guilty of nepotism and the sale of benefices and thereby caused a serious increase in the sums collected. In this lies one of the seeds of the reformation, one of whose fore-runners can be seen in William of Occam, a Minorite, who opposed John. Dante mentions John and his predecessor together in the twenty-seventh canto of the *Paradiso*, in which Peter says of them both, "I see Cahorsins and Gascons thirsting for our blood. Must that which began so loftily, end so shamefully?" John, who died at the age of ninety, was also an outstanding poet and author. In 1323 he canonized Thomas Aquinas and in 1334 he established the Feast of the Trinity. He added the third row of jewels to the tiara, the second of which had been added by Nicholas II. John's bull *Docta sanctorum*, issued in 1322, is the first important and intelligent papal utterance on church music. John founded the Order of Christ, which is bestowed in one class. Giotto painted his portrait on the altar-piece of the cathedral of Lucca.

BENEDICT XII
Jacques Fournier
20th December, 1334 to 25th April, 1342

Fournier was the son of a baker, a highly moral and just man, who was opposed to all forms of nepotism. He had risen to the position of cardinal of Santa Prisca, and had been a Cistercian monk and bishop of Pamiers and Mirepoix. He concentrated his activity on the elimination of the abuses of his predecessors, on securing a general peace, and upon reform within the church, though here his energy often failed him. By his threats, Philip V had made peace with the emperor impossible. The Pope was also powerless to prevent war breaking out between France and England in 1340, nor was he able to carry out his wish of returning to Rome where factional strife still raged. In 1334 he ordered Petrarch to compose a poem expressing the wishes of Rome. His efforts to bring the Greek Orthodox church back also met with no success. Benedict built the huge and magnificent papal castle at Avignon, which in the words of Ludwig von Pastor, "symbolizes the state of the Papacy at that time." The cathedral church which stands nearby appears small and unimportant in comparison with the castle. This opposition typifies the Avignon epoch; "the recession of the ecclesiastical element and the predominance of the worldly, warrior-prince forces." Petrarch's coronation as a poet, on 8th April, 1341, took place during Benedict's pontificate, and marked the beginning of a new epoch in the history of European culture. Petrarch, who often raised his voice to the Popes of Avignon, laid down his crown on the High Altar of St. Peter's. Paolo of Siena's beautiful and impressive bust of the Pope is in the Museo Petriano in the Vatican.

CLEMENT VI
Pierre Roger de Beaufort
7th May, 1342 to 6th December, 1352

De Beaufort was born in the castle of Beaufort in Limoges. He was a Benedictine, archbishop of Rouen and cardinal of Santi Nereo ed Achilleo, a highly cultured man and a notable diplomat, who, before the final outbreak of the Hundred Years' War, succeeded in negotiating one more armistice between France and England. He also succeeded in bringing about the election of the emperor Charles IV and of becoming master of the Minorite movement within the church. In 1345 he introduced the reform of the calendar. Luxury, nepotism and extravagance, coupled with a fiscal policy which aroused the whole of Europe, reached a new level for the papacy under Clement, and various reproaches have been made about this pope's way of life, though he was otherwise kind and helpful. It redounds greatly to his honor that he gave all possible support to the Jews during the persecutions of 1348, and offered them sanctuary in his state, even though the Bulls which he issued for their protection had, for the most part, no effect. He was a patron of the arts, and especially of Simone Martini, who had been summoned to Avignon by Benedict XII, and died there in 1344. Only fragments of Simone's frescoes remain in the papal castle, whilst his *Holy Family*, which was painted in Avignon is now in Liverpool, and his Altar of the Passion is in Antwerp. Clement endowed Petrarch, the sharpest opponent of the exile in Avignon, with a canonry in Pisa, and had him collect manuscripts of Cicero for the papal library, until, in 1343, he sent him as ambassador to the court of Naples. By his appointment of the Greek monk Barlaam, Petrarch's teacher, to the University of Rome, Clement endowed the first Western chair of Greek. The rising of the Roman people under Cola di Rienzo took place during his pontificate and Rienzo actually went to Avignon as head of a delegation. In 1348 Clement bought Avignon from Queen Joanna I of Naples, the granddaughter of Robert, the third Angevin king, who had died without a male heir. Shortly before his death St. Brigitta of Sweden wrote to the pope of her revelation of a divine punishment. A portrait of Clement is preserved in the Capella degli Spagnuoli in Florence, in the painting *The Allegory of the Church.*

INNOCENT VI
Etienne Aubert

18th December, 1352 to 6th September, 1362

Aubert was born in Mont in Limousin; he was bishop of Nyon and Clermont, and cardinal bishop of Ostia, and he was greeted on his accession by a very hopeful prophecy of St. Brigitta of Sweden. The first act of this serious-minded ruler was to clean up the court, which had fallen into such a state under his predecessor, and to revoke many of the appointments made by him. He investigated consistently the benefices of the cardinals and then extended his efforts at reform to Germany. With the object of re-founding papal authority in Rome, he sent the Spanish grandee Aegidius Albornoz, an outstanding cardinal who was described by Gregorovius as the most gifted statesman ever to sit in the College of Cardinals, to prepare for the return of the Pope. Albornoz carried out his task with intelligence, energy, and decency. He may equally justly be regarded as the "second founder of the pontifical state," in the same way as his *Constitutiones Aegidianae* can be reckoned as the "most perfect fruit of civil law-giving in the church." The Constitutiones were valid, often, it must be admitted, only in theory, down to the time of Napoleon. Cola di Rienzo returned to Rome with Albornoz and was for a short while a senator. Innocent succeeded in obtaining a ten-year armistice in the Hundred Years' War at the peace of Brétigny. He kept his nepotism within very limited bounds. In 1354, Boccaccio came to the court of Avignon as Florentine ambassador.

URBAN V
Guillaume de Grimord
28th September, 1362 to 19th December, 1370

Petrarch praised the election of Grimord, an intelligent and saintly abbot born in Grisac in Languedoc in 1309. Urban was serious-minded and filled with a sense of justice, and soon won general recognition; a Mainz chronicle refers to him as "Lux mundi." He fought continuously and successfully against abuses within the church, making a beginning in his immediate surroundings. He even demanded that his own father should return a pension granted to him by the King. The decisive act of his pontificate was the return to Rome, to which he had been induced by St. Brigitta of Sweden, Petrarch, and the emperor, Charles IV, who had come in person to Avignon. Boccaccio, who had returned to the court of Avignon as Florentine ambassador, promised Urban, as early as 1364, to provide a guard of honor if he returned to Rome. On disembarking, the Pope was greeted by Cardinal Albornoz, now an old man, whose task of restoring papal authority and the Pontifical

108

State, on which he had worked for forty years, was now complete. Urban entered Rome on 16th October, 1367, to be greeted by Petrarch with a hymn for the occasion. Charles IV's journey to Rome in 1368 for his coronation presented a picture of unity between papacy and Empire. In 1369, the Byzantine, John V, Palæologus, went to Rome to join the Roman Catholic Church and end the schism. Like his predecessors, Urban supported the arts, and began the rebuilding of Rome, which had been seriously damaged during the recent disorders. In spite of this neither the warnings of St. Brigitta nor the remonstrances of Petrarch could stop the Pope from returning once more to Avignon, where, as Brigitta had prophesied, he soon died. Petrarch complains that Urban did not allow his deathbed to be borne before the altar of St. Peter's. Urban was canonized in 1870.

GREGORY XI
Piere Roger de Beaufort
30th December, 1370 to 27th March, 1378

The nephew of Clement VI—he bears the same name—was the cardinal deacon of Santa Maria Nuova and the last French Pope in history. He was intelligent, noble and cultured, but not outstanding. At the beginning of his pontificate, Italy, under Florentine leadership, rose against the authority of the French legates. Simultaneously a powerful regenerative force entered into the history of the papacy in the person of the twenty-five year old Catherine of Siena. This girl who could neither read nor write, but whose dictated letters and works are part of the literature of Italy, was one of the greatest phenomena among all the Western saints, and her vision of the papacy equalled that of Dante before her. It is to her that the final return of the Pope to Rome is owed, for she was personally responsible for inducing Gregory to return, after she had visited him in Avignon in 1376. Vasari painted the event on a fresco in the Sala Regia in the Vatican. With the utmost clarity Catherine weighed the guilt of the Florentine rebels and of the Pope in her most famous letters, and in her efforts to make peace

109

she told both sides some bitter truths. Gregory's greatest mistake, though it was doubtless unconscious, was to send the terrible Cardinal Robert of Geneva to Italy, where in February he was responsible for the bloodbath of Cesena, thus further reducing the reputation of the papacy. As a result of this Franco Sacchetti, the poet, called Gregory, who was innocent of the whole affair, "papa gustamondo" —the corrupter of the world. The Pope, by now thoroughly incensed, did not heed the advice of Catherine, but ordered a strict blockade of Florence. He died while still trying to make peace, troubled by pangs of conscience, because he had not carried out the ecclesiastical reforms, which St. Catherine had so urgently demanded. The first thing built by Gregory after his return to Rome was the campanile of Santa Maria Maggiore, the last Romanesque campanile in the city.

URBAN VI
Bartolomeo Prignano
8th April, 1378 to 15th October, 1389

Faced with impetuous demands of the Roman people for a Roman or Italian pope, the cardinals in the midst of wild tumult, elected the archbishop of Bari, a Neapolitan who was not a cardinal. Urban was a distinguished man of great integrity, a strong opponent of all forms of simony or secularization of the clergy, yet fatally autocratic, tyrannical and ruthless. For example, he embittered the cardinals by his public reprimands, which, though justified, were nevertheless unwise. Catherine of Siena in a courageous letter to the Pope said: "justice untempered with mercy would be more unjust than injustice." Urban who had summoned Catherine to Rome did not follow her advice and appoint unobjectionable people as cardinals. In Fondi, on 13th September, some five weeks after Urban's election, thirteen cardinals with French sympathies, who had fled from Rome, elected "the butcher of Cesena," Cardinal Robert of Geneva, anti-pope, with the title "Clement VII." By this act they started the great Western schism which was to last for fifty-two years and see no less than seven anti-popes. Indirectly, Urban can be held responsible for this schism. The anti-pope found considerable support and once more took up residence in Avignon. An unparalleled obstinacy, which led him to make an undignified war on Joanna of Naples, a supporter of the anti-pope, caused Urban completely to lose sight of his true goals. His tyrannical treatment of the College of Cardinals, which had once again attained to an international membership led, in 1385, to a conspiracy of several cardinals, who intended to depose Urban. The plot miscarried and Urban committed the unprecedented atrocity of having five of the cardinals subjected to the most fearful torture and then executed, with the result that two of the remaining cardinals went over to the anti-pope. Urban died, the object of general hatred, in Rome. In 1380, St. Catherine of Siena died at the age of thirty-three: her influence had become immeasurable and today she is not only the patron saint of Rome, but also the national saint of Italy.

BONIFACE IX
Pietro Tomacelli
2nd November, 1389 to 1st October, 1404

Tomacelli, the cardinal of Santa Anastasia, a young Neapolitan of thirty, of spotless reputation, kind and intelligent in his dealings, succeeded at once in making peace with Naples, and in winning it over from the anti-pope. Nepotism, simony and fiscal measures did, however, reduce the Pope's reputation and popularity. He strengthened the curia in Rome, fortified the capital and the Vatican and restored the Castel S. Angelo. He concerned himself, too, with the administration of justice, furthered learning and cared for the poor. He proved himself a circumspect secular ruler, but, as Pope he was a failure because he did nothing to repair the schism. In 1394 the Spaniard Peter de Luna had succeeded "Clement VII" as "Benedict XIII," making the situation more serious still. Both of these anti-popes had in their time taken part in the legal election of Urban VI. Boniface decreed the Feast of the Visitation.

111

INNOCENT VII
Cosmato de' Migliorati
17th October, 1404 to 6th November, 1406

This peace-loving, experienced, single-minded yet weak Neapolitan, the cardinal archbishop of Ravenna, did not leave his mark on history, but he is famous for his encouragement of learning and for the restoration of the University of Rome, founded by Boniface VIII, to which he appointed some of the leading professors. The wide degree to which humanists were summoned into the papal service is an important factor in the history of culture. We find, for instance, Leonardo Bruni and Poggio, the vicious author of the *facetiæ* and the most scurrilous author of his time, employed by Innocent as scribes in the curia, where they wrote the most elegant Latin. Poggio retained his office under eight popes. Innocent did nothing to repair the schism.

GREGORY XII
Angelo Correr
30th November, 1406 to 4th July, 1415

Correr, a Venetian cardinal, and a man of strict personal morals, soon became dependent upon his family and was caught up in the toils of nepotism. In order to end the schism, it had been agreed before the papal election that the new Pope should resign if the anti-pope would agree to do likewise. "Benedict XIII" announced that he was ready to do this. Gregory's relatives, serving their own ends, prevented his attending the meeting which had been arranged with the anti-pope, and Gregory did not fulfill his promise. As a result of this, seven cardinals left him and in 1409 formed a third schismatic group, which declared both pope and anti-pope deposed and elected a second anti-pope, the cardinal archbishop Petros Philargi of Milan, a Greek, who called himself "Alexander V," and who died one year later. His successor "John XXIII" was the worthless, crafty, ultra-worldly Baldassare Cossa, who, with the idea of strengthening his position with the Emperor Sigismund, finally agreed to call the Council of Constance in 1414. However, he soon aroused the sharpest opposition, and was arrested after trying vainly to flee to Germany. The Council declared him deposed and interned him, first in the castle of Gottlieben near Constance, where John Hus was also a prisoner, and later in the Castle of Hausen near Mannheim. However, before "John's" flight in 1415, Gregory, the legal Pope, had decided to abdicate on his own account in order to end the schism. Before his abdication he constituted the hitherto illegal council as the sixteenth General Council, which was to be empowered to elect a pope, and which condemned the teachings of Hus and Wycliffe. Gregory became a cardinal once more and died an old man of eighty on 18th October, 1417 in Recanati where he was functioning as Legate of the Mark of Ancona. Girolamo Muziano's portrait of Gregory hangs in the Pinacotheca Vaticana.

MARTIN V
Ottone Colonna
11th November, 1417, to 20th February, 1431

This cardinal deacon of San Giorgio in Velabro, who was born in 1368 in Genezzano near Rome, was the last and the greatest Pope of the House of Colonna. His election took place in Constance after a *sedes vacans* of nearly two and a half years. The anti-pope "Benedict XIII" defied all attempts at deposition and maintained himself in his Spanish castle. Martin resided, until the beginning of 1419, in Mantua; then moved for a year to Florence, where he received "John XXIII," who, though just released from prison in rags, showed for the first time, a dignified bearing. "John" reiterated his vow of abdication and lived until December, a poor cardinal bishop, withdrawn from the world. The monument on his grave by Michelozzo and the statue by Donatello which is in the baptistry at Florence are among the most beautiful works of the early renaissance. In 1418 Martin consecrated the hospital of S. M. Novella; an event painted by Lorenzo di Bicci. Before Martin could return

113

to Rome, he managed to make peace with Joanna II, the last member of the House of Anjou, who was occupying the city. The Pope found the city half in ruins. He started an extensive program of reconstruction and for the first time summoned to Rome some of the great painters of the early renaissance, such as Gentile da Fabriano, Pisanello, and Masaccio. Lorenzo Ghiberti made eight angel-figures for Martin's famous tiara and a buckle for his pluvial. Crafts such as weaving and embroidery also enjoyed a fillip through Martin's encouragement. He was the first Pope to bestow the Golden Rose, which is still conferred upon queens from time to time. He met with great success in mastering the wave of robbery inside the Pontifical State, and demonstrated his brilliance as a political administrator. The sovereign authority of the Holy See enjoyed a new access of strength after being in a state of decrepitude for a whole century. Martin's nepotism was occasioned mainly by political necessity, though it is not to be excused for this reason. He laid the foundations of the power of the Colonnas; his great-grand niece was Vittoria Colonna, Italy's greatest woman poet and the daughter of Fabrizio Colonna, the celebrated general. In order to make peace secure, Martin brought about a reconciliation with the Orsinis, the powerful rivals of the Colonnas, but it was short-lived. After the confusion which reigned at the end of the Great Schism, during which all the anti-popes had nominated cardinals, it became necessary to nominate new cardinals, men of dignity and eminence whose choice had to be carefully considered; among the cardinals created at this time was the outstanding figure, Giuliano Cesarini. "Benedict XIII" died in his mountain retreat in 1423 after an anti-pontificate of twenty-nine years. Shortly before his death "Benedict" nominated four cardinals, of whom three now elected "Clement VIII," whilst the fourth pushing absurdity to the absolute extremity elected himself "Benedict XIV." The former remained in Spain in the center of vast political changes until, in 1429, he and his electors, who subsequently disappeared, yielded to Martin. This was the final conclusion of the Great Schism, which had lasted for fifty-two years.

Martin V is justifiably remembered in history as a peacemaker, even though he was unable to complete all the tasks which were set him: particularly that of internal church reform, though he did

114

decide to summon a reform council to Bâle in 1431. His economical mode of life was almost tantamount to greed. He lived simply and without any form of luxury in the palace of SS. Apostoli. He was responsible for the introducing of a just government into Rome, which had at last settled down after its tribulations. His magnificent tomb, carved by Simone Ghini, a pupil of Donatello, is in the Lateran basilica; the inscription extols Martin as "temporum suorum felicitas"–the joy of his time. His huge statue stands on the southern wall of the choir of Milan Cathedral, whose altar he consecrated.

EUGENIUS IV
Gabriele Condulmer
3rd March, 1431 to 23rd February, 1447

This nephew of Pope Gregory XII was born in 1383, a member of the Venetian nobility. His deeply serious attitude to life caused him, early, to join the Augustine hermits, until he was eventually elevated by his papal uncle to the see of Siena and made a cardinal. His pontificate began with an over-severe action against the House of Colonna, the relatives of his predecessor. The result of this was a rising which could however, be quashed. The seventeenth General Council which had been authorized by Martin V opened on 23rd, July 1431 in Bâle. In December, 1431, full of unjustified suspicions, Eugenius embarked on the mistaken course of declaring the council dissolved and ordering the assembly of a new one in Bologna, though not until a year and a half later. His order aroused great indignation and the secular forces took sides with the Council. Cardinal Giuliano Cesarini, one of the most captivating personalities of his time, a splendidly intelligent and single-minded man, whom Martin V had nominated as his legate to the Council, tried in vain to make Eugenius change his mind. The whole situation was bedevilled by the victory of the Hussites in Bohemia, which now made ecclesiastical reform more urgent than ever. In continuance of the policy of the Council of Constance, the new Council, under the protection of King Sigismund decreed, in 1432, the superiority of the council

115

over the Pope and ordered him to appear in Bâle with his cardinals in the following April. The prebendary deacon of Coblenz, who was later to achieve fame as the great cardinal Nicholas of Cusa, justified this almost revolutionary procedure in his much-discussed work *De concordantia catholica*—on Catholic unity. The council went even further when, in June 1432, it deprived Eugenius of the power to nominate cardinals, disputed his secular authority and demanded that in the case of his death the conclave should be moved to Bâle. Here, undeniably, were the seeds of dissolution. The conflict was settled by a Bull by Sigismund, who was crowned emperor in Rome on 31st, May 1433. The Pope annulled the decree of dissolution, authorized the council to continue the work of combating heresies, to establish peace and institute reform in the church at all levels. The tension in Bâle had given Eugenius's enemies, the Colonnas and Milan, the opportunity of distressing him and he was forced to disguise himself, flee down the Tiber in a boat during a hailstorm and take up residence in Florence. In Rome Giovanni Vitelleschi, the former robber captain, condottiere and bishop, patriarch of Alexandria and cardinal archbishop of Florence, restored order by the methods customary at the time. Meanwhile, in the council, influential factions, desirous of seeing the papal residence once more established in Avignon and now in open opposition to the Pope, were gaining the upper hand. After several of the leading members of the council, among them Nicholas of Cusa, had pledged themselves to the Pope it was possible to open a Council of Union in Ferrara on 8th, January 1438—this council is always counted as part of the Council of Bâle—in which the emperor John VIII Palæologus and other leading dignitaries from the East took part. Eugenius, whom the Council of Bâle had declared deposed on 24th, January 1438 had moved from Florence to Ferrara, whence the council moved to Florence in 1439. Here as last on 5th, July 1439, a few years before the fall of Constantinople, was realized, at least in theory, the union of the faiths, which had been desired for so many hundreds of years. The new spiritual exchange with the East was of great cultural significance and was given external expression in the elevation to the dignity of cardinal of Bessarion, the archbishop of Nicæa who had been converted to Catholicism after the

116

council. The Greco-Latin humanism of the early Renaissance finds its most complete expression in this earnest, benevolent, noble prince of the church. The library of Bessarion, who was the greatest contemporary authority on Greek thought and literature before the fall of Constantinople, forms the basis of the library of San Marco in Venice. In 1439 the Armenians, Jacobites, Nestorians and Maronites were also converted. In Bâle on 5th, November of the same year one cardinal and eleven bishops nominated the last anti-pope in history, "Felix V," Duke Amadeus VIII of Savoy. This anti-pope was a widower and the head of a semi-religious chivalric order, the Order of St. Mauritius and Lazurus on Lake Geneva. Eugenius finally succeeded in making peace on favorable terms and was able to return to Rome in September 1443; he found the city in a state of complete decay, and started rebuilding at once. New conflicts which had arisen in Germany as a result of the schism of Bâle were settled by Enea Silvio Piccolomini, later Pius II, who was at that time secretary to King Frederick III, Albrecht II's successor. Eugenius tried in vain to stem the tide of Islamic invasion, and on 10th, November 1444 after the unhappy battle of Varna, Cesarini, the cardinal legate who was accompanying the Christian army, was murdered. Eugenius certainly made political mistakes on occasions, partly through lack of experience and moderation and partly through obstinacy, but as a priest and as Pope he was filled with a quiet, lofty majesty. He had a highly-developed sense of justice, was indefatigable in his work for the poor and suffering, and lent his support to St. Bernard of Siena and St. Bernarda Romana. In spite of the fact that one of his nephews was a cardinal he was strongly opposed to simony and nepotism and did all that he could to reform the secular and the monastic clergy. The Holy College had seldom contained so many outstanding and humane cardinals as during Eugenius's pontificate. Although he was not a renaissance pope in the true sense of the word, he did all that he could to further the arts: among other things, he called upon Pisanello to continue the work of Gentile da Fabriano in the Lateran. Jean Fouquet was working in Santa Maria sopra Minerva and painted a portrait of the Pope which has been lost, Donatello was commissioned to carry out a number of works and Fra Angelico was summoned to Rome;

the latter's frescoes in the sacramental chapel in the Vatican which were begun under Eugenius and finished under Nicholas V were destroyed during the pontificate of Paul III. Eugenius also cared for the ancient monuments in Rome. The tiara which was made for him by Lorenzo Ghiberti for the final act of union seems to have been a superb piece of work. Antonio Filarete worked for twelve years on the massive middle portal of St. Peter's on Eugenius's orders. Eugenius also deserves praise, in the sphere of music, for his elevation of Guillaume Dufay, the greatest master of his time, to a canonry in Cambrai. Dufay was a Dutchman who had served in the papal chapel under Martin V and he composed among other things the motet *Ecclesiæ militantis* for the Pope's coronation, and the famous festival motet *Nuper rosarum flores* for the consecration, by the Pope, of the cathedral in Florence. Eugenius's tomb which was carved by Isaia da Pisa is in the monastery near the church of San Salvatore in Lauro. At the beginning of his pontificate, on 30th, May 1431, Joan of Arc was burnt at the stake by the English.

NICHOLAS V
Tommaso Parentucelli
6th March, 1447 to 24th March, 1455

On his election Parentucelli was Bishop of Bologna and had been a cardinal for only two and a half months. He owed allegiance to neither party and was a humanist as pious as he was famous—his election was one of the most important events in the history of the papacy. A doctor's son, Nicholas was born on 15th, November 1397, most probably in Sazana on the Ligurian coast. He began life as a humble tutor and succeeding in working his way up to become a priest and secretary to Cardinal Niccolo Albergati, the leading figure in the Councils of Ferrara and Florence. The services which Parentucelli performed at these councils through his extensive knowledge and linguistic ability led Eugenius IV to nominate him Albergati's successor as Bishop of Bologna, ambassador to Germany

118

and to create him a cardinal. It has even been averred that Eugenius prophesied that Nicholas would wear the tiara. His sole political aim was peace, and there have been few popes who have detested war to the extent which Nicholas did. He quickly came to a settlement with Naples, where, as Alphonso I, Alphonso V of Aragon had succeeded the House of Anjou and had adopted a threatening attitude toward Eugenius. The dissension which had arisen in Germany after the Council of Bâle, which both Enea Silvio Piccolomini, and in 1446, at the Reichstag in Frankfurt Nicholas himself, then a legate, had tried to settle, was finally set aside by the Concordat of Vienna on 17th, February 1448. The rump-council which was still sitting in Bâle, but which had long since been nothing but an illusion, saw itself forced to move to Lausanne by King Frederick III and here, on 7th, April 1449 "Felix V" resigned and was created cardinal of Santa Sabina by Nicholas. On April 19th the rump-council formally "elected" Nicholas pope and then dissolved itself. "Felix V" the last anti-pope died on January 7th, 1451 in his hermitage at Ripaille on Lake Geneva. Nicholas celebrated the re-establishment of peace by the Holy Year of 1450, the culmination of which was the canonization of the popular saint, Bernardino of Siena. The most famous pilgrim to visit Rome during the Holy Year was Roger van der Weyden. An outbreak of plague drove the Pope away from Rome for a time, and soon after his return an accident caused by some horses shying on the Ponte S. Angelo killed more than two hundred people and caused a nervous depression in Nicholas. At the end of the year he sent Nicholas of Cusa, the great humanist cardinal, to Germany as his legate, in order to carry out reforms there. Nicholas said of his mission that he wished to "cleanse and renew and not to destroy and trample underfoot." Simultaneously with Nicholas's activity in the West, St. John Capistrano was active in Eastern Germany at Frederick III's behest. On 16th, March 1452 Nicholas did what no pope before him had done, he crowned the King in Rome with the iron crown of Lombardy and married him to Eleanor of Portugal—on 19th March he crowned him emperor: this was the last imperial coronation to take place in Rome. The event is recorded in a painting from the school of Dirk Bouts in the Germanisches Museum in Nuremberg. The Pope's last years were darkened by two events, one of them personal, the attempt made by Stefano Porcaro to murder him in 1453, and the other, universal, the fall of Byzantium on 29th, May 1453, after the capture of Constantinople. It was an especial sort of tragedy which should have made Nicholas, the kindly, tolerant and liberal humanist the victim of a conspiracy led by another humanist possessed of ancient ideologies and drunk with republican ideas—a sort of maniacal Rienzo—to whom he had shown great kindness, and who now wished to "free" Rome by assassinating the Pope and the cardinals, and setting himself up as a tribune. The attempt failed and Porcaro and his fellow-conspirators were executed. "In fact the most peace-loving of all popes was never forced to take up arms," writes Leon Battista Alberti, the renaissance architect. Nicholas who was oversensitive and deeply wounded by the whole affair was by now in any case seriously ill and relapsed into complete dejection haunted by darkest suspicions. After the fall of Constantinople, and a few months after the unsuccessful attempt at assassination, the Pope once more called upon the Great Powers to make peace among themselves and undertake another crusade against Turkey and the increasing threat of the Ottoman empire, but he found no support among the governments of Europe. It was not until 25th, February 1455 that he was able to form, in Italy, a defensive alliance between himself, Naples, Florence, Venice and Milan, the chief powers in the country and so assured internal peace, whilst all the signatories, with the exception of the Pope, tried to further their commercial interests by finding a basis of "peaceful co-existence" with Turkey. The Imperial Diets of Regensburg, Frankfurt and Wiener-Neustadt from April 1454 to March 1455, before which Aeneas Silvio Piccolomini laid the Pope's views on the Turkish danger, abandoned the subject without any conclusive result. The last five years of his life, with all their suffering, incurable gout and other diseases, were scarcely more than a living torture. Nicholas, whose tomb in the grottoes of St. Peter's is inscribed with verses by Pius II, deserves an outstanding place in the history of learning and patronage in Europe. Even opponents of the church have recognized the greatness of his personality, his thoughts and his actions. He united the papacy and culture and so brought about the tremendous possibilities for intellectual growth. In the course of the years, this passionate bibliophile, collector and literary connoisseur increased his carefully chosen library, from the time when he had merely been a poor tutor, and with it laid the foundations of the Bibliotheca Vaticana. His envoys travelled throughout Europe, from Greece to Scandinavia, as well as in the orient. Hosts of scribes, scientists and cognoscenti worked in the Vatican under his supervision. The humanists who came to Rome, among whom were many heathens—a significant point with so essentially Christian a pope—formed a regular court of muses around their patron. Nicholas was equally great as a builder, and chief assistant was Leon Battista Alberti, the most brilliant builder of his age. There is no aspect of profane or sacred building in Rome upon which he did not exert his influence. The crowning achievement was the massive conception which he had of the new Vatican and St. Peter's in place of the old basilica of Constantine—both of them based on plans of Alberti, to whom the Pope dedicated his fundamental theoretical work *De re aedificatoria*. The rebuilding of St. Peter's had to be interrupted on the Pope's death. In the Vatican itself the wings which today comprise the Appartamento Borgia were completed and used by Nicholas. Among those who were commissioned to do work for Nicholas were the painters Benozzo Gozzoli, Benedetto Bonfigli, Bartolomeo da Foligno, Andrea del Castagna and Piero della Francesca, whose frescoes are today in the Stanza d'Eliodoro, but the most important work of all was the painting by Fra Angelico of the frescoes, depicting the legends of Laurence and Stephen, for the Capella Niccolò V. The Pope's enthusiastic support for all branches of creative art was also a great encouragement to the craftsmen of the day. One of his pet schemes, the translation of the whole of Greek literature, especially Homer, into Italian came to end on his death: Otherwise the development of the renaissance would have taken another course. Nicholas's high human qualities which far outweighed his minor weaknesses, have been greatly praised. He was incapable of hypocrisy, and his magnanimity and generosity never allowed him to resent any biting remarks which might be made against him. Gregorovius writes of him: "Seldom has a man enjoyed the pleasure of giving for noble causes to such a measure as Nicholas V," and Ludwig von Pastor: "He was probably the most generous man of his century."

CALLISTUS III
Alonso de Borja
8th, April 1455 to 6th, August 1458

The first Spanish Pope since Damasus I, a learned lawyer, he was known as Alfonso Borgia, the Italianized form of his name. He was born in 1378 and had been created a canon by the anti-pope "Benedict XIII." After being a professor at the University of Lérida, he was summoned first into the service of Alphonso V of Aragon— Alphonso I of Naples—and then into the service of Martin V. Borja brought about the submission of the anti-pope "Clement VIII," and Martin V had expressed his thanks by appointing him to the See of Valencia. After his success in achieving a reconciliation between Eugenius IV and Alphonso of Naples, the Pope made him a cardinal. A few weeks after his election he canonised St. Vincent Ferrer, for whom that highest honor had been predicted. At the outset of his pontificate, the Turkish danger was growing ever more threatening, and the aged Callistus began a crusade, with true Spanish ideological fervor, to which he pledged not only all material aid, but also his own life. Like his predecessor he strove for what he considered to be the most important prerequisite—peace among the great powers, and, to this end, he sent his legates into all the countries of Europe and dispensed church treasures as well as his own personal wealth. For reasons of economy he stopped the building program begun by Nicholas V. In its place he proceeded with the construction of a fleet, which set sail in 1456 under the command of Cardinal Luigi Scarampo, without being able to take any action against the Turks who were entering the Greek archipelago. Sultan Mohammed II, the conqueror of Constantinople, started to advance on Belgrade in 1456. Cardinal Juan Caravajal, after Eugenius IV one of the most important and noble men of the time, appeared as legate in the Hungarian outpost, together with St. John Capistrano. Both of these men gave their support to John Hunyady, the Hungarian national hero, who had been defeated by the Turks at Varna during Eugenius's pontificate. A small crusading army, which Hunyady had raised, almost entirely at his own expense —the Hungarian nobles and king had fled!—gained a victory over the Turks at Belgrade on 22nd July, 1456. In memory of this victory Callistus ordained the feast of the Transfiguration which is celebrated on August 6th. The great powers were as uninterested as ever in exploiting the victory, and the Pope and Caravajal stood alone in their efforts, after Hunyady and John Capistrano had both died, the one of the plague, and the other of his privations. The position of the Pope was made even more difficult, on the one hand by anti-Roman tendencies in Germany, and on the other by a sudden straining of his relations with Alphonso I of Naples. Nevertheless, he did all that was in his power to oppose the Turks on his own, by supporting the Albanian national hero Skanderbeg. Seen from this point of view, his pontificate shows true greatness, but on the other hand, he caused great misfortune by his fateful resurrection of nepotism, which had been unknown in the preceding twenty years. Not only was he responsible for advancing members of his unwholesome house, nearly all of whom were objectionable, but, in collusion with his twenty-five year old nephew Rodrigo de Borja, he prepared the way for Alexander VI, one of the most worthless and fearful figures to be inflicted on the papacy in the whole of its long and dramatic history. By this action Callistus heaped guilt upon himself. Even during his pontificate the terror of the Borjas began to disturb the public, with Callistus being unable or unwilling to meet it. He was widely known as a kindly, peace-loving but taciturn and dry man. In contrast to his predecessor he lacked all interest in cultural matters. He introduced the ringing of the angelus. A picture by Sano di Pietros from the Siennese academy, in which the Madonna appears to the Pope, shows the features of Callistus III, whose sarcophagus with its mortuary sculpture stands in the grottoes of St. Peter's.

PIUS II
Enea Silvio de' Piccolomini
19th, August 1458 to 15th, August 1464

De' Piccolomini came from Corsignano near Siena, where he was born on 18th October, 1405. He later renamed his place of birth Pienza. He chose the papal name of Pius not in memory of the tenth Pope after Peter, but because he was humanist and an admirer of the *pius Aeneas* of Virgil. He studied at the University of Siena and had also been a pupil of Filelfo in Florence. In 1432 in Siena, he met Cardinal Domenico Capranica, on his way to the Council at Bâle. Capranica was one of the great intellectual and humane figures of the College of Cardinals, many of whom had come to the fore during the preceding pontificates. Capranica would most probably have ascended the throne instead of Pius had he not died two days before the conclave. Piccolomini became Capranica's secretary and later served under many other princes of the church, among them Albergati, the patron of Nicholas V. After returning from a secret papal mission to the Scottish court he lived in Bâle in an anti-papal atmosphere. Of great import in the life of this young man, who had not been ordained as yet, were the life and doings of his light-hearted humanist circle of friends, who lived in a world halfway between Boccaccio and the *Sturm und Drang*. Piccolomini's two natural children, who both died young and were not heard of again, were born at this time. After his sojourn in Bâle, he entered the service of "Felix V," and in 1442 went to King Frederick, to work under Frederick's Chancellor Casper Schlick, with whom he became firm friends. In Frankfurt Frederick bestowed a poet's crown upon his secretary. Enea Silvio gave important lectures on classical poetry at the University of Vienna, and thus had a great influence upon the development of German humanism. In common with the Viennese court his political sagacity made him a supporter of Eugenius IV. In 1444 he wrote his Latin novella, *Euryalus and Lucretia*, a true imitation of Boccaccio in style, relating a love experience of his friend Schlick with a Siennese girl. In 1445, he underwent a complete moral change, and one year later he was ordained. He then became active as a political negotiator and managed to break up the League of German Princes, which had become a danger to the King and to the Pope. In 1447 he became Bishop of Trieste, in 1449 Bishop of Siena and in 1456 a cardinal. His pontificate, like that of his predecessor was completely overshadowed by a crusade. Yet he had even less success than Callistus III. He did, however, manage to make peace with Naples where he recognized Ferrante I, the bastard son of Alphonso I, as his father's successor, and arranged the betrothal of a natural daughter of the King to his nephew Antonio Piccolomini. In 1459 he called a congress of princes to Mantua in order to carry on the crusade. Interest was so slight that the Pope waited alone in Mantua for four months for the members of the congress to appear. In spite of the complete failure of his attempt, he continued his efforts, although troubled by the rejection of papal authority in France and Germany and disturbances in Bohemia. In view of the failure of his efforts and the continued advance of the Turks, he decided to give the command of the army to the most unmilitary man of the time—himself, ailing as he was—an act which in view of its complete hopelessness can only be regarded as chivalrous. A majority of the cardinals agreed to this course, the most enthusiastic being Caravajal, now an old man, who had been the co-victor of Belgrade. The whole undertaking, as holy as it was a shattering piece of quixotry, was condemned to failure from the outset. Venice alone promised some aid to the papal troops. Very ill and almost unable to move, Pius left in June 1464 for Ancona, where the little fleet was to embark and where virtually no preparation had been made. On 12th August, 1464 he received word that the Venetian fleet with the Doge on board was approaching. Dying, Pius had himself carried to the window. The Pope took leave of his crusade plan, to which he had clung to the last, with the words, "Until today I have had to do without a fleet, and now the fleet will have to do without me." His tomb stands today in Sant'Andrea della Valle in Rome. Pius's close friend Nicholas de Cusa had died on 11th August: much to the Pope's distress, a Reform Bull which Nicholas had drafted was never issued owing to the unfavorable circumstances obtaining at the time. Nicholas was well aware of the abuses in the Curia, whose lowest incarnation had always seemed to him to be Rodrigo de Borja. Pius did all that he could to stop the slave-trade and the oppression of the Jews. He opposed any idea that Councils should have precedence over the Pope or over the monarchial idea of the papacy, and recanted, of his own free will, the views which he expressed at the Council of Bâle. He canonized his great compatriot, Catherine of Siena on 29th June, 1461, and composed the office and some hymns in her honor. In the same year he undertook his remarkable effort of converting the Sultan Mohammed II by an extensive apologetic work, for which he used Nicholas of Cusa's *De cribratione al Choran*. Pius has been accused of nepotism, but in fact only two of the near and distant relatives, whom he advanced had any outstanding qualities—the cardinals Forteguerri and Todeschini-Piccolomini. This latter, an eminent prince of the church, later became Pius III. Between 1502 and 1508 Pinturicchio was commissioned by Pius III to paint his masterpiece, the great fresco cycle of the life of Pius II in the choir library of Siena Cathedral. Pius developed an extensive program of building and restoration. The rise of Pienza, his birthplace can be ascribed to him. Not only does he belong among the greatest of the popes, but he was, moreover, one of the most gifted, interesting, charming and picturesque and, almost, adventurous men in the West. There are few popes of whom such a clear and true picture can be gained from their own accounts. His works, which have run to many editions, have continued to appear right up to the present century, and his enthusiastic and lively letters belong to the literature of humanism. He is the only pope to leave his memoirs behind; these are the famous *Commentaria* written in the form of a journal, with masterly biographical portraits, penetrating descriptions, among them even one of a regatta—and a wealth of nature descriptions, without doubt among the most beautiful written before Goethe. Pius experienced nature as a Romantic, even as an Impressionist, always as a poet and a painter. Excursions, journeys, or a consistory held under ancient trees were, for him, the highest form of pleasure, and he called himself, "The lover of woods." As a famous poet, historian and critic, welding the whole of the humanistic learning of his time together in his own person, he made greater demands on the humanists than Nicholas V who was not a creative artist. Pius was the founder of the universities of Bâle, Nantes and Ingolstadt. He unfortunately only completed one part, *Asia*, of his cosmography, which was to be a geographical and ethnological description of the world as it was then known. Fragments remain of the part devoted to Europe. The Pope's universal knowledge aroused the greatest admiration. His work marks the beginning of a whole aspect of science, and among those who came under his inspiration was Columbus. Pius was simple and unassuming by nature, charming in his kindness and indefatigable in his work. He once said, "do you not know that as Pope I have to live for others and not for myself." He was for ever making gifts and seldom had any money for himself. Gregorovius characterized him briefly: "His life as Pope was without flaw; he was moderate, kind, humane and considerate."

PAUL II
Pietro Barbo
30th, August 1464 to 26th, July 1471

Paul is believed to have been born on 23rd February, 1417 in Venice and was a nephew of Eugenius IV, on his mother's side. As early as 1440 he had become cardinal deacon of Santa Maria Nuova and won great influence under Nicholas V and Callistus III, less, however, under Pius II. Paul put down the conspiracy of a group of neo-heathen literati and humanists led by Pomponius Laetus and Bartolomeo Sachi, called Platina, which was very probably directed against his life. He was responsible for the dismissal from papal service of a large number of worthless literati. Platina's posthumous revenge on Paul in his history of the Popes, has distorted the picture of this pope right up to recent years. The advance of the Turks worried Paul as much as his predecessors, but he was powerless to do anything without money. He supported the Albanian patriot, Skanderbeg, the defender of western Christianity, who had come to Rome, in his fight against Islam. Paul had disagreements with Venice and Florence, as well as with Rimini and

Louis XI of France. An attempt to unite the Russian Orthodox and the Roman Catholic Churches also took place during his pontificate. His tomb, in the Museo Petriano, of which only fragments remain, was built by Mino da Fiesole and Giovanni Dalmato and was much praised by Vasari. Nino also did the magnificent portrait bust in the Palazzo Venezia and depicted Paul in his *Last Judgment*. Paul was a peace-loving pope who showed great understanding for the common people, was always ready to help, but was, at the same time, self-possessed, reserved and suspicious. To reproach him with greed is unjustifiable. He was not a man of great culture; he had, for instance, no Latin, yet he was deeply interested in Art, and collected coins, gems and antiques. His building program was concerned mainly with practical constructions, especially sanitary ones. The most important monument to Paul in Rome is his cardinal's palace, the Palazzo Venezia—Paul was a Venetian—completed by his nephew Cardinal Marco Barbo. The Pope was constantly surrounded by wise advisers, and is free from any charge of nepotism. His nephew Marco Barbo is considered an outstanding, learned and benevolent prince of the church. Paul bestowed the biretta upon the cardinals and ordered the celebration of a jubilee every twenty-five years. During his pontificate, though through no fault of the Pope, the renaissance developed on ever more pagan lines. Paul showed great interest in the art of printing. The two German clerics and printers, Conrad Schweinheim and Arnold Pannartz brought printing, "the holy art," to Italy in 1466 and opened their first workshop in the monastery of Santa Scholastica in Subiaco, where their press can still be seen. In 1467 they moved to Rome and received every help from the Pope and the cardinals. Paul actually founded the papal publishing house, the Libreria Editrice Vaticana.

SIXTUS IV
Francesco della Rovere
9th, August 1471 to 12th, August 1484

Della Rovere was born in Celle in 1414 of a family of poor Ligurian nobles. He joined the Franciscan order at an early age and after completing his university studies became a professor at the universities of Padua, Bologna, Pavia, Siena, Florence and Perugia. In 1464 he became the minister-general of his order, in 1467 cardinal of San Pietro in Vincoli, and published a series of theological works. He was not ordained a bishop until after his election as Pope, an election which he had bought, and this is one of the most sinister episodes in papal history, by making promises. The bestowal of benefices soon began and, in giving up all that had distinguished him before his election, Sixtus introduced an evil epoch for the papacy, the results of which were unforeseeable. Equally soon after his election, Sixtus's nepotism began to assume a form which recalled the very worst precedents. The families of two brothers and four sisters were provided for most lavishly: two nephews were at once made cardinals; these were the twenty-eight year old Giuliano della Rovere, later to become Julius II, and the twenty-five year old Pietro Riario, a former Franciscan monk, who takes his place next to Rodrigo de Borja as the most scandalous example of nepotism in the history of the church. In addition to his benefices he received four bishoprics and the patriarchy of Constantinople. Riario dissipated his annual income of 2,400,000 francs on his official mistress and on orgies which recalled the decline of the Caesars. Della Rovere received as many as six bishoprics as well as numerous abbeys and benefices; he, too, was of a worldly disposition, but nevertheless he retained his dignity and used his wealth to good purpose, in patronage and in building. Riario, on the other hand, remained a parvenu, even though a generous one, and exercised an unwholesome influence upon Sixtus. When he died, at the age of twenty-eight, a victim of his own dissipation, he was given one of the most magnificent tombs of all time, the work of Mino da Fiesole. His place was then taken by his brother Girolamo, a greengrocer, who became a count, married Catherine Sforza of Milan and dominated Sixtus in a more fateful way even than his brother. According to the latest research the second figure from the left in Melozzo da Forli's famous picture of Platina's appointment as librarian to the Pinacoteca Vaticana could be Girolamo. Further nepotic appointments of cardinals were Cristofero della Rovere, and Raffaello Sansoni Riario, who later became the friend of Erasmus. Presumably it is he who is standing next to Sixtus in Melozzo's picture. There was also the incompetent Domenico della Rovere, who endowed the first right hand side chapel in Santa Maria del Popolo. Girolamo Basso della Rovere is a more praiseworthy exception. Count Girolamo's greed for land soon led to political upheavals which were expressed in the famous Pazzi conspiracy against the Medici in 1478, in Florence, and in which the Pope and Girolamo Riario took a leading part. The results of Sixtus's family politics were unrest, rebellion and war. Riario who had appropriated Forli, wanted to overthrow Ferrante I of Naples and advance on Ferrara. Sixtus exacerbated the political mischief which he had caused by indiscriminately declaring individuals anathema to him, declarations which in the rapidly changing political constellations could change at any moment to eulogies. Demands for a council were heard on all sides, but they found no favor with Sixtus. In 1481 a papal fleet won a limited success against the Turks who had taken Otranto in 1480. A year later Sixtus canonised Bonaventura. In 1476 he introduced the Feast of the Immaculate Conception on 8th, December, which Clement XI later declared a general feast. In the sphere of church politics he allowed himself to make several doubtful promises. He tried at first to modify the cruelty of the Spanish Inquisition, which began during his pontificate, but soon gave way to the pressure of the government and agreed to the appointment of the Dominican Thomas de Torquemada as Inquisitor. The pope's weak attempts at reform were soon suppressed by the "Sistine" College of cardinals. This was the college, which he himself had assembled either from family or political motives, a college from which all legendary figures such as Bessarion, Caravajal or Capranica kept their distance, and from which Cardinal Francesco Piccolomini remained as aloof as possible. Apart from Sixtus's protégés only Borja, Sforza and Cibo, Sixtus's successor, had any say in the college, which had reached the nadir of utter worldliness. The corruption and simony rampant in Sixtus's pontificate, during which he doubled, not only the taxes, but also the number of offices which could be bought, bringing their number up to six hundred and twenty five, was exceeded only by that of the Borja pope. In the economic sphere Sixtus supported a wide range of undertakings in the pontifical state. His name is connected with the Ponte Sisto, about which C. F. Meyer composed a poem, and with the refoundation of the Vatican library. Melozzo da Forli has depicted the appointment of Platina, Paul II's most bitter enemy and the author of the first great history of the Popes, as librarian, in a fresco masterpiece. This is the only remaining part of his fresco in the rooms of the library, in which Ghirlandajo also worked. The library rooms, on the building of which Sixtus spared no expense, thus continuing the work of Nicholas V, are to-day used for other purposes. Scholars of all types streamed into the papal service: he appointed painters such as Mino da Fiesole, Verrocchio, Ghirlandajo, Botticelli, Perugino, Pinturicchio, Roselli, Signorelli, and Melozzo da Forli, who was the first real court painter. Only a few fragments remain of Melozzo's monumental creation, the Ascension of Our Lord, which was in the SS. Apostoli: these are the famous angels' heads and a few apostles, and they are now in the Pinacoteca Vaticana; the figure of Christ is in the Quirinal. Sixtus rebuilt Santa Maria del Popolo and Santa Maria della Pace, his favourite church. He also completely rebuilt the great papal charity, the Ospedale di Santo Spirito, which Innocent III had founded; Umbrian murals here depict the biography of the Pope, and stand as the earliest historical murals of the renaissance. Sixtus opened the collections of antiquities, made by his predecessor, to the public, and so became the founder of the Museo Romano. Unfortunately he simultaneously destroyed a number of ancient temples, arches and tombs. Sixtus reorganized church music, and in 1484 summoned Josquin des Prés, one of the greatest musicians of all time, to Rome where he remained till 1494. As a builder and renovator Sixtus ranks as the real restorer of Rome. Other cities too owe debts to him. His name is however, most imperishably linked with the Sistine Chapel which he consecrated on 15th August, 1483. The frescoes which Sixtus had painted on the side walls by the greatest Tuscan and Umbrian masters, are full of references to the pontificate of the man who commissioned them. The twenty pictures of the Pope, between the windows, the most important of which are by Botticelli and Ghirlandajo, present the idea of the papacy through the thought which lies behind them,

131

rather than through the portrait of the man they depict. Sixtus was the first pope to have his image engraved on coins. His tomb in the grottoes of St. Peter's is one of Pollaiuolo's masterpieces. Sixtus's was essentially a discordant personality—kind to the extent of unforgivable weakness, generous, seldom insulted by criticism, and dignified in his personal life, yet a cloud of suspicion was cast upon his way of life by various literati who had been insulted by him, and especially by the opinion expressed by the contemporary historian Stefano Infessura, which for a long time influenced opinion about this pope. His inexperience did not justify the fateful consequences which his nepotism invoked—the complete secularization of the church, the withdrawal from the idea of the papacy as a spiritual power in favor of the monarchic aspect of the office, his spineless dependence on everyday politics, simony and venality. Sixtus demonstrated just how much could be concealed under the over-all cloak of the papacy. His pontificate was a misfortune for the church, a misfortune which his two successors worsened. And yet, for the arts it was an epoch of immortal greatness.

INNOCENT VIII
Giovanni Battista Cibo
29th, August 1484 to 25th, July 1492

As soon as the conclave was summoned after Sixtus's death, the corrupt Rodrigo de Borja did all in his power to become pope, while Giuliano della Rovere was only a short way behind him in his efforts to win the tiara. However, Rovere achieved the election of his protégé Cibo, the cardinal of Santa Cecilia and Bishop of Molletta, by means of simony. He was a Genoese, a relative of the Doria and was born in 1432. After studying in Padua and Rome he lived in Naples. His two natural children, Teodorina and Franceschetto were born at this time, though it must be stated that Cibo had not yet been ordained. His rise began during the pontificate of Paul II, who made him Bishop of Savona. At the beginning of his reign he was drawn into the bloody war between the Barons of Naples, where the nobility had risen up against King Ferrante I. Things reached such a pitch that Rome itself was threatened. Innocent showed to what lengths depravity and the lack of all sense of dignity and seemliness had gone when he held a magnificent wedding feast in the Vatican, on the marriage of his depraved bastard son Franceschetto with Maddalena de'Medici, the daughter of Lorenzo II Magnifico. The following year, with equal ceremony, he celebrated the wedding of his granddaughter, Battistina (the daughter of Teodorina) with Luis of Aragon. Franceschetto took up his residence in the Vatican in his capacity as the Pope's official son. Meanwhile his father-in-law Lorenzo had had his fourteen-year-old son Giovanni de'Medici, later Leo X, created a cardinal, after Sixtus IV had already appointed him a protonotary apostolic at the age of seven. The illegitimate son of the pope's brother was also created a cardinal at this time. The changing attitude was also reflected in a different treatment of the Turkish problem, for though Innocent called a congress to arrange a crusade in 1490, he found it more profitable to hold Djem, the pretender to the throne and the brother of the Sultan Bajasid II, as a hostage in the Vatican and to exert pressure by this means. Innocent's name was tainted even more by the issuance of the notorious Witch Bull in 1484, in which he sanctioned the bloody activity of two fanatical German Dominican inquisitors. The inner naiveté with which he accepted the fantastic fairy-tales made up by these two sinister figures has, more than anything else, cast a slur upon the memory of the pope and upon the reputation of the papacy, for by giving them his approval he inspired them to write in 1487 one of the most horrible literary concoctions of all time, the *Hexenhammer*, and was, too, guilty of threatening the most dire ecclesiastical punishments if the two monks were not allowed to rage unhindered. It is not however correct to assert that Innocent introduced the witch-hunt, for these had been familiar since the twelfth century; nevertheless his Bull which formed an introduction to the *Hexenhammer* stoked the fires of the new excesses. During his pontificate on 2nd, January 1491 Granada was captured and Moslem rule in Spain came to an end. Innocent who showed great dignity in death and was aware finally of his own inadequacy has his tomb in St. Peter's, which like that of his predecessor is one of Pollaiuolo's masterpieces. Columbus set out on his voyage of discovery nine days after the Pope's death, and the inscription on Innocent's tomb, which was added later, refers to the event. In the Vatican the Pope built the Palazetto del Belvedere, which was designed by Pollaiuolo and which now houses the greater part of the collection of antiquities. The once famous frescoes by Pinturicchio and Mantegna in the Belvedere have been destroyed. In 1486 the pope banned the first world congress of philosophers, of all religions, which the twenty-three-year-old humanist and philosopher, Pico della Mirandola wished to summon, at his own expense, and at the opening of which he intended to make his famous speech *On the dignity of man*. Shortly before Innocent's death, Savonarola, the famous preacher appeared and the warnings which he spoke found their true echo in the complete worldliness of the papacy.

ALEXANDER VI
Rodrigo de Borja
11th, August 1492 to 18th, August 1503

As 'Alexander V' was an anti-pope, this Alexander is really the fifth in line. The simoniac haggling for the Holy See carried on without any shame by this corrupt Borja at last proved successful. An annalist writing resignedly at the time said that in the old church a man of Borja's caliber would not even have been admitted to the lowest office of the priesthood. When his uncle, the twenty-six year old Callistus III had ordained Borja, who was born in Valencia in 1430, a cardinal, he had not even received a lower ordination. In 1460 Borja began his relationship with Vannozza Cattanei, who bore the four most notorious and well-known of his many children. The good intentions which Alexander had nursed on his election were soon forfeited and from now on his pontificate was concerned solely with the furthering of his family's interests, and especially those of his son Cesare, one of the most unwholesome and criminal figures of the whole of History. In 1493 Cesare became a cardinal, and his brother, the husband of a niece of Ferdinand the Catholic of Spain, became Duke of Gandia and Benevento. Guiffré Borja married Sanzia the natural daughter of Alphonso II of Naples, while Lucretia married Prince Alphonso of Bisceglie, the natural son of Alphonso II of Naples, after her divorce from Prince Giovanni Sforza of Pesaro. Cesare later had his brother-in-law strangled. Lucretia's third marriage was to Duke Alphonso d'Este of Ferrara. Juan Borja, whose grandson was the holy St. Francis Borja, the third general of the Order of Jesuits, whose life developed into a living atonement for the misdeeds of his evil House, was also probably murdered on Cesare's orders. Apart from Cesare, there were four other cardinals among the Borgias. The opposition against Alexander and his dynasty centered on Giuliano della Rovere, who fled in 1494 to the Court of Charles VIII of France. Charles, by virtue of his relationship with the house of Anjou, now laid claim to the Kingdom of Naples, which by marriage and treaty had allied itself to Alexander, and, supported by Duke Ludovico of Milan, he set out on his triumphal campaign through Italy. The Pope was threatened with a Council and with deposition. Charles besieged Rome on 31st January, 1494, and Alexander, who had taken refuge in the Castel S. Anglo, after being deserted by Naples, found himself forced to come to terms with him. Charles succeeded in his demands, subjugated Naples and reconciled himself with Alexander. His victory brought about, in 1495, the formation of the Holy League between Ferdinand and Isabella of Spain, the Emperor Maximilian I, Venice, Milan and the Pope. Charles returned to the North shortly afterwards, where he succeeded in breaking through the army of the League in the battle of Fornovo. In 1498 Alexander's struggle with Savonarola ended with the execution of the preacher of repentance. The Pope entered into an alliance with Louis XII of France; Cesare, who married Charlotte d'Albert of Navarre, was created Duke of Valence by the King, and from this time on is often known as the Duca Valentino. In 1499 Louis XII took Milan. In the following year Alexander divided Naples between Spain and France; Federigo, the fifth and last of the Aragon rulers yielded to Louis, Cesare conquered the whole of Romagna and separated it from the Pontifical

135

State, so that, with the Pope's agreement it could become a hereditary princedom for the Borgias, and from now on they both thought
of nothing but the secularization of the pontifical state and the
strengthening of their family's power. The Pope's nepotism developed into undisguised absolutist power politics. The next step
was the dispossession of the houses of Savelli, Caëtani and Colonna,
whose property was given as the Dukedom of Sermoneta, to Rodrigo, Lucretia's two year old son by her second marriage. A three
year old son of the pope, Juan, the so-called *Infante Romano*, who
had been rapidly legitimized, received the Dukedom of Nepi.
Meanwhile Cesare who had overrun the dukedoms of Urbino and
Camerino, nipped several conspiracies in the bud, defeated the
Orsinis and already had his eye on Tuscany. He obtained the
money for his undertakings not only from the Jubilee Year in
1500, but by selling, at a high price, nominations for cardinalates,
and by arranging the murder of cardinals, whose property was
inherited by Alexander. The wealthiest of these unfortunate men
was Michiel, a nephew of Paul II, and Cardinal Orsini was probably
another of his victims. Just as Cardinal Castellesi was about to be
poisoned, the Borja tyranny suddenly crumbled. It has never been
conclusively proved whether Cesare and Alexander were poisoned
by mistake or whether they really caught malaria. Alexander died,
Cesare, it is true, was saved, but he never succeeded in exerting
his influence again. On Columbus's return from his voyage of discovery in 1493, Alexander drew his famous line of demarcation
between Spanish and Portuguese spheres of influence in the colo-
nies. He could lay no greater claim to be counted a humanist than
could his predecessor. He had Antonio da Sangallo rebuild the
Castel S. Angelo, and widened the corridor which leads from the
castle to the Vatican, as well as the Torre Borgia. Pinturicchio
painted the magnificent frescoes in the second, third and fourth
rooms of the Appartamento Borgia, while his famous portrait of
Alexander in the Sala dei Misteri appears less idealized than Tor-
rigiani's bust in Berlin. Titian painted the Pope in his picture of
Admiral Pesaro, which is now in Antwerp. The papal chronicle of
Alexander, which was painted by Pinturicchio and which hung in
the Castel S. Angelo, has been lost. Alexander completed the

coffered ceiling in Santa Maria Maggiore, probably the most beautiful in Rome, which was begun under Callistus III and is supposed to have been gilded with the first gold brought from America to Europe. In the Jubilee Year of 1500, Michelangelo completed his Pieta in St. Peter's which distinguishes him as the greatest sculptor of his time. The purity of his work, which in Alexander's immediate entourage forms a striking contrast to the most humiliating pontificate in the whole history of the church, is typical of the range of life in this epoch. It is necessary to recognize two facts in judging Alexander's actions during his eleven year pontificate: he was an erotomaniac, who cared for nothing but the furtherance of his family's interests, and in this way he brought the church to the very edge of an abyss. The continuous decay of the church can be very clearly followed from the time of Sixtus IV onwards. If Sixtus's chief protégé Pietro Riario was considered merely "a vicious operetta figure" and if Innocent VIII officially accepted his base son into the Vatican, there appeared in Alexander's son Cesare, the tyrant whom Machiavelli glorified in his exegesis, a condottiere and cynical assassin who was out to destroy the Pontifical State and the papacy so that he might rise out of the ruins as a King. Alexander was a party to every one of his demonic son's criminal plans, for his nature was such that his essential vulgarity, which was clearly recognized by many of his contemporaries, completely overshadowed his intellectual gifts. He remained the slave of his vices to the last, a fact which no authority disputes, least of all Catholic ones. The real nadir of papal decay was reached when, on All Saints' Eve in 1501, Alexander, Lucretia, and Cesare watched in the Vatican, a ballet performance given by fifty Roman courtesans. The Borgias have been of interest throughout the succeeding centuries—today, mainly to writers of second-rate novels. Lucretia, who has been ill-served by her reputation, was the subject of a play by Victor Hugo in which the characterization was completely false. This tragedy served Gaëtano Donizetti as the idea for an opera. Alexander has again and again been cited as an argument against the papacy as an institution, but always on the wrong premises, for a papacy which could withstand a Borgia must be possessed of, and actuated by, higher forces than even this Pope was able to affect.

PIUS III
Francesco Todeschini Piccolomini
22nd, September 1503 to 18th, October 1503

Rome and the College of Cardinals presented a picture of complete confusion on the death of Alexander VI, and Cesare Borgia, who was still ill and incapable of action, was forced to leave the city. A Spaniard had as little chance as a Frenchman of becoming Pope, for everywhere there was evidence of the influence of Giuliano della Rovere, who had returned from his ten year exile. The aged nephew of Pius II, the most dignified of all the cardinals who had refused indignantly to allow himself to be bought by Alexander VI before the latter's election, was elected with no suspicion of simony. This Pope, who had served as an energetic cardinal-protector of Germany, and spoke excellent German, who was a patron of the arts and lived a life of quiet seclusion, and who was mortally ill on his election, thought only of peace and reform. He hated every form of nepotism and even forbade his nephew to come to Rome without being summoned, though he was being pressed on all sides to make him a cardinal. There was general sorrow when Pius finally succumbed to his gout and overwork. He bestowed upon the cathedral library in Siena the masterly frescoes depicting the life of Pius II, which were painted by Pinturicchio. The same artist devoted a huge fresco, also in the cathedral library, to the papal coronation of Pius III. His order to Michelangelo, whose genius Pius was quick to recognize, to carve fifteen statues for the Piccolomini altar in the cathedral at Siena was never carried out.

JULIUS II
Giuliano della Rovere
31st, October 1503 to 21st, February 1513

It has been proved that Julius, under whom the Renaissance reached its peak, achieved his election through simoniacal practices. He even sent for the hated Cesare Borgia, promised him the office

138

of Gonfaloniere or standard bearer in the church, and gained the support of the Spanish who were still allied to Cesare, before the conclave took place. Not even Alexander VI appeared before the conclave so indisputably the man to be elected, as did the sixty-year old della Rovere. Three years later, in a Papal Bull he declared simoniac election invalid and threatened the most severe punishments to simoniac electors. He was born of poor parents on 5th December, 1443 in Albinola in Savona, became a Franciscan and achieved a high degree of learning. He was elevated to the office of cardinal of San Pietro in Vincoli and appears as a superb central figure on Melozzo's fresco in the Vatican gallery. The wealth which he rapidly began to acquire he used for furthering the arts. The first change in circumstances came in Julius's changed attitude to nepotism. True he created a few Rovere-cardinals, but these were never outstanding; the best of them was Galeotto, an artists' idol, who died young, and even his nephew Francesco Maria della Rovere, the heir to the Duke of Urbino, who had received favors before Julius's election, was now kept in check. Not a single relative received any gifts worth mentioning. True, benefices and offices were still sold, though not now for personal ends, but to replenish the depleted coffers of the church, though this is no more excusable than the sale of indulgences. Against this must be reckoned Julius's great readiness to help refugees and the poor. Venice exploited the pope's position and the helplessness of Cesare in order, bit by bit, to recapture Romagna, the original part of the Pontifical State. In 1504, in August, Cesare was rendered harmless and imprisoned in Spain, while Julius obstinately set about regaining the mutilated pontifical state. Besides his diplomatic efforts he was helped by a skillful marriage policy: his nephew Niccolò della Rovere, was married to Laura Orsini, the only heir to the powerful House of Orsini. Felice, one of the Pope's three natural daughters was married to Giovanni Giordano, the head of the line of Orsini of Bracciano and his niece Lucretia Gara della Rovere married Marcantonio Colonna, of the Paliano family. Julius had neither time nor money for elaborate wedding celebrations, nor did he take part in them personally. He overthrew the tyrannical rulers of Perugia and Bologna —the Baglioni and the Bentivogli—in his triumphant campaign of

139

1506. The latter fled on the approach of this martial Pope, who returned in triumph to Rome in March 1507, after completing the chief task of the restoration of the Pontifical State. Ferdinand the Catholic of Spain and Louis XII of France, who had, up to this moment, been rivals in the Kingdom of Naples, now concluded a treaty at the Peace of Savona and stood united against the Pope. In the meanwhile, the question of the Venetian greed for land was becoming ever more acute. The enmity towards Venice which was felt throughout Europe resulted in the formation of the League of Cambrai on 10th December, 1508, between Louis XII, who was confirmed as ruler of Milan, the Emperor Maximilian I and Ferdinand the Catholic. Julius joined the League in 1509, after all efforts to settle the conflict with Venice by peaceful means had failed, and in spite of his mistrust of France. The great decree of excommunication was laid upon Venice, and in the decisive battle of Agnadello near Cremona on 14th May, 1509 she was defeated by the League troops. Julius, who had reconquered the pontifical state, now tried to drive out the French from Italy, for they had become too powerful; peace was concluded in Rome on 15th February, 1510; Venice was absolved. After years of foreign domination by the Borgias, the Pope now appeared as the incarnation of Italian national consciousness, which was opposing the foreign rule of the French. His most important ally was Switzerland under the leadership of the Bishop of Sitten, Matthäus Schiner, who remains to this day, the only Swiss cardinal. France threatened to set up Gallican self-rule, and so removed the dispute from the political to the ecclesiastical plane. Julius once more set out northwards by a series of forced marches, to take personal command of the action against France. In Bologna he received the fateful news that five treacherous cardinals had gone over to Louis XII, while, at the same time, French troops appeared at the gates of the city accompanied by the Bentivogli, thirsting for revenge; however, on the approach of the allied Swiss and Spanish troops, the French withdrew. In the winter of 1511 Julius wanted to subdue Ferrara which was allied to France. The strange portrait of the Pope in winter armour, now in the Palazzo Chigi in Rome, was painted during the siege of the key fortress of Mirandola. Since the French, under Marshal Trivulzio were once more ad-

140

vancing on Bologna, Julius had to break off the campaign and turn
back to Bologna, which was captured in the following May by
Trivulzio and so came once more into the hands of the Bentivogli.
Michelangelo's statue of the Pope, executed in 1508, in the church
of San Petronio was sacrificed to their hatred of the Pope; it was
destroyed by the Bentivogli, whereupon Alonso of Ferrara took
the metal and made it into a cannon, which he derisively called
La Giulia. Poets have sung of the tragedy of this statue, which
according to contemporary chronicles was one of the most beautiful
in the whole of Italy, if not in the whole world, and of which not
even a sketch remains. Julius fled first to Ravenna and then to
Rimini. Meanwhile, the traitorous cardinals, supported by Louis
XII and Maximilian I had demanded that a Council be summoned.
The Emperor, for his part, was working for a schism and the separation of the church from Rome. Louis XII, like Venice before him,
seized upon the tendentious pamphlet, lampoons, caricatures and
open derision of the Pope, to heighten feelings and increase the
demand for a council. At the same time, he tried to win the support
of Henry VIII of England and of Hungary. Julius returned to
Rome, a sick, but unbroken man, and there, quite independently,
he summoned the Lateran Council for April 1512, thus taking the
wind completely out of the disloyal cardinals' sails. He then fell
mortally ill, but to the surprise and terror of the whole world, he
recovered in August. It is this recovery which C. F. Meyer has
glorified in his poem *Papst Julius*. The conclusion of the Holy
League between the Pope, Ferdinand of Spain and Venice was
announced on 4th October, 1511, and in November it was joined
by Henry VIII. The four ring-leaders of the schismatic group of
cardinals were relieved of all their offices and exiled. Their "council"
met first in Pisa, then in Milan, finally fleeing to Asti and Lyons,
where it ended in oblivion. The French victory under Gaston de
Foix at Ravenna on 11th April, 1512, the threat to Rome, even to
the Pope's person, were new blows for Julius, but the French did not
exploit their victory. In June their troops faced the Swiss under
Cardinal Schiner, as well as those of the protégé Duke of Urbino,
of Venice and of Spain. But before battle commenced, they made
an ignominious withdrawal from Italy. Julius's offering up of

prayers of thanksgiving in his old titular church of San Pietro in Vincoli—in front of the chains which had bound the first pope—was one of the most magnificent symbolic acts in the history of the papacy. Raphael elevated the whole incident into the sphere of artistic revelation by painting his picture of the release of Peter from prison, in the Stanza d'Eliodoro. The Swiss must receive most credit for this release, and Julius bestowed upon them, in perpetuity, the title of "defender of the freedom of the church." In December, Maximilian I recognized the Lateran Council, a political and ecclesiastical triumph for Julius, whose last great concern was now the continued rise of Spain and the future fate of Italy. The general sorrow expressed a few months later when he was lying in state in St. Peter's showed that a truly majestic Pope had died. Julius' earlier activity within the church, which had been underrated, took second place to his political activity and the eradication of the Borgias, nor should it be forgotten that he also planned a crusade. He can be reproached with allowing politics to dominate his pontificate: but Jakob Burckhardt's verdict, that he was the savior of the papacy, will always remain valid. In Italy he was known as "Il Terribile"—"The Terrible," but always with an undertone of sublimity—for what the people understood by this term, was the powerful ruler. He could be reckless, impatient and tough, but never indecisive. The only things of importance to him were the papacy and the church after their three decades of undignified nepotism. Even more than for his political ability, Julius is remembered as one of the great art patrons of history. He gathered around him Raphael, Bramante, who became the Pope's Minister of Culture and accompanied him on his campaigns and journeys, and Michelangelo—painters of genius with an inspired patron, who for a second time raised Rome to the status of Eternal City. On 18th April, 1506 Julius laid the foundation-stone of the new St. Peter's, which Bramante had designed, at the column of St. Veronica. Bramante also started building the new papal palace, which was not completed until later, and designed the two great galleries which link the palace with the Belvedere. He, himself, finished the East gallery and the spiral staircase for Julius's summer house. In 1505, Julius appointed Michelangelo, then twenty-nine years old, the only mind which he recognized as being on an equal level with his own, to build the famous tomb of Julius. A year later, he commanded him to cast the bronze statue which was destroyed in 1511. In 1508 he formally compelled him to paint the ceiling of the Sistine Chapel. When the work was unveiled on 31st October, 1512, Julius was well aware of the part which he had played in this, the greatest revelation of the art of painting of all times. At the same time as Michelangelo was working on the Sistine Chapel, Raphael began his frescoes in the Stanzas, in two of which, the banishment of Heliodorus and the mass of Bolsena, there are portraits of the Pope; his famous portrait of the Pope hangs in the Uffizi gallery and there is a replica in the Palazzo Pitti in Florence. Michelangelo's *Moses* in San Pietro in Vincoli, the only part, but the greatest part, of the tomb of this renaissance pope, which was completed, is the most powerful memorial to Julius. Julius founded the Swiss guard on 21st January, 1506. The papal song school which he patronized is called Capella Julia to this day, whilst the name Sistine Chapel is not correct. He founded the first Arabic printing press in Fano and commissioned Sansovino to build the tombs of the cardinals Sforza and Girolamo Basso della Rovere in Santa Maria del Popolo.

LEO X
Giovanni de' Medici
9th, March 1513 to 1st, December 1521

The election of the second son of Lorenzo il Magnifico, who was born on 11th December, 1475 in Florence, was unaccompanied by any simoniacal practices and accorded with the principles laid down by Julius II. The schismatic cardinals who had been deposed by Julius II were denied the right to vote at the conclave though Leo later pardoned two of them. The cardinal deacon of Santa Maria in Domnica who was elected, was not consecrated as a priest or a bishop until shortly after his election. In contrast to his predecessor, Leo was a new type of renaissance pope—an aesthete and epicure who was generous, popular and always good-humored. He had studied under Angelo Poliziano and Marsilio Ficimo, the two great humanists at the court of the Medicis. Leo had been created a cardinal by Innocent VIII at the age of fourteen, and had returned to Florence, in 1494, as the opponent of Alexander VI for whom he did not vote. After the banishment of the Medicis, he went to Germany, the Low Countries and France, returning to Rome in 1500 where he lived in what is today called the Palazzo Madama, and gave full rein to his artistic and literary tastes. He was taken prisoner by the French in the Battle of Ravenna in 1512, but managed to escape. The power of the Medicis was restored in September—shortly before de'Medici's proverbial luck won him the tiara. Leo was sympathetically received at the beginning of his pontificate, made great efforts for peace and showed great indulgence to his enemies. France was defeated by the Swiss at the Battle of Novara on 6th June, 1513, while making a renewed attempt to capture Milan. Again Leo effected a reconciliation on all sides, and at the Lateran Council's final session of the year 1516 he was able to celebrate the admission of France, once the protector of the schismatic cardinals. On 17th October, 1513 Louis XII had decided at Lille to give way in the face of a new alliance between the emperor, England and Spain. As the head of the House of Medici, Leo combined the policies of Rome and Florence and indulged in widespread nepotism. His illegitimate cousin, Giulio, later Clement VII, became archbishop of Florence and a cardinal. Another cousin, Luigi de Rossi also became a cardinal, and Leo's brother Giulano married Filiberta, aunt of Francis I of France, became Duke of Nemours and, later, together with his cousin, Duke of Urbino, a Roman patrician. Michelangelo idealized these two protégés in the Capella Medici in Florence. Finally Innocenzo Cibo, the son of Franceschetto Cibo, and the grandson of Pope Innocent VIII also became a cardinal—he was as despicable a character as his father, but the two Dukes were generous and, to a degree, chivalrous, though politically unimportant. Giuliano died in 1516: his illegitimate son, Ippolito, later became a cardinal. Lorenzo the father of Catherine de'Medici, later to become Queen of France, revived the Dukedom of Urbino for a short time, after Leo had maliciously driven out

144

Francesco Mario della Rovre, the protégé of Julius II, who was ruling at this time. Louis XII's Franco-Spanish marriage plan and the increasing supremacy of Spain in Italy forced Leo to a new arrangement with France and England. In this he was successful and in 1514 his endless diplomacy also contrived the marriage of Mary Tudor, Henry VIII's sister, to Louis XII. Nevertheless, French plans to conquer Milan were unchanged, and Milan was once more brought under French command by Francis I of France, Louis XII's successor, in the Battle of Marignano on 13th and 14th September, 1514. After this victory, Leo decided to meet the French King in Bologna in the following December. The peace reached here assured France of the control of Milan and harmed Leo by the loss of Parma and Piacenza. Maximilian advanced into Italy in 1516 to make war on France and Venice, while Leo was busy attempting to stop an alliance between France and Spain where Charles I had ascended the throne. The Lateran Council closed on 16th March, 1517. The great wealth of suggested reforms and duties stayed on paper, for Leo, his court, and the worldly clergy did all they could to stop reform, not seeing that in Germany the great religious conflict was beginning. Instead of paying heed to the famous, impressive, and remarkably moderate speech made to the council by Pico della Mirandola, in which he advocated church reform, Leo preferred to stress the inflexible thories propounded by Boniface VIII in his Bull *Unam Sanctam*, without at the same time opening the way to internal church reform. In April 1517, a conspiracy to poison the Pope, under the leadership of the twenty-seven year old cardinal Alfonso Petrucci was unmasked. Several cardinals were involved in the plot, including Raffaelo, Riario, the protégé of Sixtus IV, and Bandinello Sauli. Petrucci was executed, but Leo generously forgave the other cardinals, although Sauli and Riario had had designs on the tiara. This tragedy aroused great attention in Europe, especially in Germany which, in any case, was in a state of ferment. Leo was guided by political and financial motives when he created thirty-one new cardinals in July 1517, until then, the greatest number ever to be created at one time. There were few really worthy people among those who were nominated. By this creation he finally renounced the figure of twenty-four cardinals and gave the pope an ascendancy over the college. On 31st October, 1517 Luther nailed up his theses on his church in Wittenberg, a happening which marked the end of unity of faith in the West. There was no one less capable than Leo of assessing the breadth and seriousness of this act, which re-echoed throughout Germany; no one less able to counter it than this kindly epicure who occupied the papal throne. Finally nothing was more significant than the concern of the Pope that Charles V should not succeed Maximilian I, which in fact happened on 28th June, 1519 in spite of all Rome's expectations, and led to the union of all the German and Spanish empires. The Bull of excommunication on Luther dates from 3rd January, 1521, but it was powerless to arrest developments. A few months later Leo bestowed upon Henry VIII the title of *Defensor fidei*, defender of the faith, in recognition of his manifesto against Luther. The rest of Leo's pontificate was filled with conflicts inside Italy and with disputes with Francis I, while the Emperor and the Pope grew closer together. An army consisting of German, Spanish, Swiss and papal soldiers recaptured Milan on 19th November, 1521 and once more put a speedy end to French domination in Lombardy. Not two weeks later Leo died of malaria; he is believed by many to have been poisoned. Julius II had left a great fortune; Leo was almost bankrupt. His funeral was miserable and his tomb, which is of no artistic value, does not even boast an inscription. Yet never before nor since has there been a pope about whom so many verses and inscriptions have been written, as Leo. Even if he did not actually say to his brother when he first became pope, "Let us enjoy the papacy, God has given it to us," at least this was the guiding principle of the life of this first pope of the Medici family. His great desire for pleasure alone sufficed to make him quite unsuited for any really great task in the world or in the papal history of his time. Yet there were no reproaches, or at least such as there were, were not slanderous, against his personal life either before or after his election. He was a spendthrift who never had enough money, yet he was indefatigable in his readiness to help the poorest of all classes. He lent his ear to any form of misfortune, and the manner in which he protected the Jews will always do him credit. His court which consisted of six hundred and eighty-three people, about four

146

times as many as under Pius II, from an archbishop to a keeper of the elephants, from musician to minor poet and court jesters, with whom Leo loved to exchange the most childish wit, cost immense sums of money—his household expenses alone were double those of his predecessor, in the region of a hundred thousand ducats a year. Thus, it is not surprising that the number of offices up for sale rose to two thousand two hundred. The sale of indulgences assumed the character of a gigantic business transaction, against which those cardinals who were aware of their duty raised protests, while Ariosto satirized the whole operation. Leo would often go hunting for weeks at a time accompanied by as many as two thousand riders, among whom were cardinals, entertainers and court players. This very musical pope—he was himself an amateur composer and musician—maintained a very well endowed "Philharmony"; musicians could easily attain to high ecclesiastical offices and benefices in his service, and he collected valuable musical instruments. He published in his *liber quindecim missarum* the most beautiful settings of the Mass that were composed in his time. Plays were constantly being produced for him and the Vatican developed into a regular court theater, where from time to time, Leo would have a particularly bad actor beaten and then give him two ducats as a consolation. In 1514 *Calandria,* an attractive work by Cardinal Bibbiena was produced and in 1515 Ariosto's *Suppositi* with decor by Baldassare Peruzzi and Raphael. Ariosto's *Negromante* was, however, banned, because its prologue derided the trade in indulgences. Even Machiavelli's *Mandragola* seems to have been performed before Leo in 1520. Worse still at the carnival of 1521, when the church was under the threat of the conflagration caused by the Reformation, and Sultan Suleiman was at the gates of Belgrade, all government business was suspended because a ballet dealing with the story of Venus and Amor was considered to be more important. Things reached such a pitch, that a Dominican described Leo as a roi-soleil. The literati were of the same mind, and their expectations were expressed by the publisher Aldo Manuzio in his first edition of the works of Plato which he dedicated to the Pope. Whole armies of literati and improvisers thronged to the papal table, received rich reward from Leo for their transitory creations, were created counts, and received titles, recommendations, posts and benefices. Out of this swarm of people, only two emerged as really important, the famous cardinals and Latin scholars Pietro Bembo and Jacopo Sadoleto: the former wrote a poem to celebrate the discovery of the Laocoön group, which is today in the Vatican. The Neapolitan poet Jacopo Sannazaro was encouraged by Leo to publish the work, *The Birth of Christ*, which he had written in his old age. Just as the three great national historians, Francesco Guicciardini, Niccolò Machiavelli—who dedicated his Discourses on the reform of Florence to Leo—and Paolo Giovio, richly enjoyed the favors of the pope, so the pope in his turn enjoyed the extravagant praise and often painful flatteries of Erasmus of Rotterdam, the greatest humanist of the time, who dedicated his edition of St. Jerome to the pope and received in return a number of favors. Christians and atheists, men with talents and men without talents dedicated their work to Leo, who accepted everything indiscriminately. Jacob Burckhardt has referred, with justice, to Leo's patronages as being "casual, and having all the traits of a lottery." On the other hand it would be wrong for us to underestimate the value of the inspiration which the Pope gave to art—either wittingly or unwittingly. The greatest artist associated with his name was Raphael, who was responsible for the picture of Leo and his two cardinal protégés in the Palazzo Pitti in Florence; a picture which flatters Leo's natural ugliness. Raphael also worked in the Stanzas, where, in his picture of Leo the Great's meeting with Attila, he no longer painted the Pope as Julius II, but as Leo, who also appears on the frescoes in the Stanza dell' Incendio, the majority of which were completed by Raphael's pupils; they depict events from the lives of Leo III and Leo IV, but also bear reference to events during Leo X's pontificate. While Raphael's most famous pupil, Giulio Romano, was working in the Sala di Constantino, Raphael himself designed the cartoons for the famous carpets in the Pinacoteca Vaticana and painted the loggias. Leo's patronage was effected more in the sphere of art than literature; however, if his patronage is compared with Julius II's, then it becomes clear that Leo was not inspired by any central ideal, but that his chief concern was for the decorative and aesthetic. In spite of this, his fame as a patron has endured. Called to the Holy See at a fateful point in history, he emerges as a double-tongued diplomat without any inner greatness. The deeds which Ariosto had expected of him in the seventeenth canto of *Orlando Furioso* were beyond his capability. His deceit, which was typical of the Medicis, his diplomatic cleverness, and his egotistical behavior, displayed especially in the war with Urbino, aroused the indignation and the just criticism of many contemporaries.

HADRIAN VI
Hadrian Florensz
9th, January 1522 to 14th, September 1523

At the conclave, both Cardinal Wolsey, Henry VIII's ambitious chancellor and Giulio de'Medici cast hopeful eyes on the tiara, yet it was a man of poor parents, born in Utrecht in 1459, the serious, eminently moral Bishop of Tortosa, a former tutor of Charles V, and Erasmus's teacher, who was elected pope. The new Pope who did not arrive in Rome until August, had been appointed a cardinal through the influence of Charles V. After the brilliance of the last pontificate the Romans were not very glad to see a German professor, the last foreigner to occupy the Holy See, come to them as Pope. The general opposition grew as Hadrian reduced the size of the court and dismissed the poets who had been sponging off his predecessor, but it was when Hadrian started to reform the corrupt curia and do away with the sale of offices and eject all forms of nepotism, that he finally engendered real hatred. The plague which broke out in Rome in the Fall of 1522, which the Pope courageously braved out, slowed up his reforms. In September, he sent a legate to the Imperial Diet in Nuremberg, first, to demand the enforcement of the sentence of outlawry passed upon Luther, and then to present a confession of guilt for the schism, an act of strength which marks the first step in the counter-reformation, a step answered by Luther in a pamphlet against Hadrian. Without declaring his support for either side Hadrian tried to achieve unity between Charles V and

Francis I, in order to oppose the irresistible advance of the Turks, who had captured Rhodes in December, 1522. As he achieved nothing in this way, he tried to raise the necessary means for a campaign against the Turks himself, and especially for the defense of Hungary which was under an especial danger. It was his fate to find himself forced to sell offices and promises to raise money for this purpose, when for any other he would never have been prepared to do this. In order to achieve the peace which he so much desired, he issued a Bull, in 1523, ordering an armistice and threatening the severest ecclesiastical punishments for disobedience. The emergency forced Hadrian to ally himself with the Emperor, Henry VIII, the Archduke Ferdinand later to become King and Emperor, Milan, Florence, Genoa, Siena and Lucca, against Francis I, who was threatening him with the fate of Boniface VIII, and was once more starting to arm against Lombardy. The pontificate of this Pope, who was modest and pious, filled with the purest of motives and a high sense of duty, and uninterested in art, was filled with true tragedy. In the Rome of Leo X he remained a stranger to his death, mocked in life, and insulted in death—a "burnt offering to Roman derision" as Burckhardt says. On his tomb in the German national church of Santa Maria dell' Anima are inscribed the words: "Alas, how much depends upon the age in which even the most outstanding man is active."

CLEMENT VII
Giulio de' Medici
19th, November 1523 to 25th, September 1534

This protégé of Leo X had had a successful career and under both Leo and Hadrian he had proved his worth as a leading counselor. His election was celebrated by Vittoria Colonna, Italy's greatest woman poet. Clement was born in 1475, the natural son of Giuliano, the brother of Lorenzo il Magnifico: he was a serious studious person, the complete opposite of Leo X. He had long since laid aside the rather looser morals of his youth, and began his pontificate by trying to make peace among the great powers, but in contrast to his attitude as a cardinal, he now took up a neutral position, instead of supporting the Emperor. When Francis I captured Milan in October 1524 Clement changed his attitude and made a treaty with him and with Venice. After the Battle of Pavia on 24th February, 1525, in the course of which the King was taken prisoner, Clement, who was on the point of allowing Francis to march through the pontifical state, in order to attack Naples, once again changed his mind, concluded a treaty with the imperial governor of Naples and promised help to Milan. At the same time, the curia was busy working out an anti-imperial treaty which would counter Spanish attempts at world domination. When Francis I, after earnestly assuring him that he had renounced his claims to Milan, was finally released in 1526, both he and Clement considered the peace invalid. The upshot of this was the formation of the Holy League of Cognac on 22nd May, 1526, an alliance which included Francis I, Venice, Milan and nominally, at least, and only after much vacillation—of great significance for the assessment of his character—the Pope. Clement no longer held the view that peace should be his only aim; he armed energetically and took up an aggressive attitude towards the Emperor who was making efforts to mediate; whereupon the Emperor replied in the same tone. There was a sharp division between the two factions and, with the Emperor's connivance, an attack was launched on the Vatican and St. Peter's under the leadership of Cardinal Pompeo Colonna, the head of the House of Colonna which was traditionally loyal to the Emperor, his nephew Vespasiano and Ascanio, the brother of the poet Vittoria. This attack was a prelude to a number of terrible events, among them the destruction of the Hungarian army by the Turks at the Battle of Mohacs on 29th August, 1526 and the occupation of Hungary. After the attack Cardinal Pompeo was relieved of his office, and Ferrara who had always been the enemy of the Pope went over to the Emperor. There was no longer any talk of the effectiveness of the League. Clement who, on this score, was a man of great integrity, had twice refused to create cardinals for money and when he was finally driven to this expedient, there was no money left among the six nominees to meet Clement's needs for halting the advance

151

on Rome of the imperial general Constable Charles of Bourbon, who had deserted France, and for forcing him to withdraw from the city. Bourbon fell on 6th May, 1527 during the attack on Rome; the army which consisted of Spanish marauders and German mercenaries at once burst into the city, murdering and plundering, in an action more terrible than any since the attack on Rome by the Vandals. The heroic Swiss Guard defended the Pope, who had fled into the Castel S. Angelo, almost to the last man. Among those who were manning the guns in the castle was Benvenuto Cellini. This terrible event, one of the most cruel outrages of all time, went down in history as Sacco di Roma; it was the end of the golden age of the Renaissance. Thousands of people, tortured to death, littered the streets of the burning city—St. Peter's and the Sistine Chapel were used as stables, and the kerchief of St. Veronica, the holiest relic of St. Peter's was offered for sale by the mob in the taverns of the city. Clement was taken prisoner on 5th June and for seven months he was held under the most severe conditions. In order to be able to raise at least part of the immense sums which the Emperor demanded of him, Cellini, who was also a prisoner in the Castel S. Angelo, melted down the tiaras, the gold plate, and golden chalices in an improvised wind furnace near the statue of the angel inside the fortress. In order to meet further demands the Pope had to beg for loans at a high rate of interest, and pawn the last of his possessions. In Rome, hunger and pestilence raged. Clement was finally released on 6th December, and fled to Orvieto, where he lived in the utmost poverty with a few of his cardinals. He raised justifiable complaints against his so-called friends of the League, especially Francis I, for forsaking him. French troops advanced on Naples whereupon the troops who had plundered Rome moved southward after destroying two thirds of the houses in the town and laying waste the countryside for fifty miles around. The rest of their work of looting they left to the leaders of robber bands In June, Clement moved to Viterbo and the victorious French army was at the gates of Naples. The secession of the Genoese fleet, under the famous Italian admiral Andrea Doria, to the Emperor and th outbreak of plague forced the French to beat a retreat, in the cours of which they were completely destroyed. The Pope was still uncertain as to his best course, but saw his greatest hope in Charles V, at whose request he returned to Rome in 1528. "A miserable corpse, torn to shreds, presents itself to our sight," in these words he described the appearance of Rome to Charles V, who meanwhile was making Clement realize how dependent he was on him. The Pope soon adopted a neutral position again. However, when on the one hand the League no longer regarded him as an ally, the Emperor, on the other, announced his intention of coming for a personal discussion of the situation with the Pope, and Clement was feeling justifiably hopeful of support from the Emperor for the restoration of the Medicis' power, the whole situation changed again. On 29th June 1529 Charles V and Clement concluded the Peace of Barcelona and in the face of this new political grouping, Francis I felt himself forced to submit to the Emperor. The peace which was signed on 5th August 1529 in Cambrai is known as the "Ladies' Peace," in memory of Louise the Queen Mother of Savoy and Margaret of Austria, the Emperor's aunt and the governor of the Netherlands, who were the moving spirits behind it. On 23rd December a peace was signed in Bologna between the Pope, the Emperor, the Emperor's brother, Ferdinand I of Austria, Venice, Milan, Mantua, Savoy and a number of smaller powers. Naples formally fell to Charles V, who received the iron crown of Lombardy on 22nd February, 1530 and on 24th February became the last emperor to receive the imperial crown from the hands of the pope, although this was not in Rome. Florence capitulated on 12th August and the Medici returned to the city. Clement granted an amnesty to all the enemies of his house. Alessandro, his protégé, the natural son of Lorenzo of Urbino, did become the hereditary duke, but Clement remained the true ruler of the city. Francis I prevented the Pope from summoning a council, but Clement who was determined to prevent excessive imperial influence in Italy promised the King the hand of Catherina de' Medici, the sister of Alessandro, for his son, the future Henry II. Henry VIII's marriage to Anne Boleyn in January 1533, was the begininng of the separation of the Church of England from Rome. In the same period, Sweden, Denmark and important parts of Switzerland were lost to the Roman Catholic Church. The pope married his great niece Catherina to Henry in Marseilles on 12th October. Francis I was not afraid to discuss a possible Franco-Turkish alliance with the horrified Pope. Clement died after an illness lasting for several months. He is buried near his cousin Leo X in Santa Maria sopra Minerva. His pontificate was a misfortune for the church, and his blameless life should not deceive us into thinking that this pope always worked single-mindedly for the interests of the church. He was cold and indecisive, a crafty diplomat, never completely frank, always afraid, forever vacillating in his concern for the political situation and never able to see the larger perspectives. Even the Sacco di Roma did not suffice to make him realize that as pope he had tasks to fulfill, other than political maneuvering. The poet Francesco Berni passed a crushing verdict on him which contains these lines:

> His reign was rich in seeking every way,
> In change of mind and trying to be wise,
> In ifs and buts and noes and ayes,
> With nothing ever done, but always much to say.

When a decision had to be taken, the interests of the Medicis were often the deciding factor—especially the interests of the cardinal protégé Ippolito de' Medici, and the equally corrupt Duke Alessandro. No one had a word of praise for Clement except Pietro Aretino the journalist who was his creature and received payment for his efforts. Even this did not prevent his abusing Clement when the latter was held prisoner in the Castel S. Angelo, treatment which caused the pope to burst into tears. Clement deserves honor for his protection of the Jews and his opposition to any form of forced attempts at conversion: this explains John III of Portugal's enmity towards him. Because of the circumstances of his pontificate, he could only give limited support to the arts, among others that of the goldsmith which achieved it highest expression with Cellini as its leading exponent, whose autobiography which was translated by Goethe, completely mirrors the period of Clement's pontificate. Machiavelli's great history of Florence appeared in 1432; the work is dedicated to Clement by whom it had been commissioned while he was still a cardinal. The court painter Sebastian del Piombo painted his master and the portraits are now in the gallery in Parma and in the National Museum in Naples. The Pope forgave Michelangelo for the part he had played as commander of the fortress of Florence in 1530 during the fight against the Medicis, and gave him several important commissions, among them the building of the tombs of the Medicis in San Lorenzo and the Bibliotheca Laurenziana. Toward the end of his life the Pope set the titanic genius of his compatriot the task of creating in the Sistine Chapel, the painting of the Day of Judgment, though the work was not finished during the pontificate of this unhappy pope.

PAUL III
Alessandro Farnese
13th October, 1534 to 10th November, 1549

This former cardinal, the last one living who had been created by Alexander VI, was elected after a surprisingly short conclave. He was born in 1468 either in Camino or in Rome and had studied under the celebrated Pomponius Lætus. He owed his rise to the Borgia Pope, who thought in this way to show thanks for the favors so richly bestowed upon him by Farnese's sister, the famous Giulia La Bella. Farnese, who became cardinal deacon of San Cosma e Damiano at the age of twenty-five, was made Bishop of Parma in 1509 by Julius II, who had legitimized two of his illegitimate sons —whether he also legitimized the third son and his daughter is not known. Of these sons, the eldest, Pier Luigi, was to achieve a tragic fame. Farnese had undergone a spiritual change since his translation to the bishopric of Parma, and from being the thoroughly worldly cardinal, who was not ordained a priest until 1519, he became a serious prince of the church with an earnest desire for reform. Speaking later of his unsuccessful attempt to obtain the tiara at the conclave of 1523, he said that Clement VII had robbed him of ten years of his pontificate, but he remained loyal to

Clement, whilst Pier Luigi went over to the side of the Emperor and even took part in the Sacco di Roma; he was excommunicated, but his father pleaded successfully for his absolution. In 1524 Farnese, the gifted statesman and cardinal, who was widely beloved, became Bishop of Ostia. His election as Pope caused joy on all sides, especially in Germany where he was known to support the wish to hold a council. Great strength of will and high intellectual capacity were still alive in this rather ill man of sixty-seven, and instead of his early death, which many had expected, his contemporaries were to experience the longest pontificate of the century. Paul, unfortunately, at once entered upon an orgy of nepotism: his grandson Alessandro Farnese, the son of Pier Luigi, and Guido Ascanio Sforza, the son of the Pope's daughter Constanza, boys of fourteen and sixteen became cardinals; later they were joined by the fifteen-year-old Ranuccio, also a son of Pier Luigi, and by Niccolò Caetani. Alessandro grew up into an excellent man, and though at first completely worldly he later sobered down completely. The Pope appointed his son, Pier Luigi, as Gonfaloniere of the church. In 1535 Paul pointed out the necessity for a council, but this was extremely unwelcome to the worldly-minded cardinals, who showed the utmost superficiality in their views upon Germany. The Protestant princes supported by Henry VIII and Francis I rejected the proposition that a council be summoned. On 26th June, 1535 the English king made the first sacrifice to his schism by executing the martyr Bishop, John Fisher, who had been created a cardinal only one month before his death; two years later on 6th July the second martyr, Thomas More, was beheaded. Both were canonized in 1935 by Pius XI. Paul's nominations for cardinals in 1535 show a discernible change towards the idea of reform. More and more outstanding men were coming into the college, which had merely served political ends under the Medicis and thus it was that Gaspero Contarini, the former Venetian ambassador in Rome and one of the most arresting and outstanding personalities of his day became a cardinal. On his advice Paul created two reform cardinals in 1536 —Jacopo Sadoleto and the English nobleman Reginald Pole, a greatnephew of Edward IV and Richard III. Henry VIII took vengeance by beheading Pole's eighty-year-old mother. Gian Pietro Car-

afa, later to be Paul IV, also received the red hat. Pole and Contarini belonged to Vittoria Colonna's most intimate circle of friends,
and the Pope commissioned Contarini to sit as the head of a commission of cardinals which was to work out recommendations for
reform and whose recommendations were first to be implemented
in Rome and among the leaders of the Universal Church. In March
1536 on his return from his expedition in Tunis, Charles V made a
long speech in the Consistory in which he attacked Francis I and
vainly tried to woo the Pope away from his policy of neutrality.
Meanwhile the Turkish danger had become more pressing and at
the end of July 1537 the Osmans attacked Apulia, only to withdraw
again soon afterwards when they discovered that their ally, Francis
I "the most Christian King" was not, contrary to their expectations, prepared to invade Italy from the North. Venice which was
threatened from Corfu now joined forces with the Emperor and the
Pope. In order to realize his plans for a council Paul had to mediate
between the emperor, who had invaded France in July 1537, and
Francis I; again, as so often in the past years, the negotiations
hinged on Milan and Savoy. A new Holy League was signed on 8th
February, 1538 in Rome and people were already talking of Charles
V's sitting on the throne of Constantinople. In Nice on June 18,
1538 Paul managed by dint of his personal intervention to bring
about, at least, a ten years' armistice between the Emperor and
Francis I. Paul made a marriage contract with the Emperor; Margaret, the natural daughter of Charles and the widow of Alessandro
de' Medici, who had been murdered in the preceding year, was now
to marry the Pope's grandson Ottaviano Farnese. Nine months later
after the Turkish naval victory of Prevesa the League dissolved and
Venice made a separate peace. In the same year, all hope of a
Council was lost because of the numerous seats of opposition and
the lack of interest on the part of the great powers. The Pope's time
was absorbed for the moment with internal conflicts and the German
question, and at this time Ignatius Loyola, the leading figure of
the counter-reformation appeared in Rome; he and his companions
had been working in the city towards the ideals of reform and
charity since 1538. Loyola's masterpiece, the *Exercises* of 1541,
met with the full approval of the Pope, who confirmed the new

157

order. The Bull calling for a council issued in 1542 again met with general disapproval, especially from Charles V who again reproached the Pope with his role of neutral mediator—and also from Francis I who was allied to the Turks, and who was threatening the Pope that he would secede from Rome, like the English, while at the same time declaring war on Charles V. The Pope met the Emperor in Busseto in June 1543, discussed the Milanese question and expressed the hope that in view of his constant need of money, the emperor would agree to sell Milan to Ottaviano Farnese, for whom the Pope just had purchased the dukedom of Camarino. In spite of the interests of nepotism, the Pope still regarded the establishment of peace as his highest duty. The council which had been called to Trent had to be postponed and the whole situation, from which only the German Protestants benefited, was in the balance. Meanwhile, Paul, without surrendering his neutrality was inclining toward Francis I who was trying to make good his past mistakes. At the same time the Emperor offended the Pope by making an alliance with Henry VIII and threatening him through his protégé cardinal Alessandro Farnese with the fate of Clement VII. The peace which was concluded at Crespy on 17th September, 1544 altered the whole situation and both monarchs now expressed a desire that the council would be convened. Such a favorable political constellation misled the Pope into crowning his nepotism with terrifying indelibility by bestowing Parma and Piacenza as a united dukedom upon his son Pier Luigi. The Council of Trent which was opened on 13th December, 1545, as the penultimate General Council, marked the official beginning of the counter-reformation. In March of the same year Luther had poured out the venom of his hatred against the Pope in his work *Wider das Papsttum* (Against the Papacy). In the last years of the Pope's life the disputes with the emperor grew more and more acute and Paul turned towards France and to all the powers who were opposed to the Spanish and the imperial powers in Italy. Henry VIII died in January 1547 and the Pope, in Perugia, was praising his good fortune, after assisting the emperor in the wars of Schmalkalden, Pier Luigi was assassinated in Piacenza with the connivance of the Emperor who intended to retake Parma and Piacenza. The final upset of his life was the flight of his spoilt godson, Ottaviano, from Rome, who, in order to retain Parma, threatened to ally himself with the emperor. On his deathbed, Paul confessed to the guilt of his nepotism. His impressive tomb in St. Peter's is the work of Guglielmo della Porta, who also carved the marble busts of the Pope in the National Museum in Naples. Paul was characteristic of this transitional period in the papacy, for the old and the new were united in his character in a curious paradox. Titian painted the Pope, as an old man, in three of his most famous portraits, the most important of which shows Paul with Alessandro and Ottaviano: these hang in the National Museum in Naples, where his portrait of the Pope as a cardinal and his portrait with Pier Luigi also hang. Dignity, great intelligence, knowing cunning, calculation and deliberation all speak from his penetrating eyes. Paul, the master diplomat, was always the winner in an argument, in which he would allow everyone to express his point of view before he himself came to an independent verdict. He always showed consideration for others. Scarcely any other pope has enjoyed such confidence. Yet, when in 1546, he believed that he had a presentiment of death, it was typical of him to go and discuss the question of his successor, in the deepest confidence, with Vittoria Colonna, whose family were his most bitter enemies and that, as Pope with an unbiased relationship to all parties, he should express his thoughts to the greatest woman in all Italy, who in 1541 had addressed two sonnets to him, begging him not to persecute her family. His nepotism was a complete expression of the renaissance, as was his practice of seeking the advice of astrologers as to the best time to undertake any action, his magnificent festivals in the Vatican with musicians, entertainers, singers, dancers and jesters, and the lack of concern with which he celebrated the baptism of his great-grandsons, the twins of Ottaviano and Margaret, on the day of his coronation. What was new, however, was the way in which he used his important powers for the changing reform of the church, and so quitted the path of his predecessors. In 1539 he created the aged Pietro Bembo, the last great humanist of Italian literature, a cardinal. In 1542 he founded the Holy Office for the combatting of heresy, yet he wished the inquisition to be applied with mercy. He tried to convince those who had gone astray, by intellectual means. By means of two short edicts he became the first Pope to stand up for the rights of the Indians who had been persecuted and enslaved by the conquistadores: that the edicts had no effect was not his fault.

Rabelais derided the Pope; Pietro Aretino, according to the needs of the day either defamed him or praised him. Ariosto placed a monument to him in the forty-sixth canto of *Orlando* and Copernicus dedicated his epoch-making work *On the revolution of the heavenly bodies*, to him. He was the last great patron of the late renaissance. His beautiful statue, which stands as a monument to his building activity in Rome stands today in Santa Maria in Aracoeli. After the emperor's visit in 1536 he commissioned Michelangelo to produce plans for the complete remodelling of the capitol, which had presented a rather unworthy appearance to Charles V. Nevertheless in Paul's pontificate all that was done was to move the statue of Marcus Aurelius from the Lateran to the Capitol square and to erect the double staircase to the palace in Rome, the Palazzo Farnese, which had been started by Antonio de Sangallo; in the Sistine Chapel he painted the Last Judgment, which was unveiled on 31st October, 1541, and then the frescoes in the Capella Paolina which Sangallo had built for Paul. The Pope then commissioned Sangallo to build the Scala Regia between the Sistine Chapel and the Capella Paolina, but this was not completed till 1573. During the course of the building, the sacramental chapel which Fra Angelico had built for Nicholas V was demolished. The state rooms of the Castel S. Angelo were built during his pontificate. The palace which the Pope had built at Santa Maria near Aracoeli was demolished in 1886 to make way for the Vittoriano. Vasari, who wrote his *Life of an Artist* during Paul's pontificate, painted his frescoes, glorifying the reign of the pope, in the Sala dei cenro giorno of the Cancellaria. In 1547 Paul finally transferred the direction of the building of St. Peter's to Michelangelo; its most splendid creation, the cupola, symbol of the Eternal City, was to arch over a new era for the church and the papacy.

JULIUS III
Giovanni Maria Ciocchi del Monte
7 February 1550 to 23rd March 1555

Del Monte who was born on 10th September 1487, had gone to
the court of Julius II through the influence of his uncle Antonio del
Monte, the archbishop of Siponto. This uncle, who had been raised
to the status of cardinal, gave up his archbishopric in favor of his
nephew. In 1527 Clement VII, at the time of his capitulation, had
to put up del Monte as a hostage together with a number of others.
Del Monte was twice led to the gallows and threatened with death.
In 1536 Paul III created him cardinal of San Vitale and designated him the first president of the Council of Trent in 1545. Although he was at first conscientious and industrious, Julius later gave
himself over to worldly pursuits, and his peasant behaviour, which he
had formerly laid aside, now became unpleasantly obvious. He is
typified by a round of bull-fights, carnival celebrations, endless parties, hunts and gambling for high stakes. Two of his relatives received the purple. One of them, Roberto de'Nobili, was an excellent
man, the other, Fulvio della Crogna, a vicious figure. Julius was
guilty of an act which showed a scorn of his contemporaries and
brought disgrace upon the college of cardinals, when he gave the
keeper of his apes, a lad of seventeen, a worthless creature who had
risen up from the gutter, the name of del Monte, and created him a
cardinal in defiance of the protests of all the other cardinals. The
appointment gave rise to the worst rumors, which could not however
be proved. The Tridentium continued its work in 1551 after a temporary interruption. Politically Julius remained neutral and conciliatory like his predecessor. England under Mary the Catholic, the
daughter of Henry VIII and the wife of Philip II of Spain, returned
for a time to the Catholic church. The Pope entered upon a war
with Ottavio Farnese, the grandson of Paul III, which was both
damaging to the reputation of the papacy and time-wasting. Julius
never understood the gravity of the times in which he lived, and
after Paul III a man was needed quite different from this uncertain,
spiritless, pleasure-loving pope, who was at the mercy of any change

161

of mood. In Rome he is recalled by the Villa Giulia, which is today the Etruscan Museum; otherwise there are no monuments to his pontificate. In 1551 he summoned Palestrina to St. Peter's as choirmaster. Palestrina dedicated the volume of his masses to the Pope in 1554, and the title woodcut shows him kneeling in the act of presenting them to the Pope.

MARCELLUS II
Marcello Cervini
9th April, 1555 to 1st May 1555

Marcellus was born in Montepulciano on 6th May 1501. He early acquired an extensive education, and also worked at arboriculture, bookbinding, drawing, carving and modelling. In Siena he studied astronomy, mathematics, architecture and archaeology. He and his father were commissioned by Clement VII to produce a work on calendar reform. Cervini later became companion to cardinal Alessandro Farnese, later Paul III, and was responsible for the education of the protégé of cardinal Alessandro. He served them both successfully as secretary. In 1539, the pope made him cardinal of Santa Croce in Jerusalem, an action which was greeted with lively satisfaction by the reform party. He was an excellent administrator of the various sees which were allocated to him. In spite of the tremendous number of offices which he held, he never forgot that he was a scholar and in this capacity he did great services to the Vatican library. Michelangelo respected his extensive knowledge in the field of architecture. Innumerable research workers gained his support— from the commentator on Homer to the author of a work on fish. He refused to allow his relatives even to set foot in Rome. The few days which the pontificate of this excellent pope lasted were devoted to reform and justice. When he died the historian Onofrio Panvinio quoted the lovely words by Virgil: "Fate simply wanted to show him," and on his grave the poet Faustus Sabaeus wrote: "It is not the grave which honors the ashes, but the ashes which honor the tomb." Marcellus's name also lives on in music, for Palestrina wrote his most famous mass to the memory of this saintly pope; the Missa Papae Marcelli. One of the pope's sisters became the mother of St. Roberto Bellarmin. The splendid portrait of Cardinal Cervini by Francesco Salviati hangs in the Galleria Borghese in Rome.

PAUL IV
Gian Pietro Carafa
23rd May, 1555 to 18th August, 1559

Paul was born on 28th June, 1476 in Naples; he studied theology and became Alexander VI's chamberlain, he subsequently became Bishop of Chieti, thanks to the furtherance of Julius II. In 1513 Leo X sent him as his legate to Henry VIII. In England he met Erasmus, whom he inspired to publish the works of St. Jerome. In 1515 he became Nuntius to the court of Ferdinand the Catholic, in Madrid where his hatred of Spain, a mark of the House of Carafa, deepened, although Charles V bestowed on him the achbishopric of Brindisi as well as his see at Chieti. Hadrian VI called him to Rome, and under Clement VII he resigned his bishoprics so that together with St. Gaetano of Tiene he might form the reform order of the Theatines in 1524. In 1536 he became a cardinal and the dean of the college.

Paul was the soul of the reform in its most severe expression. The purity of his priesthood corresponds to an equal degree of self-assuredness, iron will and energy. Even under Paul III he was considered the driving force of the inquisition, and later Cardinal Girolamo Seripando, the gifted general of the Augustine hermits, said jokingly: "May God grant that he will carry through for the reform of the church what Paul III said he wished, for Paul III spoke not acted, Marcellus did what he was able, and said nothing. If only Paul IV were to talk and act—were to do what he said." Seripando's hopes were at first to remain unfulfilled. One of Paul's first acts was to raise his protégé, Carlo Carafa, a brutish adventurer without conscience, and a condottiere, to the rank of cardinal

163

deacon and secretary of state. Carlo soon had his uncle completely in his power. A man of low blackmailing character, he looked after the house of Carafa most generously and strove, like Cesare Borgia, for a princedom. The Pope and the cardinal were guided by one thought and one thought only in their policies; hatred of Spain, Charles V, and after his abdication in 1556, Philip II—a hatred which degenerated into a wild passion. The protégé had in fact served for many years with the imperial army, but had felt himself slighted. In December 1555 Paul allied himself to France, taking no notice of the fact that by so doing he was aiding the Protestants, was helping the Turks and engaging Lutheran mercenaries. On Philip II's order, the Duke of Alba forestalled their plan to start an unprovoked war, by advancing from Naples and threatening the pontifical state. Alba's victory at Paliano, at the same time as the Spanish victory at St. Quentin in Flanders, as well as the threat of a new Sacco di Roma forced Paul to make the Peace of Cava in Palestrina, which was sealed on 12th September 1557. Shortly before this he had planned to "depose" Philip. The conditions which the King imposed for the settlement proved as moderate as the damages of the campaign which he had provoked were serious for Paul—quite apart from the damage which his reputation had suffered. In other ways, too, the beginning of his pontificate was not convincing. In contrast to Marcellus II, Paul lived in princely style and made Giovanni, cardinal Carafa's deceitful brother, the Duke of Paliano. Two other protégés, however, Alfonso and Diomede proved worthy members of the College of Cardinals, and other less important protégés also received preferment—Paul had committed exactly the errors with which he had reproached other popes. After the political bankruptcy of the Spanish campaign, Paul devoted himself to reform, without showing any interest in continuing the Council of Trent. He began to take stern action against the corrupt clergy and to suppress simoniac movements towards the election of a new pope. His efforts had a decisive influence upon the later decrees of the Council of Trent. But, whatever credit he may have deserved for this has been overshadowed in history by the reputation which he gained as the pope responsible for the most terrible inquisition. Ignoring the elementary teachings of Christianity, this

164

pitiless man, who was filled with hatred, raised the inquisition up to the position of his favorite authority and swore the fearful oath that: "even if my own father were a heretic, I would gather the wood, to burn him with my own hands." Cardinal Seripando wrote "At the outset, this court, like the nature of Paul III, was moderate and mild, but later, chiefly, as a result of Carafa's inhuman severity it gained such significance, that people believed that nowhere on earth were more terrible and fearful verdicts passed." If worldliness had reached its peak under the Renaissance popes, reform swung to the other and no less questionable extreme and it took time for the scales, in the inexorable march of history, to reach equilibrium again. Paul did not hesitate during the perpetual sniffing out of heretics, which had become second nature to him, to accuse, along with other innocent people, two cardinals who had done great service to the church: Giovanni Morone and Reginald Pole, who was once more living in England. For a long time he had persecuted them both with his personal hatred. Morone whom only the Jesuits were courageous enough to support, was imprisoned in the Castel S. Angelo, from which he was released only after Paul's death. Pole refused to make an appearance in Rome and the touching vindication of himself which expresses his sorrowful disappointment at Paul's behaviour is one of the most shaming documents written about him and contains, indirectly, the sharpest indictments. St. Peter Canisius, the first German Jesuit, declared that the Index of Forbidden Books which Paul set up was a stumbling block, and Cardinal Ghislieri, who was undeniably a strict leader of the Roman inquisition, maintained that Paul, by banning Ariosto's *Cento novelle antiche* and his *Orlando Furioso,* had merely made himself ridiculous. The Index in this form was later revoked. The Jews who so often found in the Pope a source of succour and justice were sent back into the ghetto by this tyrant, who degraded them still further with his order that they should wear yellow hats. At the beginning of 1559 Paul at last learned of the criminal treason of Cardinal Carafa, who together with all the other protégés was mercilessly hounded out of Rome. The Pope died in the knowledge that he had compromised his work of reform by his nepotism. The curse of the population which was freed from terror by his death followed him into the grave. The inquisition building was burned to the ground, Paul's statue on the capitol was torn down, its head rolled through the city and finally cast into the Tiber. Paul's pontificate in spite of all that was correct, justifiable and praiseworthy about his reforms, marked a step back into the time of Boniface VIII. Like Boniface he inflicted punishment upon the world—like Boniface, he treated the princes of the earth as immature schoolchildren, who were supposed to accept orders from him which were as arrogant as they were rhetorical. Under the icy severity of the Carafa Pope, all the arts and all intellectual activity had to perish. The world has scarcely been able to find one likeable trait in this stony, ascetic man who knew neither his fellow beings nor the power of moderation.

PIUS IV
Giovanni Angelo de' Medici
25 December, 1559 to 9th December, 1565

In spite of all the excesses against the Carafas the College of Cardinals recalled Carlo Carafa, the protégé who had been deposed, and restored him to his office. Morone, too, was released from prison and joined the conclave, which after deliberating for three and half months elected the cardinal of Santa Pudenziana. Pius who was not related to the Florentine Medicis, and up to this time had never made great impression, was the son of a notary and was born on 31st March, 1499 in Milan. After studying medicine, philosophy and law in Pavia and Milan he came to Rome, where thanks to his patron who was later Paul III, he soon became a high administrative official. After a period of very changeable activity, Medici rose ever more quickly. He has been shown to have had, before 1542, two illegitimate daughters and one illegitimate son, who never achieved any importance. Suspicions which have been raised as to Medici's mode of life as a cardinal and indeed as Pope have never been proved and can neither be confirmed nor denied. Medici was ordained in 1545 and a year later he became the archbishop of Ragusa: he was very active politically and became a cardinal in

1549. Under Paul IV he retired to his new see of Foligno. The election of this cardinal who was friendly, lively, contended and well-loved for his charitable acts, and yet of a simple nature aroused general pleasure. Pius at once set about establishing good relations with the princes, and furthering his protégés, the Hohenems—or Altemps as they were also called—the Serbelloni, the Borromeos and others. Altogether twenty-eight protégés appeared in Rome. One of them has gone down in the church as one of the greatest saints: Carlo Borromeo, the son of a sister of the pope and his favorite nephew. In 1560 at the age of twenty-one together with another protégé, Gian Antonio Serbelloni, he received the purple as cardinal of SS Vito e Modesto and also became Secretary of State. The sudden death of his brother Federigo, whom the pope had selected to found a princely house, put Carlo, the good influence in this pontificate, onto the path which was finally to lead him to develop into a saint. He became a priest with the title of Santa Prassesse, where the table at which he fed the poor of Rome can still be seen. At the beginning of his pontificate, Pius tried the Carafas, after the notorious Duke Giovanni of Paliano, supported by his brother, Cardinal Carlo, had had his wife murdered. Both were executed with their accomplices. Cardinal Alfonso Carafa, who was arrested at the same time, but who was innocent was released, and died at the age of twenty-four, in his archbishopric of Naples, a completely broken man. The scandalous cardinal Innocent del Monte, the protégé of Julius III, who had also been imprisoned was spared but sent into exile. The tragedy spelt the end of territorial nepotism. After Pius IV all protégés, in so far as they existed at all, were satisfied with social distinctions and titles of the nobility. On 3rd and 4th December, 1563, the final session of the Council of Trent took place after so many changing and fateful fortunes. It was unable to restore unity of belief, but the fault for this lies not with the Council but with the delays of the years immediately after the appearance of Luther. On the other hand it did achieve considerable significance for the renewal of the Catholic doctrine and way of life, which could be sensed on all sides. In collaboration with the Council, Pius sought the greatest mildness in carrying on the inquisition whose autonomous position of power can only be understood against the background of the ferment of a time in which questions of faith stood in the forefront of thought, and heresies generally had a fateful effect on the life of the state. The massacre of Vassy in 1562 and the apostate movement marked the beginning of the French religious wars, the main guilt of which must be borne by the policies of Catherine de' Medici. In December 1564 there was a conspiracy against the pope's life: the murderer was betrayed and executed. Pius, whose taxation policy in Rome caused the greatest discontent distinguished himself by his sober intelligence and moderation, which stood the counter-reformation in very good stead. His patronage was bestowed more liberally on the plastic arts than on the literary. He commissioned Piero Ligorio to complete the Belvedere court in the Vatican according to Bramante's design, and also to build the great niche which had presumably already been designed by Michelangelo, in which, since the time of Pius V, the gigantic and venerable pine cone, which was mentioned by Dante, has stood. During the carnival of 1556 the massive courtyard which did not then contain the huge library wing, was inaugurated by a great tournament. In 1563 Giovanni da Udine completed his paintings in the Loggia della Cosmografia. The casket ceiling of the Sala della Concistoro Segreto was also worked on Pius' orders, and the Sala dei Papi were enhanced. However, nothing has done so much to keep the name of this papal builder alive as the building conceived as a resting place, the Casino Pio IV. This building stands in the grounds of the Vatican and is today the home of the papal academy of sciences. One of the most costly buildings of all time, it is particularly important as it is the only completely preserved secular building of the period of transition between the renaissance and the Baroque. Pius commissioned Michelangelo to design the Porta Pia, laid the foundation stone himself and then handed the work of building over to the master. He had the Porta del Popolo rebuilt and commissioned the building, also by Michelangelo, of the church of Santa Maria degli Angeli in the thermal springs of Diocletian on the Piazza Esedra, which was completed in 1566. The pope's tomb is in the church. Under Pius' protection, the eighty-six year old Michelangelo remained the builder in charge of St. Peter's. In 1564 this great man who had served ten popes and who had done more than any other artist for the glory of Rome, the church, and the papacy, died. The Pope's plan of having him buried in St. Peter's, the place of his most sublime activity as a builder, and of raising up a memorial to him there, came to nothing because Michelangelo in his will had asked to be taken back to Florence. Pius insisted that Michelangelo's ideas and plans for St. Peter's should be carried out. The Pope's last great idea, the building of colonnades in front of St. Peter's, was not realized until much later, by Bernini. Pius is the only pope, who together with Carlo Borromeo, has appeared in an opera: in Hans Pfitzner's legend *Palestrina*, with its underlying theme of the reform of the church according to the decisions of the Council of Trent.

PIUS V
Antonio Michele Ghislieri
7th January, 1566 to 1st May, 1572

The reform cardinal Carlo Borromeo was the driving force behind the election of Ghislieri. Ghislieri was born of poor parents in Savoy on 17th January, 1504, and as a boy worked as a shepherd. A patron made possible his entry into the Dominican order when he was fourteen. This exemplary member of the order soon became a prior, and the Inquisitor of Como. In Rome, in 1550, he met the future Paul IV and gained his support. Ghislieri's passionate faith refused to allow him to undertake a dangerous journey into the Protestant province of Chur in Switzerland, because he wished to have the joy of dying a martyr's death in the Dominican habit. Julius III summoned him to Rome and appointed him General Commissar of the Inquisition. He fulfilled this function in Rome after Paul IV, in spite of his protests, had appointed him to the see of Sutri and Nepi, and made him, in 1552, cardinal of Santa Maria sopra Minerva, and later of Santa Sabina. Pius IV limited his authority as Grand Inquisitor. As Pope this ascetic man, stern, conscientious and completely unworldly, wore his hair shirt beneath his papal robes and, as far as his duties would allow, continued to live the life of a monk. Twice a year he made a pilgrimage on foot

169

to the seven arch-basilicas. Without his tiara and chair he carried the Holy of Holies through the streets in the Corpus Christi procession. His first act after his coronation was to dismiss his predecessor's court jester. Only the urgent pleas of the cardinals moved him to make a cardinal of an insignificant nephew who was a Dominican. He appointed another nephew commandant of the bodyguard, but dismissed him when his way of life aroused unfavorable comment. The cardinal protégé was forbidden, among other things, to wear silken robes. Pius started at once on the task of reforming Roman morals. His good intentions often drove him so far that it was said that he wanted to turn the whole of Rome into a monastery. He took care, with an iron severity, that justice should really speak the word of the law. As to the inquisition, he went back to the edicts of Paul IV, yet even if, in the strict fulfillment of the decrees of the Council of Trent, a certain severity and even executions re-entered the courts of the inquisition, Pius was far from emulating the régime of terror of Paul IV, who greedily accepted every denunciation at its face value; on the other hand, his methods were certainly often far removed from the greatness of Pius IV's. He pressed for the unity of belief in Italy and spared the country political upsets and civil wars like those of the Huguenots in France. Yet a Capucin father pointed out to the Pope, who always listened humbly to the points of view of others, even if these were expressions of criticism, that for every passage in the Bible praising God's justice, there were ten others which praised his mercy. On the political side Pius's pontificate was filled with disputes over the demands for a state church raised by Philip II of Spain, with the risings in the Netherlands, the French religious wars, which had broken out under Pius IV, and the persecution of the Catholics which was taking place in England within the framework of the changes brought about by the establishment of a state church under Elizabeth I. In France, where political and religious demands were inextricably linked together through the politics of Catherine de'Medici, who lacked all interest in religious matters, the Huguenots had been granted religious freedom by the Peace of St. Germain on 8th August, 1570. In the same year, Pius published his Bull of excommunication on Elizabeth I—it is the last Bull of Excommunication and "deposition" to be issued against a ruling monarch. The only result of the Bull was to sharpen the Catholic persecutions which now exceeded the bounds of imaginable cruelty. In Germany, the Emperor, who had long had leanings towards Protestantism, agreed to the religious peace of Augsburg in 1555. Pius demanded that this peace be broken, and it was only with difficulty that he was restrained from pressing his demand and forcing the Emperor into open warfare with Rome.

Tension was increased when Pius bestowed the dignity of a grand-duke upon Duke Cosimo of Florence, as the only Italian prince: as feudal lord, Maximilian refused him the right to do this. The great event of this pontificate was the formation of the Holy League, on 20th May, 1571 between the Pope, Spain, and Venice, which was directed against the powerful Turkish armies now once more advancing. With the famous Don Juan of Austria, the natural son of Charles V, as High Commander, and Marcantonio Colonna, a nephew of Vittoria Colonna as the commander of the papal troops, and Admiral Sebastiano Vernier as commander of the Venetian fleet, the Turks were completely defeated at the sea battle of Lepanto on 7th October, 1571, one of the greatest victories over Islam. The festival which the Pope proclaimed in thanks, Our Dear Lady of the Victory, is celebrated on 7th October. Gregory XIII called it the Feast of the Rosary, and Clement XI prescribed it for the whole church. The Pope's faithful idealism did immeasurable service to the West with this victory. Venice, however, entered into a treacherous and separate peace with the Turks in 1573 and gave up Cyprus, which had spurred on the original advance of the League. Voltaire said mockingly that it seemed as if the Turks had won the victory of Lepanto. Like all the Holy Leagues of former popes the League of 1571 split up because of the special interests of the individual powers composing it. The greatest artists who celebrated Lepanto in their art were the fifty-nine year old Titian, whose allegory is in Madrid; Paolo Veronese, whose two works hang in the Academy and in the Doge's Palace in Venice; and Tintoretto whose work was destroyed by fire in 1867. In memory of the battle, the Pope donated a coffered ceiling to the church of Santa Maria in Aracoeli. Vasari was commissioned by the pope to paint his frescoes of the founding of the League and of the sea fight in the Sala Regia of the Vatican. Pius, who died after a painful illness wore his monk's habit even on his death bed. His grave, endowed by Sixtus V, is in Santa Maria Maggiore. Even if many of the pope's action have to be understood against the background of the desperate religious situation of his time, and the pope's lack of political understanding and human sympathy, there can be no doubt that he lived the life of a saint. In questions of faith he paid no heed to human wishes and demands, and he would have been ready to give his life for the church if occasion had arisen. "Thanks to his indefatigable energy, the dead letter of the Council began gradually to come alive again, and the countenance of the whole church began to be renewed," writes Ludwig von Pastro. Pius had little understanding for art, especially for antiquities. In his pontificate Jacopo Vignola received the order to build the Jesuit church, Il Gesù, in Rome, an endowment of the cardinal protégé, Allessandro Farnese. Pius was canonized on 22nd May, 1712.

GREGORY XIII
Ugo Boncompagni
13th, May 1572 to 10th, April 1585

The election of this unselfish, gentle lawyer who was born in Bologna on 1st January, 1502 was welcomed on all sides. He had begun his career as a professor of jurisprudence at the university of Bologna, had then held several minor offices in Rome and Trento and had become vice-legate. After holding a further office in Turin he was appointed cardinal of San Sisto in 1565 and in the same year Pius IV sent him with a mission to Madrid. Under Pius V he continued to perform his duties, and as a lawyer he was constantly opposing the severity of the Pope; on the insistence of the cardinals he made a good-humored though insignificant nephew a cardinal who was for a long time thought of as the poorest of the cardinals. For his son Giacomo, who was born ten years before Gregory was ordained, he purchased a dukedom and a county outside the Pontifical State. Giacomo spent his life as a patron of the arts, appointed Palestrina as his concertmaster and was friendly with Tasso. Gregory's work of reform, in which he came strongly under the influence of Cardinal Borromeo, came at a time when many of the saints were also busy: in Rome Philip Neri, the patron saint of Rome and the friend of the proletariat founded the oratory within the framework of whose teaching outstanding laymen were brought to a new religious and spiritual revival and trained to act as lay apostles to carry St. Philip Neri's message to others. One of Philip's most assiduous pupils was the great cardinal, Cesare Baronius, who wrote for him the history of the Popes. In 1576 Gregory summoned the Jesuit, Roberto Bellarmin, the nephew of Marcellus II and a professor in Louvain, to Rome. Here he developed his rich literary theological activity and served as the chief teacher at the priestly seminaries which Gregory had set up for Germany and England, the Germanicum-Hungaricum and the Anglicanum. At the same time Spain produced in Theresa of Avila one of the greatest women and saints of all time, whose Carmelite rule was confirmed by Gregory in 1580. St. John of the Cross, another classic writer of mysticism and a figure in the literature of the world, worked together with St. Theresa. Politically Gregory's pontificate began on 23rd and 24th August, 1572, with the massacre of St. Bartholomew's Eve, in which Catherine de' Medici, through her son Charles IX, who was completely dominated by her, crowned her sinister policies by the murder of the leading Huguenots. Her atrocity forms a parallel to the cruelties meted out over the years by the Huguenots to the Catholics. Gregory celebrated what he genuinely believed to be the victory of the Catholic cause in France with a festival Te Deum—but not, as has often been maintained, because he rejoiced at the crime, whose motives had been completely falsely represented to him. When he learned the truth the Pope burst into tears and cried: "I weep for this act of the King, which is illegal and which is against God's will." True, the danger of a Huguenot invasion was eliminated, but the hopes which Rome had pinned on the happening soon showed themselves to be deceptive and the Huguenot wars continued in the same way as before, just as the complete lack of religious acumen continued at the court of Catherine de'

173

Medici. Things did not improve even when Charles IX was succeeded by his weakling of a brother, the last Valois, Henry III. The rejection of the acceptance of the decrees of the Council of Trent which Gregory had demanded marked a decisive strengthening of so-called gallicanism, French ecclesiastical independence. While the Pope was active with his work of the counter-reformation in many European countries which had gone over to Protestantism, his attitude towards England and towards Elizabeth I was weak at a number of points, and is shown up in a rather unfortunate light. The position which he took up, even though it did not arise from any flaw in his character, was unworthy of a pope: after having unsuccessfully urged Philip II to embark upon a war of intervention against England, he supported the miserably unsuccessful plan of an atheistic adventurer for a rising Ireland; this resulted in a renewal of Elizabeth's persecution of the Catholics. Later Gregory gave his approval to a plan for murdering the Queen which had been advanced by a few English noblemen, and even if political assassination was a commonplace at this time, and Elizabeth had formed plans for assassinating the Pope in 1581, Gregory as a Pope of the counter-reformation should have set himself above the view current among many of his contemporaries that a person who had been excommunicated was automatically an outlaw. Under Gregory's pontificate the Catholic missions in Asia, Africa, and America began to assume world-wide significance: as missionaries the Jesuits performed inestimable services both for learning and for religion. In Rome, which Montaigne describes so colorfully and vividly in his journal for 1580 and 1581, Gregory developed a considerable and many-sided building-program, although he is not reckoned among the great papal patrons of art. Masters like Giacomo Vignola, Giacomo della Porta, Bartolomeo Ammanati, Martino Lunghi, Giorgio Vasari and Federigo Zuccari served under the pope. Lunghi was in charge of the building of St. Peter's which was now rapidly approaching completion. He was also commissioned to build the Chiesa Nuova, known as Santa Maria in Vallicella, which is for the priests of the oratory. Many Roman fountains were built at this time, among them the enchanting Fontana della Tartarughe in the Piazza del Popolo. The furnishing of the capitol according to

174

the designs of Michelangelo made significant progress. Here, too, Gregory commissioned Porta and Lunghi to work, and in 1579 the latter built the belfry of the Palace of the Senators. In 1575 the Pope ordered work to begin on the Palace of the Quirinal. In the Sala Regia, Vasari painted a number of pictures, among them the excommunication of Frederick II by Gregory IX, the return of Gregory XI from Avignon, the battle of Lepanto and three frescoes depicting the Massacre of St. Bartholomew. The Sala di Bologna in the Vatican also bears witness to Gregory's activity, for it was on his initiative that one of the most important frescoes in the Vatican was begun: the Galleria delle Carte Geografiche with the sixteen monumental painted charts by Ignazio Danti, which are of equal value as works of art and as documents. The Pope's most important act and the one which had great historical significance was the Gregorian reform of the calendar. The reform was not introduced into all the countries of Western Europe until the 18th century, and some orthodox countries only introduced it after the first World War.

Gregory died at the age of eighty-four. The lively pontificate of this industrious and pious pope, who was filled with an active charity, marks a decisive period in the papacy of the counter-reformation. Gregory is buried in the Capella Gregoriana in St. Peter's.

SIXTUS V
Felice Peretti
24th, April 1585 to 27th, August 1590

The new pope sprang from very humble origins: he was born on 13th December, 1521 and, having become a Franciscan, gained a considerable degree of fame as a preacher and a strict advocate of reform. Paul IV appointed him inquisitor of Venice and Paul V appointed him vicar-general of the Franciscan conventuals, at the same time making him Bishop of Santa Agata near Goti. When Peretti became a cardinal in 1570 he took the name of Montalto. Under Gregory XIII he was condemned to inactivity, as neither of them could tolerate the other. His anger towards Gregory is understandable when it is remembered that the murder of his nephew by his wife Vittoria Accorombona, the heroine of Stendhal's and Tieck's novels of the same name, went unavenged. Sixtus, who had always hoped for the tiara, made one of his first acts as Pope the bestowal of the red hat upon his fifteen-year old nephew Alessandro Peretti-Montalto, who later developed into an excellent personality. He also provided for other relatives, but never at the expense of the state. Two of his great-nieces married into the Orsini and Colonna families. He appointed the heads of the two families to take turns in the office of assistant to the papal throne, the highest office which could be bestowed upon a layman. Sixtus's pontificate began with the most severe and ruthless measures against banditry, which imposed the death sentence even upon the main accomplices of thieves. Two years later the security of the Pontifical State was assured. With Draconian severity Sixtus imposed the death penalty for incest, procuration, abortion, sodomy and adultery, and he did not spare those who were closest to him. At the same time, he organized a fleet to defend the coasts against the corsairs. He took great pains to see that Rome was well provisioned, undertook the draining of the Pontine marshes, encouraged agriculture, furthered the woolen and silk industries, and in 1589 the state treasury was in possession of four million scudi, partly as the result of a temporarily successful, yet basically unhealthy financial policy, and partly as the result of the sale of offices. He was responsible for finally fixing the number of cardinals at seventy—six cardinal bishops, fifty cardinal priests, and fourteen cardinal deacons—the present-day composition of the college. The organization of the curia and the congregations which he carried out in 1588 is, with a few alterations demanded by the times, still in force.

After the assassination of Henry III in 1589, Henry of Navarre, the last Valois and leader of the Huguenots, came to the throne of France as Henry IV, the first of the Bourbons. Since Henry had promised to protect the Catholics, Sixtus took no action, but preferred to wait; Philip II however demanded action against Henry, and invaded France, only to suffer defeat at Ivry. Sixtus, a man of considerable political insight, who was bothered by the superiority of Spain, had realized that Rome's independence could only be maintained if there was a balance of power among the Catholic powers. England demanded quite a different attitude on the Pope's part. Sixtus saw in Elizabeth the strongest enemy of the counter-reformation, and yet he respected her capabilities as a ruler. He had no scruples about summoning Spain to make war on England, even though he rejected her policy towards France. On 18th February, 1587, Mary Stuart, the Catholic claimant of the English throne was beheaded after she had nominated Philip II, shortly before her death, as the heir of her dominions. Pope Urban VIII later wrote a poem on her death. In July, Sixtus and Philip II agreed upon a war to win back England for the old faith. These high-falutin plans of the Spanish Armada were destroyed in the English Channel between 31st July and 8th August, 1588, thus rocking Spanish imperial power to its very foundations. This defeat crushed any hope that Sixtus may have had of England's returning to the old unity of faith. After the defeat Sixtus no longer felt obliged to pay to Spain the sums of money which he had promised to contribute to the war as part of the agreement between himself and Philip.

Sixtus is buried in the "Sistine Chapel" of Santa Maria Maggiore, which he had commissioned in 1586 from Domenico Fontana; he also transferred the body of Pius V to this chapel. His heart—and from this time on the hearts of all popes up to Leo XIII—was taken to SS Vicenzo ed Anastasio. Sixtus belongs to those popes who are attractive less by nature of their human qualities, than through the importance and admiration which they gain as rulers. The idea which he held of having the right to act as the guardian of the whole world and having the right to decide in matters temporal and spiritual, was not in keeping with the times. In this way and in this way only he was emulating Paul IV and Boniface VIII, to whom in all other ways he was superior. He even placed on the Index the *Disputations*, the masterpiece of Roberto Bellarmin, the Jesuit and later cardinal, because in this work Bellarmin took up a different and more mature attitude than Sixtus, and only recognized an indirect papal power in temporal matters. As a statesman Sixtus belongs among the great figures of his century. He retained his Franciscan mode of life even as Pope, and he was a prudent ruler of the Roman people, in whose memory he lives on in innumberable anecdotes and legends as "Papa Sisto." Intrepidity, strength of will, clarity of understanding and impartiality distinguished his character more than mercy and goodness. In this he had much in common with Julius II. His pontificate was of outstanding importance for art and learning. Among other things he furthered the future Cardinal Cesare Baronius's great history of the church which had been suggested by St. Philip Neri. Baronius dedicated to the Pope the first two volumes of this work, which is one of the masterpieces of Western historical writing, a treasure trove for the student of medieval history. Tasso, too, enjoyed the personal protection of the Pope, whose building program the poet celebrated in enthusiastic verse, especially Sixtus's greatest work, the huge aqueducts of the Aqua Felice, with which in the literal sense of the word he again embraced the seven hills of Rome. Sixtus consecrated the columns of Trajan and Marcus Aurelius to the apostles Peter and Paul, and so began his transformation of heathen monuments into Christian ones. He enhanced the appearance of the city by the building of new streets and squares: the Via Sistina is named after him. He had the huge obelisk of Caligula from Heliopolis, which for years had lain half in ruins near St. Peter's, erected on St. Peter's square. This work of engineering genius was carried out by Domenico Fontana, the Pope's chief builder, and Sixtus bestowed the title Cavalleria della guglia—knight of the obelisk—on him. Sixtus had the famous words, that have now become a Catholic hymn: Christus vincit, Christus regnat, Christus imperat, engraved on the foot of the obelisk, which itself is not without significance for the papacy. It had already witnessed the martyrdom of St. Peter and seen the living torches formed by the early Christian martyrs in Nero's circus, the heights and the depths, the pomp and the shame of the papacy—a dumb witness to immeasurable historical dramas in a millennium and a half. Sixtus also had other obelisks in Rome dug up and placed before Santa Croce, the Lateran, in front of Santa Maria Maggiore and on the Piazza del Popolo. In 1568 he commissioned Fontana to build the Lateran palace, which today houses a number of important museums, but which caused the reckless demolition of some ancient and medieval monuments. Frescoes in the Palace glorify the life and works of the Pope. In the Vatican, Sixtus divided the Belvedere court into two by the building of the present library, and another of his works was the Salone di Sisto V with its magnificent frescoes in praise of the greatness of books, which is the most costly book exhibition room in the world. In 1589 Fontana started to build the new Vatican palace, which was completed and furnished during the pontificates of the succeeding popes. The most powerful undertaking of this super-active Pope was the building of the cupola of St. Peter's by della Porta and Fontana according to Michelangelo's designs, twenty-five years after his death. On 14th May, 1590, the last stone, blessed by Sixtus and bearing his name was laid in the cupola after a thanksgiving mass had been sung. On this day an eighth hill was added to the seven hills of Rome, as an eternal symbol. In the spire of the Lateran the following words stand in gold mosaic: Sancti Petri Gloriae Sixtus Pontifex Maximus V Anno 1590. A picture of Sixtus V painted by a member of the Roman school hangs in the Pinacoteca Vaticana.

URBAN VII
Giambattista Castagna
15th, September 1590 to 27th, September 1590

The election of the former Nuncius in Madrid, the cardinal of San Marcello, who was born on 4th August, 1521 in Rome, met with approval on all sides, but on the second day after his election the new Pope fell ill. Many hopes were buried with him. A portrait of Urban by an anonymous painter is in the Sala dei Foconi in the Vatican.

GREGORY XIV
Niccolò Sfondrati
5th, December 1590 to 16th, October 1591

The so-called "papal prophecies" of Malachia seem to have arisen during the *sedes vacans* after the death of Urban VII, and

179

the back-dating of them to the time of Celestinus II is a forgery.
The origins of these mottoes, which bear on the individual pontificates right up to the present day, can no longer be determined.

The *sedes vacans*, which Tasso lamented in a sonnet, came to
an end with the election of the cardinal of Cremona, who was also
praised by Tasso in one of his most beautiful poems. Gregory, who
was born on 11th February 1535 in Milan, studied law and was a
friend of St. Carlo Borromeo and St. Philip Neri. In Rome this
saintly, peaceful and very sick cardinal lived a very retired life.
Completely inexperienced in politics he made the mistake of immediately appointing a nephew, who was equally inexperienced,
to be a cardinal and secretary of state; this nephew soon showed
himself to be a presumptuous upstart who quickly aroused the
displeasure of the cardinals. The policy of maintaining the balance
of power, so skillfully carried out by Sixtus V, was given up, to the
benefit of Spain and the detriment of Henry IV of France. Gregory
made the disastrous decision of giving Spain military aid against
the French king. The whole plan miscarried and made the most
drastic inroads into the fortune which Sixtus V had so carefully
amassed. The pope's work within the church continued on the lines
of the counter-reformation pursued by his predecessors. Palestrina
dedicated a collection of motets to his old patron, who died after
suffering the greatest agony. Gregory had the lantern placed on
the cupola of St. Peter's which had been completed under Sixtus
V's patronage.

INNOCENT IX
Gian Antonio Facchinetti
29th October, 1591 to 30th December, 1591

No doubt the cardinals chose this ailing old man because he was
as acceptable to Philip II as his predecessor had been, while the
cardinals sought to conceal their hatred for Spain in order to
gain time. Innocent was so infirm that in Rome he was known as
"the clinical pontiff." Nonetheless, he developed a lively course of

action which kept his policies in line with those of his predecessors. Like a builder, he followed the plan of Sixtus V. Always kindly, dignified, and religiously frugal, he was mourned at his death as an upright man.

CLEMENT VIII
Ippolito Aldobrandini
30th January, 1592 to 3rd March, 1605

Descended from a family which had emigrated from Florence to Rome, he was born in Fano on February 24th, 1536. Alessandro Farnese, the supreme nepotist as Paul III, made it possible for him to study law. Advancing in the papal service, Aldobrandini became Cardinal of San Pancrazio in 1585 and proved his diplomatic talent in the question of the succession to the Polish throne after the death of King Stephen Bathory. Although as a cardinal he had been strongly critical of nepotism, as Pope he fell into the same evil, when, after long deliberation and much urging from the cardinals, he elevated his two nephews, Cinzio Passeri-Aldobrandini and Pietro Aldobrandini, to the offices of Cardinal and Secretary of State. Both were admirable men. Pietro, the builder of the Villa Aldobrandini in Frascati, played a prominent political role as a skillful diplomat. Likewise Cinzio gained prominence as an important patron of the arts, the man with whom the true patronage of the Baroque began. The "Aldobrandini wedding", which was excavated at that time, was named after him. The worldly protégé Gian Frumesco was a good soldier and an intelligent administrator. Clement would not accept the formation of a princedom for his family. The French question, which was still precariously balanced, presented the pope with an urgent problem, but the combined political wisdom of the Pope and Henry IV finally achieved a solution in 1595 when Henry IV was converted to Catholicism. His reception into communion with the church and the final recognition of Henry as the legal king dealt a serious blow to Philip II's Spanish empire. The papacy, too, now saw itself slowly being relieved of an unbearable pressure: Clement was able to intervene as a mediator and peacemaker and was especially able to contribute to the internal peace of the church in France. However, he did encounter some difficulties, as Henry IV would not accept the decrees of the Council of Trent in order not to alienate the Huguenots and the Gallicans: the Edict of Nantes of 30th, April, 1598 was decisive in securing religious freedom for Catholics and Calvinists. France was soon to produce, in François de Sales, the first of a whole line of saints who completely changed the face of the Catholic religion in France during the Grand Siècle. The Pope was able to enlarge the Pontifical State by incorporating Ferrara, when the legitimate line of the House of Este died out: he resided there for six months soon after. Clement's relationship with Spain, where Philip III had succeeded Philip II remained tense; he was not allowed to form a League against the advancing Turks, nor did the position in England alter when, in 1603, Elizabeth I was succeeded by James I, the son of Mary Queen of Scots, who defended his crafty religious policy in a letter to the cardinal Roberto Bellarmin. Inside the church Clement found himself faced throughout Europe with a host of problems, outstanding among which was the complicated struggle over the question of Grace between the Jesuits and the Dominicans. Finally two further events took place during Clement's pontificate which were to exercise people in later years; the executions of Giordano Bruno the famous heretic, and of the parricide Beatrice Cenci. Both of these cases drew the pope into a conflict of opposing ideas—in the case of Beatrice, completely unjustifiably, for the picture of this youthful murderess in no way corresponds to the idealized figure of persecuted innocence which Shelley portrays in *The Cenci* a verdict which has been repeated time and time again by dramatists and novelists. Clement and the two cardinal protégés developed an extensive scheme of patronage: Pietro supported, especially, Gianbattista Marini, the founder of baroque literature. Batista Guarini was also one of the many pupils of Cardinal Cinzio's academy: he was the author of the pastoral drama *I pastor fido,* a work important in the history of music for the large number of times that it has been set to music. In addition to these there were Luca Marenzio, the composer, and classical writer of madrigals, and above all, Tasso whose *Gerusalemme liberata* became the real epic of the counter-reformation. The revision of *Gerusalemme liberata*, which was an artistic failure and the *Discorsi del poema eroico*—A Discourse on the Heroic Poem —were dedicated to Cinzio, who right to the end did all in his power to help the unfortunate poet: he it was who personally brought him the pope's blessing as he lay on his deathbed in Sant' Onofrio on the Gianicolo. While still a cardinal Clement had been the poet's patron and in 1592 he gave him quarters in the Vatican —it was here that Tasso wrote his religious poem on the creation of the world. The breviary owes one of its most beautiful hymns to this pope who was so receptive to poetry: the *Pater superni luminis,* which was composed as part of a papal wager. In 1597 Orlando di Lasso dedicated his last work, *The Tears of St. Peter's,* to Clement. Cesare Baronius whose immense history of the church was making important strides, became head of the Vatican library, which enjoyed the Pope's especial support. In 1596 Giacomo della Porta, Fontana's successor, finished the Vatican palace. In 1593 the golden ball and the cross were placed upon the cupola of St. Peter's, whilst Cavaliere d'Arpino was busy with the designs for the mosaics inside. The new papal altar, still without its structure, was consecrated by Clement under the cupola on 26th June, 1594. The Capella Clementina, which stands opposite the Capella Gregoriana is called after him. Cardinal Varionius was the chief adviser for the pictorial decoration of the altar. After Porta's death Clement appointed Carlo Marata to take charg of building operations. He also commissioned a number of works in the Lateran basilica. In the Palace of the Vatican he built the Sala del Consistoro and the Sala Clementina. One of the Pope's most significant acts was to insist upon the completion of the buildings begun by Michelangelo, though he never lived to see them finished. The cardinals, too, vied with each other in building and furnishing churches. In Clement's pontificate the Dominican poet-philosopher Thomas Campanella, who had been influenced by Thomas More, wrote his *City of the Sun* (1602), portraying the powerful Utopia of a universal Catholic monarchy. Clement, a pious, conscientious, just, and peace-loving Pope is buried in the Capella Borghese of

183

Santa Maria Maggiore, which was erected by Paul V. In remarkable contrast, but probably partially as a result of ill-health, circumspection, restlessness and often indecision opposed each other in his make-up. He listened to criticism with an open mind. This charitable Pope delighted in taking his simple meal together with a number of Roman poor, whom he would often serve himself.

LEO XI
Alessandro de' Medici-Ottaviano
1st April, 1605 to 27th April, 1605

The Spanish faction in the College of Cardinals prevented the election of the great Cesare Baronius, yet Spain was equally dissatisfied with the election of de' Medici. Leo was a son of a niece of Leo X and was born in Florence on 2nd June, 1535. He was an excellent man who had been a pupil of St. Philip Neri, later becoming bishop of Pistoia and archbishop of Florence. In 1583 Gregory made him a cardinal. His election was approved on all sides and there was great sorrow on his dying so shortly after. He enjoyed a great reputation as a patron of the arts. The Villa Medici on the Monte Pincio in Rome is named after him. The portrait of Leo by Antonio Scalvati hangs in the Sala dei Foconi in the Vatican.

PAUL V
Camillo Borghese
16th May, 1605 to 28th January, 1621

Paul was born in Rome of a Siennese family who had taken up their residence there, studied law and entered upon the career of a priest. Clement VIII sent the knowledgeable and intelligent prelate as ambassador to the court of Philip II, and on the successful completion of his mission there in 1596, made him a cardinal and Bishop of Jesi; he later made him Vicar of Rome. Shortly after his election Paul made his twenty-seven year old nephew Scipione Safarelli a cardinal and gave him the name Borghese. This protégé who was later to achieve such popularity and whose joviality Bernini has expressed so convincingly in his two famous busts in the Villa Borghese at Rome, had many pleasing traits of character and avoided any unorthodox behavior. He made a name for himself as a typical baroque patron of the arts, a collector and the builder of the Villa Borghese, but he was not an outstanding secretary of state. Borghese put the huge income which Paul secured for him to the best use and there is no such proof that he led a doubtful life. Two brothers and other relatives of the Pope's younger brother founded the House of the Princes of Borghese. At the beginning of the pontificate there was a sharp dispute with Venice upon which the interdict was placed, because of the measures taken there toward the creation of a state church and the persecutions which were taking place. The complications threatened to lead to a war, in which the English and German Protestant rulers had promised to support Venice: Henry IV of France finally succeeded in making a compromise peace, out of which neither the Pope nor Venice emerged victorious. The conflict had demonstrated that the power of the papal interdict over a state was broken, and that historical development had gone beyond the rigidity of this last resort. Paul remained neutral in his dealings with France, in spite of the fact that Henry tried to influence him against Spain and in spite of the fact that Paul had equally little desire to witness Spain's superiority. The situation did not become tense until Maria de' Medici became regent for her son Louis XIII after the murder of Henry IV in 1610. There was a rapprochement between the two powers in the next year, followed by the formation of a Defense League made possible by the double marriage which was arranged on the one hand between the heir to the Spanish throne, later Philip IV and Louis XIII's sister Isabella, and on the other between Louis XIII and Philip's sister Anna. Paul's nuncios exerted a decisive influence on both of these events. Even if at the same time anti-papal writings were appearing in France, Paul had the satisfaction of knowing that, in 1615, under the leadership of Cardinal Jacques du Perron, the French clergy declared the decrees of the Council of Trent to be binding, and so set out on the path of revival. In England in 1605 the Gunpowder Plot, a desperate act strongly disapproved of by the church, but with its origins among Catholics led to new difficulties: James I's accusations that Paul was the originator of the plot were quite unscrupulous: on the contrary, Paul expressed to the King his horror at the affair and even demanded the punishment of some Jesuits if they had actually been connected with the plot, but instead, Henry Garnet, the noble leader of the English Jesuits, who was just as innocent as his fellow brothers, was most cruelly executed. The plot was the signal for new persecutions, which spread as far as Ireland. The last years of the pontificate saw the fraternal quarrel in the House of Hapsburg and following the uprising in Bohemia, the outbreak of the Thirty Years' War. A few weeks after the Battle of the Weisser Berg, a victory for the Roman Catholic Church, the Pope died. He is buried in the Capella Paolina of Santa Maria Maggiore, which he himself donated. A man of unblemished life, pious, of modest needs, without passion and completely unselfish, Paul damaged his reputatioon only by his nepotism, for his generosity was only directed towards his own family. St. Peter's was finally completed during his pontificate, and Michelangelo's plan for a central building was given up. Carlo Maderna, whom Paul had summoned to Rome, built the Long House. In 1615 the anteroom to the Confessio was built. After the steps to the Square of St. Peter's had been laid out in 1617 and the statues of the apostles dating from Pius II's time had been erected, this great work, upon which generations of men had been employed could really be considered complete. In contrast to the demolitions carried out by Bramante at the beginning of the reconstruction, Paul saved anything which was of the least value. In Rome several new churches were built, and two new rooms were constructed in the library of the Vatican. The Quirinal was also extended. In 1612 Paul ordered the restoration of the old Trajan aqueduct, the Aqua Paola, as a counterpart to the Aqua Felice, and had built for himself on the Gianicolo, the incomparable water citadel which has been praised in verse by both Goethe and von Platen. Paul is also responsible for numerous fountains, among them the Aqua Acetose, built in the city. The Palazzo Borghese was not built by Paul but purchased by him and extended. He also had the first two fountains on St. Peter's Square built by Maderna. In the Villa

Borghese is Bernini's bust of the Pope as well as a portrait of him after an original of Caravaggio.

GREGORY XV
Alessandro Ludovisi
9th February, 1621 to 8th July, 1623

Born on the 9th January, 1554 of an old Bologna family, Ludovisi was consecrated a priest on the completion of his studies in Rome and entered the papal service under his compatriot Gregory XIII. Under Clement VIII this quiet, unbiased and learned prelate seized every possible opportunity for playing the role of peaceful mediator in difficult political situations. In 1612 he became Archbishop of Bologna and in 1616 a cardinal. He worked intensively towards reform in his diocese. Ludoviso Ludovisi, his protégé, who at the age of twenty-five had already proved himself as a priest, showed himself a man of gifts and integrity, and was of great value as an assistant to the pope, who was a sick man. In Rome he is best remembered as the donor of the church of Sant' Ignazio, and as the benefactor and collector from whose estate the Hera Ludovisi in the Thermae museum comes. The co-operation between Gregory, the wise counsellor, and his active protégé, both high-minded men, was exemplary at the time. The Pope achieved the transfer of the electorship of the Palatine to the Duke Maxmilian of Bavaria, and received in thanks the gift of the university library of Heidelberg —the Bibliotheca Palatina. In the so-called Veltlin question which threatened to lead to war between France and the Hapsburg power, Gregory mediated, initially, with some success. Richelieu who, in 1622 had become a cardinal, destroyed the Pope's work by occupying Veltlin—it was the period of the struggles of Jürg Jenatsch. Gregory crowned his comprehensive work within the church by his canonization on 12th March, 1622 of Ignatius Loyola, Philip Neri, Teresa of Avila and Francis Xavier, the apostle of Eastern Asia. In the same year he constituted the Propaganda Fide, a turning point in missionary history. Gregory, one of the most likeable of the Popes, is buried in Sant' Ignazio. The most well-known portrait of him is the bust by Bernini.

URBAN VIII
Maffeo Barberini
6th August, 1623 to 29th July, 1644

After the Aldobrandini, the Borghese and the Ludovisi, Urban marks the beginning of the rise to power of the Barberinis. He was born in Florence on 5th April, 1568, studied law and was Nuncius in Paris, where he was created a cardinal in 1606. Paul V bestowed the See of Spoleto on him. This wealthy cardinal kept a large establishment in Rome and was known as a literary connoisseur. He had hoped for the tiara in 1621. His nepotism knew no bounds; his twenty-six year old nephew Francesco Barberini, his twenty-year old brother, the Pope's own brother (a Capucine father, Antonio the Elder), as well as a nephew Lorenzo Magalotti, were all created cardinals. Francesco was a likeable person and was also a great patron of the arts, as was his less balanced brother; Antonio the Elder continued to live his strictly ascetic and industrious existence; Taddeo, the worldly brother of the cardinals was the founder of the princely house. None of these protégés exerted any influence upon Urban. Urban's pontificate coincided with the decisive phases of the Thirty Years' War, in the course of which he gave a small amount of financial aid to the Catholic powers. The successes on the Catholic side led the Emperor Ferdinand II to issue an edict of restitution in 1629, calling on the Protestant powers to restore any church property which they had confiscated. The complete execution of the edict and Germany's return to the unity of faith which had been planned did not come about. At about the same time, in October 1628, La Rochelle, the stronghold of French Calvinism, fell, and Calvinism in France ceased to be a political and military force. Richelieu was now able to concentrate, by means which he considered suitable, upon the destruction of the House of Hapsburg and the establishment of French absolutism. The Mantuan War of Succession, after the Gonzagas had died out, brought about a new turn of events: France and the Emperor as the main powers, the Duchess of Lorraine and the Duke of Guastalla—both supported by Spain, as the third and fourth parties to the dispute, all laid claim to Mantua. In spite of his sympathy for France, Urban remained neutral, but did raise an army, when the emperor made a victorious advance and after plundering Mantua, threatened a Sacco di Roma like that of 1527; Vienna accused the pope of bias in favor of Spain. Richelieu was working towards a system of treaties against the Hapsburgs and achieved far-reaching political successes at the Peace of Ratisbon in 1630, especially in the Mantua succession struggle. A year later he made a treaty, directed against the Emperor, with the Swede, Gustavus Adolphus, who was at that time, in Germany. In this way it came about that a cardinal assisted in the final victory of Protestantism in Germany. Urban now directed his modest financial aid to the Emperor and tried in vain to separate Richelieu and Gustavus Adolphus, hoping at the same time to reconcile Richelieu with the Emperor. Urban's reluctance to come out entirely on the side of the Emperor laid him open to some very bitter reproaches, but he did not seek a personal treaty, merely a common front against Gustavus Adolphus, whose death at Lützen in 1632 caused general rejoicing in Rome. However, far from achieving peace, Urban now witnessed a strengthening of the Emperor's power after the Peace of Prague in 1635 and the declaration of war by Richelieu, who up till now had been content to wage a "cold war." Ferdinand III, the son of Ferdinand II called the Imperial Diet to Ratisbon in 1640 and made concessions to the Protestants. In spite of the Pope's endeavors the war continued. Richelieu died on 4th December, 1642, leaving the field to his pupil Mazarin, whom he had succeeded in having created a cardinal in 1640, and who was even less concerned with ecclesiastical and religious scruples than was his master. Urban was quite unable to counter an enemy of the caliber of Richelieu, the Machiavelli in purple, and the cardinal showed him that the era of Rome's ability to mediate for peace was now over. Although there can be no doubt of Urban's desire for peace, he failed to take those decisions which the Thirty Years' War had need of. Instead of taking money from Sixtus V's treasury and placing it at the disposal of the German Catholics he preferred to squander it on a miserable little war with Odoardo Farnese, whose dukedom of Castro was coveted by Urban's protégés. The money that might have served the Catholics to win back lost provinces, disappeared into the pockets of the

Barberinis, the richest landowners in the Pontifical State. At precisely the time when Richelieu was idolizing the absolute state, the French church gained with one of the greatest saints of all time in Vincent de Paul, who received the Bull of approbation from Urban for his Lazarite foundation, in 1633, but only after great difficulty. The notorious trial by the inquisition of Galileo Galilei took place during Urban's pontificate. Originally Urban had been kindly disposed towards the great man, and the tragic mistake of the narrow-minded inquisitors, who were unable to recognize Galileo's genius and who threatened the aged man with the rack, has long been recognized. True, Urban let Galileo return to Florence, but his equivocal behavior towards him does not do him any credit. The inquisition, itself, grew aware of its complete failure, and drew its own conclusions for the future. Jansenism which was to cause the papacy great difficulties, also had its beginnings in Urban's pontificate. The Pope was very active within the church: he had a great understanding for music and in 1629 appointed Gregorio Allegri to the Sistine Chapel, whose famous *Miserere* for two choirs was not allowed to be copied; and was not published until 1770 when Mozart wrote it down after a single hearing. Girolamo Frescobaldi was organist at St. Peter's in Urban's time. The Pope who had great talents as a poet and author was just as benevolent to the literati as were the protégés. The cardinal protégé, and with him the whole of Rome, entertained the Puritan John Milton as the most honored guest in the year 1638. Urban vied with his protégés in making Rome more beautiful. The Baroque found its most powerful expression in his pontificate in the hands of Lorenzo Bernini, the creator of the bust of the Pope in the Barberini Palace. After Urban had consecrated St. Peter's on 18th November, 1626, a work to which in the course of a hundred and forty years, twenty popes had contributed, Bernini made the massive ciborium above the papal altar in the Confessio. This work which was completed in 1633 marks the beginning of his international reputation: his works in Rome can scarcely be numbered. Under Urban he completed the Palazzo Barberini. He perpetuated the memory of the Pope in the huge bronze monuments of the Palazzo dei Conservatori, and on his tomb. Among the great artists who worked for the Pope and

190

his protégés were Domenichino and Andrea Sacchi. Van Dyck painted Urban shortly before the papal election, but the portrait has been lost. He is shown, however, in a beautiful portrait by Giuseppe Abbatini in the Barberini Palace. Poussin and Lorrain finally settled in Rome, and Velasquez was greatly admired by Francesco Barberini. In 1626 he built the summer castle, Castello Gondolfo, to the designs of Carlo Maderna, and wrote some distichs in praise of it. Urban had many fine qualities, a wide knowledge of humanity, and diplomatic talents; he led a simple life, loved to go riding for hours on end, and liked to recite his verses to a musical accompaniment. He only realized the economic excrescences of his nepotism shortly before his death.

INNOCENT X
Giambattista Pamphili
15th, September 1644 to 7th, January 1655

Like so many other families the Pamphilis were elevated during the pontificate of Innocent X, who was born on 7th, February, 1574, and became the princely House of Doria-Pamphili. In common with most of his predecessors the Pope began life as a lawyer. Through his maternal grandmother he was descended from Juan Borgia, the Infante Romano, who was the illegitimate son of Alexander VI. Clement VIII appointed him consistorial advocate and he proved his worth under Urban in missions to France and Spain, until he was finally created Cardinal of Sant' Eusebio in 1629. He was an open critic of Urban's unfortunate Castro war, the outcome of which he prophesied. Because of the strict caution which he always exercised he was known as "Mr. It can't be done." Innocent did not learn the lesson of Urban's nepotism, but neither the insignificant Cardinal Camillo, who soon returned to his worldly life, nor the equally ineffective Francesco Maidalchini, nor the mediocre Camillo Astalli-Pamphili ever achieved any significance at all. It was the Pope's sister-in-law, Olimpia Maidalchini, Camillo's mother and one of the most revolting women in Rome at this time, who soon established herself in a position of unfettered power rather like that of Marozia in the tenth century: she dominated the Pope so completely that she was known mockingly as the "Papessa." Diplomats and prelates wooed the favor of this presumptuous intriguer, who filled the Vatican with her quarrels and debased the papacy during the closing years of the Thirty Years' War. The Pope was inclining more and more to the support of Spain. His election was of itself a defeat for Mazarin, who then reconciled himself with the Barberini protégés, although they had voted for Innocent. Innocent began an action against the Barberinis, in which the Castro War once more played a leading part and the three brothers fearing the same fate as the protégés of Paul IV fled to France. Their property was confiscated and France even threatened to declare war on the Pontifical State: in the face of this, Innocent had no choice but to capitulate to the demands of Mazarin and pardon the Barberini. The Peace of Westphalia was concluded in Münster on 24th, October 1648; it was a triumph for Mazarin, but meant new losses for the Catholics in Germany, against which Innocent protested in vain. It is because of this that he has been, quite wrongly, accused of wishing to continue the war. Mazarin was now on the way to becoming all-powerful, while the Pope was protecting his chief opponent, the adventurous Cardinal de Retz, who has achieved great fame with his memoirs; as a result Innocent found himself torn backwards and forwards between the French and Spanish factions. A few months before the conclusion of the peace treaty, the revolution in Naples against the power of Spain, which Auber was later to celebrate in his opera *La Muette de Portici,* collapsed and Innocent who was, on paper, the feudal lord of Naples was relieved at the Spanish victory and the failure of Mazarin's plans to acquire the kingdom: nevertheless he protested vehemently against the inhuman revenge which the Spaniards wreaked on the Neapolitans. At the end of 1649, after the execution of Charles I, new persecutions of the Catholics began in England, especially after the subjugation of Ireland. The most important decision which Innocent took within the church was the condemnation of Jansenism in France: the movement brought forth a powerful ally in the genius of Pascal, whose letters which appeared under the

192

title of *Provinciales* are a major work of French literature. Innocent achieved a miserable fame by his campaign against Castro, the princedom of the Farnese, an undertaking in which his predecessor had failed and for which he had been criticized by Innocent. Castro was taken after a siege lasting for three months and was razed to the ground together with all its churches. Urbino had come into the possession of the Pontifical State in Urban VIII's pontificate, now Castro and one or two small possessions were also annexed to it. Innocent's reign was not marked by any kind of splendor, nor were there any marks of greatness in the Pope's character, which was a mixture of good-nature and coldness, suspicion and reserve, greed and moodiness and surliness and vehemence. When he died the avaricious Maidalchini stole the remains of all that she could lay her hands on, then declared herself a widow without means and she and her son refused to buy Innocent a coffin, in spite of the gifts which he had showered upon them: and so the corpse was left to rot for days in a damp sacristy. A wretched grave in the church of Sant' Agnese on the Piazza Navona, which had been built a short time before by Innocent, holds the remains of this luckless Pamphili pope, who lives on in the magnificent portrait painted by Velasquez in 1650, which does a great deal to flatter the repellent ugliness of this pope. Bernini was commissioned by the Pope to build the magnificent four-jet fountain on the Piazza Navona and the triton on the fountain opposite the Palazzo Pamphili, where Innocent lived as a cardinal, and where the Maidalchini later took up residence. Borromini worked on the restoration of the Lateran basilica. One of the most outstanding buildings of the whole century is the Villa Pamphili, which was built by the protégé Camillo Pamphili.

ALEXANDER VII
Fabio Chigi
7th April, 1655 to 22nd May, 1667

Alexander who was born on 13th, February, 1599 in Siena belonged to the family of wealthy bankers, whose founder Agostino

Chigi, the friend of Raphael and of Leo X, built the Villa Farnese. After studying law, philosophy, the history of art and theology, he went to Rome, where he entered the service of the church and was ordained a priest in 1635. In 1639 Urban sent him as his nuncio to Cologne, where he spent thirteen years in that office and earned great esteem for his intelligence, frankness and modesty. Innocent appointed him his representative at the Peace conference in Münster, where he successfully accomplished some of the most difficult tasks imaginable. In 1651 Innocent appointed him his secretary of state and a year later created him a cardinal. Chigi's guiding principle was to do a lot and say little. His election was opposed by Mazarin. Alexander had a coffin and skull made by Bernini, placed in his room as a constant reminder of human frailty: his first official acts after his election were the banishment for life of Olimpia Maidalchini and the appointment of Cardinal Giulio Rospigliosi as secretary of state. Unfortunately, he quickly abandoned his good intentions with regard to nepotism, though the cardinals brought a great deal of pressure to bear upon him and persuaded him to appoint his protégés. His nephew Flavio Chigi became a cardinal at the age of twenty-seven, after the completion of his theological studies. Another more distant relative also became a cardinal and other protégés received secular offices, yet in spite of these gifts, Alexander did contrive to keep his nepotism within reasonable bounds; his own court was of a strictly spiritual kind, but later on when he was a sick man he was unable to keep the encroachments of his worldly protégés at bay. On 23rd, December 1655, the ex-queen Christine of Sweden, the daughter of Gustavus Adolphus, who had been converted to Catholicism made her entry into Rome, as a crowned *enfant terrible* and someone whom the popes could not always easily tolerate. Alexander who, as nuncio, had once protested against the Peace of Westphalia, which had been signed in her name, received her in Rome with great magnificence. Relations with France were meanwhile developing along the worst possible lines—not only up to the time of Mazarin's death in 1661, and was leading his country towards the dangerous goal of absolutism. The Peace of the Pyrenees had finally put an end to the old rivalry

194

between France and Spain, to the advantage of the former: besides this, France's position had been strengthened by the nonaggression pact signed between Mazarin and Cromwell. Spain was finished as a world power. Louis XIV and his ambassador, the Duke of Créqui, demonstrated their power in a manner most humiliating to Alexander: they took possession of the pontifical estates in Avignon, prepared an attack on the Pontifical State, and Louis as the "most Christian King" forced the "Peace" of Pisa upon the Pope in 1664, in which besides other personal and degrading conditions a series of interferences with the Pontifical State were confirmed: Avignon was not to be restored until these conditions had been fulfilled. Within the church Alexander condemned Jansenism as well as forty-five propositions of the casuistic moral theory of the Jesuits called probabilism, which in case of doubt as to whether something is or is not permissible decides that it is. This was the central problem which had led Pascal to write his *Lettres Provinciales*. As a patron of the arts, Alexander's chief protégé was Bernini, who produced, among innumerable other works of art, two statues for the Capella Chigi in Santa Maria del Popolo, and in 1665 the magnificent Scala Regia in the Vatican with its statue of Constantine: he crowned his architectural achievements with the colonnades which he built for St. Peter's Square between the years 1657 and 1667 and which are a triumph of baroque lay-out. St. Peter's Square has from that time been the eternal *Venite* of the papacy to the whole Catholic population of the world. Even before the completion of St. Peter's Square, Bernini had built the Cattedra above the apse. Alexander's tomb, on the other hand, was not completed until the pontificate of Innocent XI.

CLEMENT IX
Giulio Rospigliosi
20th June, 1667 to 9th December, 1669

If anything is to be regretted about Clement's pontificate, then it is its brevity. Rospigliosi was born on 28th, January 1600 in

Pistoia; he studied philosophy and theology in Pisa and taught there for two years. After a creditable career in Rome he was appointed nuncio in Spain in 1644; he returned after nine years. Alexander appointed him secretary of state and, in 1657, made him cardinal of San Sisto; his works and his character gained Rospigliosi the highest regard from all factions. Above all he won fame in the history of the opera, for, as a librettist, he was a decisive inspiration to the Roman opera of his day and anticipated Neapolitan *opéra comique* by a hundred years. During his term as nuncio he seems to have had Lope de Vega as his adviser on matters connected with the stage. Stefano Landi set Rospigliosi's *Sant' Alessio* to music and the first performance, with Bernini's décor, took place at the opening of the Barberini's private theater; the text of the opera showed a greater profundity than was common at the time. Other operas followed; in 1635 *Santa Teodora*, later *San Bonifazio* and *San Eustachio*. In 1639, in Milton's presence, the first performance of *Chi soffre, speri* was given with music by Virilio Mazzochi and Marco Marazzoli: it was the beginning of the Opera Buffa. Calderon's influence could be seen in *Dal male il bene* and Bernini again did the décor and Antonio Maria Abbatini composed the music for *La comica del cielo*, which had a great success at its first performance in 1688. Rospigliosi even persuaded Alexander VII to erect a theater on the site of the former prison, To di Nona. Among his works is a sonnet in praise of the art of the famous prima donna, Leonora Baroni, whom Milton also praised enthusiastically. Clement directed his activities as pope to the achievement of peace: shortly before his election, Louis XIV had attacked the Spanish Netherlands and Clement whose election was welcomed by both Spain and France was recognized as a mediator, in which role he emphasized the renewed danger from Turkey. Peace was concluded at Aix-la-Chapelle on 2nd, May 1668: France was allowed to retain part of her conquests and had, in fact, yielded less because of the Pope's mediations than because of the Triple Alliance between England, Holland and Sweden. However, the King allowed Clement to take the main credit for the peace and Bernini celebrated the occasion with a gigantic firework display in

Rome. The fall of Candia in Crete, the last bulwark against the Turks which the Venetians were defending against superior forces was a tragic blow for Clement: he had sought help on all sides and had himself contributed all that he could, and in addition his nephew, Vicenzo Rospigliosi, was in command of the fleet. Even Louis XIV sent help, though under another flag, as he did not wish to break off relations with the Turks but in spite of everything Candia was forced to surrender on 6th April, 1669 and thirty thousand Christians and a hundred thousand Turks perished in Crete. Byron called this tragedy, in which Clement's failing strength finally gave out, the "Troy of Venice." The news that Louis XIV had been guilty of a sudden volte-face and had received the Sultan's ambassador in solemn audience, was spared him. The people honored the dead man, who had done so much for them, like a saint; he is buried in Santa Maria Maggiore. There have been few popes possessed of such priestly qualities, so blameless an outlook, such strength of character, goodness, culture, inner nobility and sense of justice as Clement. Although he had a few protégés, he dealt nepotism a fatal blow by refusing to allow them to receive any money from the state, so that they were forced to live from the income which they received from their offices, all of which were excellently administered: they were not allowed to assume the title Don. Clement was not responsible for making the Rospigliosis into a princely house: the elevation was effected by the marriage of one of his nephews to a Pallavicini. His nephew Jacopo Rospigliosi, whom he made a cardinal was already internuncio in Brussels on Clement's election, and would have retained his cardinalate on these grounds. A few of his relatives were permitted to stay in Rome, but had to leave again after Clement's death. All were agreed that no papal family had ever distinguished itself so greatly, by its thoughtful and modest bearing, as Rospigliosi. Carlo Maratta has captured the most important traits of Clement's character in his portrait which hangs in the Pinacoteca Vaticana. A portrait of the Pope by Baciccio hangs in the Barberini Palace, one which shows him as a cardinal hangs in the Corsini Palace. Perhaps the motto: *Aliis non sibi Clemens*—consideration for others and not for himself—best sums up the Pope's char-

197

acter. He loved to visit and succor the poor, and served thirteen of them, every day, in the Vatican.

CLEMENT X
Emilio Altieri
29th, April 1670 to 22nd, July 1676

This Roman patrician who was already eighty years old when he was elected, was born on 13th July, 1590 and became a priest after a short but successful career as a lawyer. After spending a short time at the nunciature in Poland he became Bishop of Camerino, a see which he administered excellently: he became a cardinal shortly before his predecessor's death. After his election he bestowed the name Altieri upon Cardinal Paluzzi, whose nephew had married Clement's niece, the last heir of the Altieri, and so made Paluzzi an "adopted" protégé. Paluzzi who was both talented and experienced dominated the aged Pope without difficulty and amassed great wealth for his family. Only one important event took place during Clement's pontificate: the victory, at Chocim on the Dniester on 11th November, 1673, of John Sobieski, the "lion of the North," over the Turks who were advancing on Poland. Sobieski, who was elected King of Poland, defeated the Turks again a year later at Lemberg and wiped out their army. Europe was threatened with the danger of a new war when Spain began to defend her possessions: the Emperor Leopold I advanced to the Rhine and France declared war. The Pope immediately began to make efforts to re-establish peace, but he met with no success: Turkey once more threatened Poland and no less a person than Leibnitz called upon Louis XIV to march against the Turks in Egypt and so draw them out of Europe. This gentle, honest and simple Pope did not live to see peace return. He is buried in the Capella Altieri in Santa Maria sopra Minerva: it was he who commissioned Bernini to make the costly ciborium in the sacramental chapel of St. Peter's. In 1671 he canonized Gaëtano di Tiene, the founder of the reform order of the Theatines, Francis Borgia, the general of the Jesuit order and the great-nephew of Alexander VI, and Rosa of Lima, the first South American saint.

198

INNOCENT XI
Benedetto Odescalchi
21st, September 1676 to 12th, August 1689

Odescalchi was born on 19th, May 1611 in Como: he originally intended to become an army officer, but went instead to Naples to study law and then became a priest. The Barberini protégés smoothed his path to a successful career. Innocent X took him into the College of cardinals when he was only twenty-four—not, as some have maintained, because Odescalchi had succeeded in bribing Olimpia Maidalchini, but because Innocent valued certain traits in his character, especially his love for the poor and his conscientiousness. Odescalchi enhanced his reputation both when he was Bishop of Novara and later in times of pestilence and flood when he was living a life of complete withdrawal and devotion to charitable works, in Rome. He had no desire to be elected Pope; later he was to have three thousand requiems read for a cardinal who had opposed the election. Many touching details have been handed down about this modest Pope, who for ten years wore the same ragged soutane and who avoided any demonstration of popular esteem. He made it quite clear to his relatives, from the start, that they could expect nothing from him and that they should carry on with their work, yet it was typical of the cardinals that they were able, by their opposition, to make the Bull, which the Pope had drawn up forbidding nepotism, impossible to publish. The good offices of Charles II of England had made it possible to start peace negotiations in the war which Louis XIV had begun during Clement's pontificate and, in Nijmegen on 10th August, 1678, peace was made between France and the Netherlands: France made peace with Spain on 12th, September and with the Emperor Leopold I on 5th February, 1679. From all these peace settlements Louis XIV emerged victorious and in full possession of his power. The tremendous achievement of the Papal nuncio Luigi Bevilacqua in bringing about the peace is never once mentioned in the documents. Innocent was happy to renounce any claim to mention: much more important to him was the central aim of the papacy, the destruction of the Turks. The chief opponent of Innocent's plan was Louis XIV who was

199

actually inciting the Turks to march against Austria. In 1683 Innocent managed to arrange a treaty between John Sobieski and the Emperor Leopold I and gave this alliance his full support; on 12th, September, 1683 allied troops who were under the overall command of Sobieski and the direct command of Duke Charles of Lorraine wiped out the Turkish forces near Vienna: Innocent prescribed the feast of *The Name of Mary* for the whole church as a perpetual memorial to this victory. The victories of Ofen and Belgrade in 1686 and 1688 inflicted new and severe losses upon the Turks, and in order to support them Louis XIV attacked Germany, thus forcing the Emperor back on to the defensive. The reign of the Stuarts in England came to an end in 1688 when James II was exiled and William of Orange came to the English throne. James II who had become a Catholic was deposed because he tried to lead the English back to Catholicism in a clumsy, absolutist and intolerant manner. Innocent now found himself in a curious position, for a ruler who was friendly to France and a Catholic, was displaced by one who was a Protestant and an opponent of the Pope's chief enemy, Louis XIV. Until quite recently the Pope was accused, on the basis of forged documents, probably of French origin, of having known of William's intention and even of supporting it out of enmity towards Louis XIV, but it has now been proved that he was taken completely by surprise by the turn of events, just as, on the other hand, he had disapproved of James II's mistaken Catholic policy, however sorry he may have felt for him as a person. There is no question of his having given his support to William. Relations between Louis XIV and the Pope were rapidly coming to a head, and Gallican moves towards the establishment of a state church in France were beginning to take on a serious aspect. At this time, too, a movement was set on foot to convert, often by means of force, non-Catholics, and Calvinism was seriously weakened, until, in 1685, the King acting from political motives and following up his successes in the war against the Huguenots, revoked the Edict of Nantes, which, under Henry IV, had assured them freedom of belief and equal rights with the Catholics. Innocent is said to have remarked: "What is the sense of it all, if all the bishops are schismatic?" He feared a complete break with Rome of the sort which had taken place in England and refused all the concessions which the King demanded for his "services," at the same time denouncing the use of force as a means of conversion and ostentatiously singling out French bishops who had opposed such use of force. At this time Louis' ambassadors to Rome were behaving like extraterritorial potentates: the King provoked the Pope more and more and tried to enthrone someone of his own choice as archbishop of the powerful archdiocese of Cologne. When the attempt proved unsuccessful, he arrested the papal nuncio in Paris, occupied Avignon and threatened to summon a council and invade the Pontifical State. Innocent was one of the most important popes of the century. He dealt with the political situation of his time with great strength of character, always working from first principles, in spite of the fact that never having been a nuncio, he had little or no political experience. His strictness in reform, his admittedly often petty scrupulousness, his great thrift, his earnest nature, which though often clouded by melancholy was never ungenerous and his generally loveable character, won him great popularity in Rome. It was not until he was dead that people suddenly realized that a great pope had passed away and one who had spent his life trying to achieve peace on earth and one who hated dishonesty. He made mistakes, it is true, but he was always sincere, and if he was often prevented from taking advice, it was because he was suspicious of the selfishness of others. His steadfastness in the face of Louis XIV's absolute power has called forth the highest admiration from posterity and any mention of the champions of freedom in Europe must include Innocent. He was keen to receive the idea of a crusade. His idealism, nobility and moderation soon won the unqualified recognition of the German Protestants, and his untarnished honesty was a source of untold power to the papacy. Little was done to support the arts during his pontificate; Bernini was called upon to convert the Lateran palace into a poorhouse. Innocent, who was a shrewd administrator, brought order into the finances of the State and augmented them. His tomb and that of Queen Christine of Sweden, who predeceased him by four months, after she had spent many years in Rome, are in St. Peter's. Clement XI inaugurated the process of Innocent's canonization, but it was stopped under Benedict XIV by the French government. Not until October 7, 1956 did the beatification finally take place.

ALEXANDER VIII
Pietro Ottoboni
6th October, 1689 to 1st February, 1691

Ottoboni was born in Venice on 22nd April, 1610, and began his ecclesiastical career under Urban VIII, on the completion of his legal studies. In 1652, Innocent X created this experienced administrative lawyer a cardinal, and in 1654 made him Bishop of Brescia. His diligence, intelligence, kindness, and the blamelessness of his life made him an outstanding personality. However, nepotism, which was reviving, darkened the picture, for with jovial unconcern this eighty year old pope said, "Let us hurry, the eleventh hour has already struck." Working on this principle, he at once summoned his relatives from Venice and showered riches upon them; dukedoms were bought, advantageous marriages made, and his protégés Marco and Pietro Ottoboni were made cardinals. The twenty-two year old Pietro was a great patron of the theater and his friend Handel who later lived in Rome wrote numerous works for him. Pietro's own opera *Columbus* is reputed to have had no success. His office as secretary of state made few demands upon him. The Pope showed himself compliant to the demands of Louis XIV; Avignon was again evacuated, but Alexander did not change the papal attitude toward Gallicanism. He secured parts of the rich estate of Queen Christine for the Vatican library. He is buried in St. Peter's in a pompous and tasteless tomb.

INNOCENT XII
Antonio Pignatelli
12th July, 1691 to 27th September, 1700

Innocent came from a Southern Italian family of princes and was born on 13th March, 1615. He was nuncio in Poland and Vienna under Alexander VII and Clement IX: Clement X made him Bishop of Lecce and entrusted him with a number of offices. He was created a cardinal by Innocent X and became archbishop of Naples, where Pignatelli's government was known as the Golden Age. Innocent is remembered in history chiefly for the Bull *Romanum decet Pontificem* of 22nd July, 1692 which forbade nepotism for all time. It was calculated that since the reign of Paul V alone, protégés had received seven million scudi from the state coffers, apart from their other sources of income. In future every pope and cardinal was to have to swear to obey the Bull. Innumerable expensive offices were discontinued and their renewal forbidden: relatives of the pope were permitted to become cardinals only if they were considered to have deserved the office through their services to the church, and even so their incomes were not to exceed twelve thousand scudi. Poor relatives were to be treated in exactly the same way as other needy persons. The Bull met with enthusiastic approval throughout the Catholic world and even some Protestants were strongly impressed. The Pope also took very decided measures to improve the education of the clergy and of the monks. Faced by the Grand Alliance, with whom he was at war, and troubled by the question of the Spanish succession which struck very close to him, Louis XIV decided that it would be advisable to renounce his old enmity with Rome, under which many popes had had to suffer and also to make some concessions with regard to Gallicanism, without actually giving it up. Innocent declared his support for the French succession in Spain, where after the death of the last Hapsburg, Charles II, the Bourbon rule had begun witth Philip V, the grandson of Louis XIV and the great-grandson of Philip IV of Spain. Innocent, during whose pontificate Prince Eugene defeated the Turks at Zenta on 11th September, 1697, is buried in St. Peter's. This benevolent Pope devoted his life to charity and to the alleviation of need.

CLEMENT XI
Gian Francesco Albani
23rd November, 1700 to 19th March, 1721

Albani was born on 22nd July, 1649 in Urbino and received a distinguished philosophical, theological, legal, and literary education: he also acquired a knowledge of classical languages and played a leading part in the learned academy of Queen Christine in Rome. He was twenty-eight when he entered the service of the church and was made a cardinal deacon in 1690 by Alexander VIII. He was most decisively opposed to his election as Pope and was only prevailed on to accept it after the most serious representations had been made to him. He was determined to abide by the Bull issued by his predecessor forbidding nepotism: his nephew Anibale Albani, who had proved himself in a number of diplomatic missions did not receive his appointment as cardinal until 1711 and then only as a result of pressure exerted by the other cardinals, while his brother Alessandro, one of the greatest patrons of art of the century and the patron of Winckelmann, was not made a cardinal until Innocent XIII's pontificate. The Albani did not receive one scudo of support during the whole twenty-one years of Clement's pontificate, not even from the Pope's private fortune, from which it was later discovered, he had distributed one million scudi to the poor. When Louis XIV tried to secure the succession to the French throne for his grandson Philip V, who had already been recognized as the heir to the Spanish throne and the first Bourbon ruler of Spain—a thing made impossible by the testament of Charles II the last of the Hapsburg line—the emperor Leopold I, William III of England, and the Netherlands concluded the second Grand Alliance. This was the beginning of the War of the Spanish Succession. The Pope's attempts to mediate were made more difficult by the claims to Naples which were being made simultaneously by the Emperor and Philip V, the advance of French troops to Milan, the surrender of Mantua to Louis XIV, the invasion of Ferrara at the emperor's instigation, and an unsuccessful attempt by the emperor's supporters to organize a rising in Naples and overthrow the Spanish. Thus Clement was forced out of his position of neutrality and into the arms of the French, a situation which seriously prejudiced his chances to mediate, especially as he was linked even more closely to France by his support for the Stuart pretender "James III," the son of James II, who had been exiled, and who enjoyed the support of Louis XIV. The Pope's attitude jeopardized still further the position of Catholics in England. The tension between Rome and Vienna increased when, in 1703, the Emperor proclaimed his son, Charles III, King of Spain, and again two years later when a papal general at the evacuation of the papal possessions by the Austrian and French armies, treacherously allowed the French to march in again. The struggle started in 1705 when Joseph I had succeeded Leopold I, although Clement had never really supported the French-Spanish claims and genuinely sought a reconciliation with Joseph. The whole situation suddenly underwent a radical change: Charles III succeeded in driving Philip V out of Madrid in 1706 and had himself proclaimed King, while the French had not only suffered severe defeats in the Netherlands, but had also been beaten in the same year at Turin, by Prince Eugene and driven out of Italy by him. In 1707 imperial troops were at the gates of Rome. Clement was powerless to prevent their marching through the Pontifical State: he also refused to recognize Charles III as the King of Spain. After the capture of Naples by imperial forces in July 1707 Austria had possession of Italy with all the consequences which this entailed for a Pope, and in 1708 the Pope and the Emperor were at war. Joseph I issued a manifesto against the Pope, denying his right to secular power and Imperial troops advanced on Rome. Clement had to bow to force and made peace on 15th January, 1709 with very moderate conditions, thus bringing the last war in history between the Pope and the Emperor to a close. Among other conditions, was the recognition of Charles III and the right of free passage through the Pontifical State for the Imperial army. The unhappy Clement was not in a position to validate any more demands and Philip V began to take ecclesiastical reprisals without the support of Louis XIV. The situations which resulted set the Pope a diversity of problems: the death of Joseph I in 1711, the succession of his brother, who declined the Spanish throne, the Peace of Utrecht in 1713 and of Rastatt in the following year, which finished the War of the Spanish Succession, the recognition of Frederick I of Brandenburg, as the first King of Prussia, by France and Spain, the cession of Sicily to Duke Victor Amadeus III of Savoy. At the same time, too, a rearmed Turkey declared war on Venice. Clement sought aid in any form whatsoever, while the Turks were advancing and threatening Italy. In April 1716 the Turks were defeated by Prince

Eugene at Peterwardein. Clement sent the prince, who crowned his victory with a further success, a costly hat and a consecrated sword and prescribed for the whole church the Feast of the Rosary, which Gregory had introduced as a mark of thanksgiving for the victory of Lepanto. On 16th August, 1717 Prince Eugene captured Belgrade. Soon afterwards an attack by Philip V and his wily minister, Cardinal Alberoni, on Sardinia made any further progress impossible. Clement who had promised the Emperor peace in Italy while he was fighting the Turks was bitterly accused by Vienna and even suspected of having a secret understanding with Spain. The sorely-tried and disappointed Clement tried in vain to demonstrate that these reproaches were unjustified. Alberoni captured Sicily, which had been handed over to the Duke of Savoy, in 1718. The quite justifiable fear of a resuscitation of Spanish power led to the formation of a Quadruple Alliance between the Emperor, England, Holland and France. This alliance led to the downfall of Alberoni after which Philip joined it. In spite of all the ancient feudal rights of the Pope, the Emperor received Sicily and Victor Amadeus of Savoy became the first King of Sardinia and Savoy. Shortly before his death Philip V made peace with Rome. No less agitated than the political happenings were the dogmatic disputes with Jansenism, which Clement had to face during his long pontificate. He was very active in the missionary field, where the famous quarrel with the Jesuits of Eastern Asia over the accommodation of Christianity to pagan practices led to unpleasant differences of opinion. In the social sphere the pope deserves great praise for his penal reform, into which he introduced the revolutionary idea of correction of prisoners instead of punishment. Science, archaeology and museums received great assistance from the pope. Clement built SS. Apostoli, the last baroque church in Rome. The Pope died after great suffering: an unpretentious marble tablet with a few simple words covers his tomb in the choir chapel of St. Peter's. One of his last words was: "Only that is great which is great in the eyes of God." A long prayer which he wrote characterizes most impressively his reverent personality. He scarcely enjoyed a peaceful moment during his pontificate: he bore all the insults aimed at him with the quiet dignity or true greatness. By his indefatigable work to stabilize its defense, he made, like Innocent IX before him, decisive contributions to the salvation of Western Europe from the Turks.

INNOCENT XIII
Michelangelo dei Conti
8th May, 1721 to 7th March, 1724

Conti came from Innocent III's family, in whose honor he chose his name: he was born on 13th May, 1665 in Poli, and was educated by the Jesuits after which he held several gubernatorial posts, and became nuncio in Switzerland and in Lisbon. Clement XI made him a cardinal in 1706 and he enjoyed the reputation of being a clever diplomat and a man of irreproachable character. He was already a sick man when he was elected. He bestowed Naples and Sicily upon Charles VI, who was already occupying them both. He was the first pope openly to admit his opposition to the Jesuits, who were hated by a number of people. He accused them of disobedience in their missionary work in China, in a decree which presaged the breaking up of their order. In the liturgy he ordained the Feast of the Name of Jesus for the whole church. He is buried in St. Peter's, but no monument has ever been erected to him. He gave a great deal of valuable material to the Vatican library.

BENEDICT XIII
Pietro Francesco Orsini
29th May, 1724 to 21st February, 1730

Benedict is the last pope of the House of Orsini. He was born in Gravina near Bari, the son of a Duke, on 2nd February, 1649, renounced his princely heritage, much against the will of his parents, and entered the Dominican order, where he took the name of Vicenzo Maria. He studied philosophy, theology, and above all else, ecclesiastical history in Naples, Bologna and Venice. He would not accept the red hat until he had been forced to do so by the general of his order and Clement X in 1672. Three years later he became archbishop of Siponto, in 1680 of Cesena and in 1683 of Benevento. He was inexhaustible in works of charity; even in the Vatican he continued to live the life of a simple brother, full of good works, who refused to use the state apartments, and who had a cell built in the back building. His main desire was to exercise pastoral care. His complete lack of experience in all wordly affairs, especially in questions of government, led him to take the fateful decision, with which his name has been tainted, to make a certain Niccolò Coscia a cardinal-archbishop-presumptive against the wishes of many of the cardinals. He reposed his whole trust in him and the upstart whose rise had been so meteoric abused it witth complete shamelessness. Benedict was soon surrounded by a clique of extortioners, who bought their offices from Coscia just as in the days of papal decay, and there was no form of corruption in which he was not willing to indulge in order to enrich himself, so that after a single year he had extorted two million scudi. The Pope refused to heed any warnings about his favorite, although the state deficit soon reached the sum of one hundred and twenty thousand scudi. No happenings of historical importance mark Benedict's pontificate; within the church disputes with the Jansenites continued. In 1726 the Pope canonized, among others, Aloisius Gonzaga, John of the Cross and Stanislaus Kostks and in 1728 Margaret of Cortona and John Nepomuk. He is buried in Santa Maria sopra Minerva. The pontifical office was far beyond his powers. Saintliness and pettiness were the two opposing poles of his character. Two busts of him by Pietro Bracci are in the Palazzo Venezia.

CLEMENT XII
Lorenzo Corsini
12th July, 1730 to 6th February, 1740

It was pure chance that enabled Coscia to escape Roman Lynch law and make his escape. In 1732 he was seized and after being deprived of his office, he was condemned to ten years imprisonment for extortion and forgery. In the conclave, one cardinal dared to vote for him, whereupon a sonnet containing some very bitter truths began to circulate among the electors. The new pope was a scion of the Florentine nobility, to which St. Andreas Corsini had also belonged, and was born on 7th April, 1652. After completing his legal studies in Pisa, he became a priest at the age of thirty-two. He worked in Rome under Alexander VIII, and Clement XI bestowed the purple upon him. Corsini who was considered a brilliant patron of the arts, was already ill when he was elected, and two years later he lost his sight. He made his nephew, Neri Corsini, who was also a great patron of the arts and built the Palazzo Corsini, a cardinal but did not permit him to exert any influence over him, nor did he give the already wealthy man any further riches. In 1733 Spain, France and Sardinia united to drive the Emperor Charles VI out of Italy. In the fall Charles was forced to evacuate Lombardy which then fell to Charles Emmanuel of Sardinia. Clement's warning to the combatants to make peace went unheeded and in 1734 the Spaniards once more landed in Italy, while Clement was powerless to prevent their marching through the Pontifical State to the south and capturing Naples, where the Infant, Don Carlos of Spain, the stepson of Philip V became King of Naples and Sicily with the title of Charles III. In order to win Clement over to his side he installed the Pope's nephew Bartolomeo Corsini, as his representative in Sicily. Austria for her part scarcely made any show of resistance. The political relationship between the emperor and Louis XV of France changed once more, without reference to the Pope, in the Peace of Vienna in 1735: almost the whole of Lombardy was restored to Charles VI, as well as Parma and Piacenza which were irrevocably lost to the Pontifical State. Troops marched backwards and forwards across the Pontifical State at will and no one took the slightest notice of the Pope's protests. In Rome, Spanish recruiting sergeants were able to recruit troops without hindrance, until the populace stormed the houses of the Piazza di Spagna, among them that of the Spanish Embassy, in order to free their fellow citizens who were imprisoned there. Spanish troops were encamped around Rome, murdered, ex-

209

torted and even erected gallows. Madrid and Naples tried every means at their disposal to extract ecclesiastical concessions from Clement, who, seriously ill, was spared no humiliation: the two governments even went to the length of breaking off diplomatic relations with him. Neither the extortion from the Pope of the investment of Charles III with Naples, nor the concordat with Spain led to peace within the church: in fact both things only worked to the Pope's disadvantage. The devastations caused by the imperial and the Spanish troops and the decrease in population posed problems for the Pontifical State which equaled those caused by the breakdown of the rule of law. Within the church the most important events were the canonization of Vincent de Paul and the first papal condemnation of freemasonry, in 1738. Clement achieved lasting gains in Ravenna which was completely depressed, and where the once omnipotent Spanish ex-minister, cardinal Alberoni was striving to improve his bad reputation. One of the greatest hydraulic works of the century was carried out in the city, which freed it from the danger of flooding, and the ship-canal to the sea was later completed together with the harbor which bears Corsini's name. His memory is still alive in the city today. The small republic of San Marino owes its freedom and independence to Clement. The Pope was also responsible for great services to art and learning, even though for the last years of his life he was almost completely bed-ridden. In this way his politically tragic pontificate achieved new splendor. By purchasing the busts of the emperors from the collection of the well-known cardinal Alessandro Albani, he laid the foundations of the Capitoline Museum, which was inaugurated in 1734 as the first archeological museum in Europe. Among the great amount of building undertaken by the Pope, the Fontana Trevi and the façade of the Lateran basilica are outstanding, the latter was not finished when Clement died. The Pope's second great foundation in the Lateran is the Capella Corsini which is dedicated to St. Andreas Corsini—one of the most beautiful chapels in the world, and an impressive work of the transitional period which led to classicism. Clement is buried here—a high-minded, passionless, just, kind and upright pope, whose pontificate was a long vale of suffering. There is a bust of the Pope by Pietro Bracci in the Villa Borghese.

210

BENEDICT XIV
Prospero Lambertini
17th August, 1740 to 3rd May, 1758

Benedict was one of the most splendid popes ever to ascend the pontifical throne. He was born in Bologna on 31st May, 1675 of a poverty-stricken family, received an excellent legal and theological education and modelled his literary style on Dante, Tasso, and Ariosto. He wanted a legal career and entered Clement XI's service as a consistorial lawyer: at the time he wrote a work of lasting value:—*On the Beatification and Canonization of the Servants of God.* He had the ability to combine great knowledge with common sense, so that Benedict XIII who appointed him archbishop of Ancona and made him a cardinal in 1728, always used to ask on any matters of importance: "What does the doctor think about it?" The newly-created cardinal wrote to a friend: "You may be sure that it is only my color which I am changing in this metamorphosis; I am still the same Lambertini." Clement XII bestowed the archbishopric of Bologna upon him, where he awakened boundless admiration and, in spite of the amount of work he had to do, still found time for writing. As Pope he forbade his brothers to come to Rome, had one of his nephews educated according to the strictest precepts of the Jesuits, and when, late in life, his sister bore no children, he said disappointedly: "I thought the 'razza de caglioni' (the band of idiots) had died out." Considering the political developments and the anti-ecclesiastical bias of the Age of Enlightenment, Benedict distinguished wisely between what he considered inalienable and what was merely conditioned by the times, and he let fall anything which could have been upheld only by damaging the whole structure. And yet he anticipated the revolutions which were threatening at the time and played his part, at least, in postponing them then. He concluded concordats with Savoy, Spain, Naples and Portugal, and though his predecessors had withheld recognition from Frederick II of Prussia, he granted it and so brought to an end a number of embarrassing situations; although there were still to be a number of disputes within the church. Shortly after Benedict had ascended the throne, the Emperor Charles VI died, and soon afterwards the

War of the Austrian Succession broke out. Benedict recognized Maria Theresa's right of succession on the grounds of the Pragmatic Sanction and he even undertook to be the godfather of her eldest son, the heir apparent, Joseph. However, in Frankfurt in 1742 the Elector Charles Albert of Bavaria, the son-in-law of Joseph I, was elected Emperor with the title of Charles VII and was crowned in Prague: Benedict had to recognize the election. Meanwhile, Spanish troops had landed in Italy, in order to snatch Lombardy from the hard-pressed Maria Theresa, who now turned against the pope, marched into the Bologna area, while Neapolitan troops forced their way through the Pontifical State, to join up with the Spaniards. With bitter humor the Pope wrote that he had every provocation to write a work on the martyrdom of neutrality. Enemy troops were encamped all over the Pontifical State, and its position became desperate when, in 1744 Maria Theresa gave the order for the recapture of Naples; whereupon Spanish, Neapolitan and Austrian troops looked upon the Pontifical State as a kind of no-man's land which was fair game for all forms of looting. At the same time they started a blockade of Rome. The Austrian troops then received orders to give up the whole undertaking, but they remained in the Pontifical State for a further winter. After the death of Charles VII, Maria Theresa's husband, the Grand Duke of Tuscany was elected Emperor on 13th September, 1745 with the title Franz I, and was recognized by the Pope, who once more showed with what felicity he could act in setting aside differences which threatened peace. The Peace of Aix-la-Chapelle of 18th October, 1748 ended the War of the Austrian Succession and secured peace in Italy for the next forty years. When Frederick II of Prussia began the Seven Years' War in 1756, Benedict refused to agree that the King should call his war of conquest a religious war, but at the same time he was glad to see France and Austria form an alliance after their hundred year long period of enmity. Within the church, Jansenism and the Jesuit question posed the Pope many problems: he gave special attention to the missions, the reorganization of his completely shattered finances, and the reconstruction of his unhappy State. He lived modestly and demanded that others do likewise, he gladly denied himself the pleasures of re-visiting his home town, so as to

212

save the costs of the journey and give the money to the poor and he also reduced the size of his small army, of whose uselessness he was convinced. He supported the people against the great landowners and speculators, was concerned with every branch of the economy and made his authority as a lawmaker felt on all sides. The Pope undertook a great deal of restoration in Rome. The most important work which he supported was the construction of an art gallery in the Palazzo dei Conservatori and the enrichment of the Capitoline Museum, in which Winckelmann who had been living in Rome since 1744 received so many profound impressions. His pontificate saw no great masters at work and he was concerned more with preservation than with creation. Out of the academies which Benedict founded, there remain the Accademia Litturgica and the Accademia Romana di Archelogia. He created new chairs of higher mathematics and chemistry, and chemistry and physics laboratories at the University of Rome: he lent his special support to natural sciences and experimental physics, and almost two centuries before other universities had taken the decision, this pope who was quite unprejudiced, created chairs for two women professors. Besides this he endowed an anatomical museum and a chair of anatomy in his home town. Among the many great artists and scientists whom he supported, Antonio Muratori, the father of the study of Italian history, and Giovanni Battista Piranese were outstanding. Pietro Metastasio, who had studied jurisprudence under Benedict and had become the Viennese court-poet and the leading opera librettist of the century, could not be persuaded to come to Rome. Innumerable writers, in all countries, honored the Pope by dedicating or by sending their works to him: Voltaire who composed a Latin distich on the portrait of the Pope, sent him his *Mahomet*; Benedict expressed his thanks by sending him two gold medallions, and only learned later that he was dealing with a man who hated the church; he later forbade the production of *Mahomet* in Rome. He also corresponded with Pierre Louis Maupertuis, the famous physicist. When Gluck gave the first performance of his opera *Antigone* on 9th February, 1756, Benedict conferred upon him the distinction of the Order of the Golden Spur, after which Gluck referred to himself as a knight. Benedict presented the Vatican library with a number of costly treasures, and instituted work on the publication of the catalogue of manuscripts. Montesquieu gave him the honorary title of the Scholars' Pope. As a canon lawyer his historical method was far in advance of the parallel developement in profane law. Benedict died at the age of eighty-three after great suffering. His last words were: "I am going in silence and oblivion to the one place which belongs to me." His over-ornate tomb in St. Peter's is quite out of keeping with the character of this touchingly modest Lambertini pope. Horace Walpole's son erected a statue to him in his gallery and praised him in verse as a priest beloved by the Catholics and esteemed by the Protestants, without vainglory or selfishness, a prince without favorites, a pope without nepotism and a scholar without pride. When Benedict, insusceptible to flattery, read the poem, he remarked that he was like the statues in St. Peter's—only bearable when seen from a distance. Jan Pitt, a relative of the great William Pitt and a Protestant like Walpole, placed a bust of Benedict in his palace with the inscription: "Jan Pitt, who never had anything good to say about the Roman priest raised this monument in honor of Pope Benedict XIV." Inexhaustible goodness and never-failing sense of humor, frankness, and honesty, the great nobility of spirit and healthy sarcasm formed the basis of the Pope's character. The Romans used to see him with his walking-cane in his hand, walking through the city talking to the people. He was never offended by personal insults. When a minor poet derided him in a satire, he corrected the miserable verses, sent them back and expressed his hope that they would now sell better. He took a real delight in the brilliant caricatures drawn by Pier Leone Ghezzi, which spared neither him nor the cardinals; he gladly suffered public criticism of the government and kept himself informed of it. His letters have a special charm in their mixture of seriousness and humor, criticism and robustness, sense of responsibility and consideration for the weaknesses of others, modesty and mockery. Papa Lambertini has never been forgotten in Italy especially in Rome. It Macaulay called him the best and wisest of St. Peter's two hundred and fifty successors, to his people he was the most humane. He was acclaimed by believers and by atheists as a stage figure during the nineteen-thirties, and he was also portrayed in the film *Il Cardinale Lambertini*. His portrait, by Crespi, hangs in the Vatican.

CLEMENT XIII
Carlo Rezzonico
6th July, 1758 to 2nd February, 1769

Rezzonico was born on 7th March, 1693 in Venice, studied law and theology in Padua and entered the curia after his ordination. He held various offices under Clement XI: Clement XII made him a cardinal and Benedict XIV bestowed the see of Padua on him. He was noted for his devotion to duty, his piety and his goodness. In the Seven Years' War, which, like his predecessor, Clement refused to recognize as a religious war, he was on the side of Maria Theresa, but he worked all the time for the conclusion of a quick peace, which finally succeeded at Hubertusberg in 1763. In 1765, after the death of the emperor, Francis I, he recognized the succession of Joseph as Maria Theresa's regent. He was faced with a number of difficult problems within the church after the death of Frederick Augustus II of Poland, where Catherine the Great placed Stanislaus Poniatowski on the throne. Essentially, however, his pontificate was taken up with the Jesuit problem. During Benedict XIV's pontificate a fatal threat had been gathering over the heads of this order, which was hated on all sides and by a large part of the College of cardinals. Personal desire for revenge upon the Jesuits and their own objective guilt led to cruel persecutions in Portugal under the minister Pombal, who was an enemy of the church. The Order was first expelled from Portugal, then from Spain and Naples and from Spanish Parma and Piacenza: in France, however, it was merely dissolved and banned. Clement's protests only served to worsen the position of the Order and even led to the occupation of parts of the Pontifical State, while the Bourbon monarchies pressed their demands for a categorical ban to be placed on the Order. The final affliction came to Clement with the publication of a work by Febronius, the pseudonym of

Nicholas Houtheim, suffragan bishop of Trier, which attacked the Pope's supreme authority and started controversies throughout Europe. The series of tragic disappointments caused the heart attack which killed this noble but nervous Pope. His tomb in St. Peter's, one of Canova's masterpieces, was not finished until 1792. Clement bore the oppositions and enmities of his pontificate with an almost heroic calm, even if he did make mistakes through his lack of human understanding. He was well aware that the Jesuits were out to strike at the papacy itself and he was ready to forfeit his own estates and more, if in this way he could secure peace within the church. In the midst of all his own misfortunes he found time to show his concern for the misfortunes which a famine had visited upon his subordinates. The insults which were hurled at him, even after his death, did nothing to sully his reputation. Clement was painted several times: his portrait by Raphael Mengs, whom the Pope invested with the order of the Golden Spur, hangs today in Milan: Goethe praised this work in his *Italienische Reise* as the master's greatest work. Mengs's second portrait of the Pope hangs in the art gallery in Bologna and the third complete one is in the Stockholm Museum. The Villa Albani in Rome, in which Mengs painted his Parnassus, was completed during Clement's pontificate; cardinal Alessandro Albani made it into one of the most beautiful collections of antiquities in the world. In 1763, the Pope appointed Winckelmann as commissioner for ancient monuments and so enabled him to write his *Geschichte der Kunst des Altertums*—a History of Ancient Art—which made him the founder of the science of archaeology. In 1756 he gave his approbation to the Feast of the Sacred Heart of Jesus, which was extended to the whole Church by Pius IX in 1856.

CLEMENT XIV
Lorenzo Ganganelli
19th May, 1769 to 22nd September, 1774

The conclave, during which Joseph II arrived in Rome unexpectedly and incognito, was completely dominated by the Jesuit problem, which was coming to a head. Joseph was the first emperor to come to Rome since Charles V: on the day after his arrival, the emperor visited the cardinals in the conclave and did little to conceal the fact that he and his mother would raise no objections to the dissolution of the Order of Jesuits. He spoke with contempt of the cardinals. Clement was born on 31st October, 1705 in Sant' Arcangelo near Rimini, the son of a doctor. At eighteen he entered the Franciscan order, was later appointed adviser to Benedict XIV in Rome. In 1759 Clement XIII made him a cardinal, partly because Ganganelli was friendly towards the Jesuits. The new cardinal made no secret of his wish to become Pope and when he saw that this would be impossible if he continued to support the Jesuits, he swung over, to the great disappointment of Clement XIII, to the anti-Jesuit camp. Under pressure from the Bourbon powers, whom Maria Theresa had reluctantly joined, Clement issued the notorious papal brief *Dominus ac Redemptor,* on 21st July, 1773: the brief is a masterpiece of guilty conscience. The last general of the order, Lorenzo Ricci, a worthy personality was imprisoned in the Castel S. Angelo together with his closest associates, all of whom were aged men like himself. Clement appointed as the "examining magistrate" an obscure Monsignore Alfani who proved to be both cruel and greedy and pounced upon the estates of the Jesuits in order to fill his own pockets. Nothing could be proved against Ricci, yet this miserable man was held in prison without a formal verdict or proofs of his guilt until death finally released him from his suffering in 1775. Pius VI had tried in vain to have him released to his home town, but Spain who addressed Rome only in tones of command would not allow it. Clement supported the work of Raphael, Mengs, and Piranesi, who dedicated his city plan and his work on the pillars of Trajan to him. In April, 1770 the young Mozart who was accompanied by his father arrived in Rome, and wrote down the famous *Miserere* by Allegri, after only one hearing: the Pope invested him with the Order of the Golden Spur. Clement extended the collections of antiquities in the Vatican by extensive purchases and founded what is today the Museo Clementino. The Pope was not poisoned, as has often been suggested. He is buried in SS. Apostoli and his tomb, like that of

217

his predecessor, which was built later, is one of Canova's master-pieces. His character shows up in the most unfavorable possible light. Only the enemies of the Jesuits heaped the most embarrassing flattery upon him and finally termed him a worker of miracles: in fact Clement was a man of mediocre intellect, weak-willed, un-reliable and suspicious, whose actions were conditioned by ambi-tion and fear, yet he was ready to listen to any rumor, was always engaged in some secret activity, and was filled with low cunning. He had a special skill in the concealment of his true intentions. Politically he was under the thumb of the Bourbon monarchies. The only people who enjoyed his confidence were a Franciscan monk named Bontempi, the son of a cook, who soon achieved a position of great power and earned general hatred, and the grain profiteer Niccolò Buschi, who was no less hated. When Clement died, satires were written not only against him but against his two venal creatures.

PIUS VI
Gianangelo, Count Braschi
15th February, 1775 to 29th August, 1799

Braschi who was born on 25th December, 1717 in Cesena, studied law and was ordained at the age of thirty-six. Benedict XIV took him into the curia, Clement XIII appointed him treasurer and Clement XIV made him a cardinal. Braschi disapproved of conditions under Clement and his favorites and devoted all his energies to his diocese of Subiaco. In defiance of the regulations laid down by Innocent XII, Pius revived the practice of nepotism: his nephew Romoaldo Onesti-Braschi became a cardinal and was highly respected for his quiet benevolence. His brother, on the other hand, an uncultured avaricious man, whom the Pope made a duke by the purchase of Nemi, was generally hated for his extreme arrogance. Even the draining of the Pontine marshes, which was energetically undertaken by the Pope had as its real aim, the acquisition of cheap land for his protégé, who deported himself like a renaissance prince. Even the long-forgotten cere-

218

monies of nepotism were revived. In spite of the poor financial position of the Pontifical State, Braschi built himself the Palazzo Braschi on the Piazza Navona. Pius tried, unsuccessfully, to continue his predecessor's policy towards the princes. Specialized interests for the establishment of a state church, and an increased enmity towards the church in both Sicily and Austria caused the Pope troubles which were to have serious consequences. The development of Josephinism in Austria sent him to Vienna in 1782, but he failed to arrive at any sort of understanding on essential points. The Pope was powerless to oppose the ideologies of the French Revolution, which were making themselves felt in the Pontifical State. Cagliostro, who prophesied the fall of the Pope was condemned to death by the Inquisition, but his sentence was mitigated by the Pope to one of life imprisonment: Alfieri wrote his tragedies against which Rome protested in vain, but the really acute danger came in 1796 when Bonaparte took over command of the Italian troops. Since there was no question of defending the Pontifical State, Pius decided to negotiate, and the negotiations led to the Peace of Bologna on 23rd June, 1796. When hostilities again broke out Pius hoped for aid from Austria, but he was doomed to disappointment and was forced to make peace again at Tolentino on 19th February, 1797, when he finally renounced his claim to Avignon and paid in addition the sum of six million scudi. In the course of revolutionary disturbances in Rome, the French general, Duphot was murdered. On 9th January, 1798, General Berthier occupied Rome, announced the conditions of capitulation and on 15th February declared the Pope deposed and the Republic founded. In reply to the eighty year old Pope's plea to be allowed to die in Rome—he was mortally sick—General Haller gave the famous answer, "You can die anywhere". On 20th February the Pope was taken away as a prisoner. Bonaparte assembled five hundred vehicles to remove the invaluable art treasures of the city as booty and they were not restored to Rome until after his final defeat. The Pope's long and tragic suffering ended in Valence. Braschi, the last of the protégés had, meanwhile, established himself in Rome as burgomaster and clad in the revolutionary cockade. No humiliation was spared the Pope, whose last words

219

were words of forgiveness to his enemies, who thought that they saw in him the last pope. It was not until 1802 that Pius VII was allowed to bring his predecessor's body back to Rome. Canova carved the magnificent statue of the Pope in the Confessio in St. Peter's. Pius, to whom Goethe referred as "a most beautiful and dignified man" was in reality an unbalanced character, in whom an excess of zeal often gave the appearance of severity. He was vain and ambitious and laid great store by external appearances, but he took his office seriously and has often been praised for his great energy. The final tragedy of his life removed all the dross from the picture of his character and he died as the one who had suffered most for the sake of the papacy in this period of change. He did very much to further learning: among other things, he built the sacristy of St. Peter's and extended the Vatican archaeological museum, which since then has been known as the Museo Clementino. His pontificate witnessed a huge number of excavations and the resulting discoveries were of the highest import. Great masters like David and Canova drew their inspiration from the museums of antiquities, which Goethe referred to simply as "The Museum". This was the beginning of the great period of Germano-Roman cultural life, which may be said to have begun when, in 1789, Goethe and his circle of friends gathered around the Duchess Anna Amalia of Weimar, who was highly thought of by the Pope, at the Villa Malta. The Duchess was painted by Angelica Kauffmann beneath the cypresses of the Villa D'Este, while Herder read to her from *Tasso*. The portrait of Pius in the Vatican was painted by Mengs. In the Rosselli collection in Milan there hangs a beautiful painting by Francesco Guardi which shows Pius and the Doge of Venice on the island of St. George.

PIUS VII
Barnaba, Count Chiaramonti
14th March, 1800 to 20th August, 1823

A new era for the papacy began in the island monastery of San Giorgio Maggiore in Venice in the year 1800, when thirty-five cardinals elected the Benedictine monk, Chiaramonti. He was born in Cesena on 14th August, 1742, became a monk and then taught philosophy, theology and canon law in Parma and Rome, where Pius IV first made him Bishop of Tivoli in 1782 and in 1785 a cardinal and Bishop of Imola. He at first resisted his election to the papacy but later accepted it. The secretary of the conclave, Ercole Consalvi, who was later to become famous as the first cardinal secretary of state of modern times was the one who did most to persuade him. Pius forbade his protégé ever to come to Rome, which he entered in triumph in July. His first task was the re-organization of the Pontifical State which had been restored at the Peace of Lunéville, though reduced in size. He set about his task moderately and progressively: on 15th July, 1801 he concluded a concordat with Napoleon which had a great effect throughout the church and in 1804 he went to Paris to crown Napoleon emperor. "The Holy Father was sent for like a chaplain summoned by his master to say Mass", wrote Consalvi in his memoirs. The memorable ceremony of 2nd December, 1804 has been recorded for posterity in David's famous painting. Magnificent presents and utter humiliation were heaped upon the Pope, who was spied on from all sides and who was not allowed to return to Rome until April 1805. Napoleon's attacks on the Pontifical State which began soon after led to endless conflicts: Pius stood up courageously to the Emperor's ultimatum and refused to surrender any of his rights. Görres and Humboldt have given high praise to his courage and strength of character. On 2nd February, 1808, the French occupied Rome, Pius declared himself ready for martyrdom, looked upon himself as a prisoner in the Quirinal and refused to fly to Sicily. On 10th July the tricolor was flying over the Castel S. Angelo and heralds proclaimed the end of papal rule. On the same day, the Pope excommunicated Napoleon and the invaders. He was arrested by French bailiffs on 6th July and taken on a forty days journey to Savona, where he was to live in exile. All the cardinals were banished to Paris. The terror reigned in Rome, while in France Napoleon subjected the Church to every possible form of force. Pius rejected every demand made upon him, without flinching. On 9th July, 1812 the Pope who was seriously ill with a kidney complaint was moved to

Fontainebleau. In 1813 Napoleon succeeded in tricking a convention out of him, which Pius revoked after he learned of the true circumstances. Before Napoleon took up his position against the allied troops, who were advancing on Paris in 1814, he sent the Pope back to Rome and restored his lands to him. On 20th May, twenty days after his oppressor had set foot in Elba, Pius the apostolic pilgrim made his triumphal entry into Rome, with tears in his eyes. Princes drew his carriage through scenes of tremendous jubilation and children bearing palms preceded him. The day was celebrated by Catholics and Protestants in the whole of Europe. In the course of the Hundred Days, the Pope had to flee to Genoa, because of the danger which threatened him from Murat, who was in Naples. After the final exile of Napoleon to St. Helena, the Pope became the protector of Napoleon's family, especially the aged Letitia and he tried too to ease the burden of the Emperor's exile. At the Congress of Vienna, Consalvi succeeded in gaining recognition for the Pope as a temporal ruler. From now on Pius was only concerned with the reconstruction of the Pontifical State, the Catholic Church in Europe and the international missionary work, which had been disrupted. In 1814 he re-formed the Order of Jesuits. Pius continued the tradition of papal patronage filled as Canova said, "with a boundless love of art". Consalvi, the protector of the composer, Domenico Cimarosa, and of Canova formed a happy complement to his master's patronage. An extensive building and reconstruction program was now begun in Rome: Pius completed the Museo Chiaramonti in the Vatican and the Galeria Lapidara, both of which had been begun before his deportation and with Canova's co-operation the rebuilding of the Braccio Nuovo was completed between 1817 and 1822. Successful excavations enriched the collections in the museums and the booty which had been taken to France in 1798 was restored. The old Pinacoteca Vaticana and the Bibliotheca Chiaramonti were also founded. There was no branch of learning and art which did not benefit from the Pope's munificence. Four days before his death, the basilica of San Paolo fuori la mura burned down, but in order to spare the dying man, who was delirious and murmuring, "Fontainebleau—Savona", Pius was not told of the occurrence. For three nights the faithful Consalvi who had suffered with his master through one of the most tragic epochs in history of the papacy, watched by his bedside. Consalvi later had Pius' tomb erected in St. Peter's. No note of disharmony disturbed the general mourning on Pius' death. His statesmanship and his intellect were just as praiseworthy as his unselfish generosity, his loveable modesty and his greatness as a priest. The most important portraits of the Pope were painted by David and by Thomas Lawrence, who also painted the famous portrait of Consalvi.

LEO XII
Annibale, Count della Genga
28th September, 1823 to 10th February, 1829

Della Genga was born on 22nd August, 1760 at the castle of Genga near Spoleto and was appointed secretary and canon of St. Peter's by Pius VI and, in 1786, archbishop and nuncio in Cologne. He occupied important diplomatic posts and became a cardinal and Bishop of Sinagaglia, until the Pope summoned him to Rome in 1820 to take office as cardinal-vicar. In the conclave, the enemies of Consalvi and his progressive ideas won the upper hand. Leo's pontificate was a reaction against the modern and tolerant ideas of Pius VII and Consalvi. Wise decrees made in the last pontificate were annulled, the inquisition and the system of informants flourished. Leo even forbade smallpox vaccination, which had been introduced by Consalvi, and the resulting increase in the death rate was of no consequence to him. On all sides, administrative and legal decrees which were long out of date were revived. The Jews, who were once more enclosed in the ghetto and who, among other humiliations, were subjected to the inquisition, emigrated, if they were wealthy, thus upsetting the financial stability of the state. A cruel cardinal legate, of the type which had been unthinkable for years, condemned five hundred people to death, prison or exile in Romagna within the space of three months. The inhabitants of Ravenna fled the city in the face of these barbaric executions. Leo's memory is more hallowed for his interest in art, culture and church reform, than for his ability in government. He is buried in St. Peter's. In spite of some good qualities—he was opposed to nepotism—his personality and his pontificate were characterized by narrow-mindedness, pettiness and obstinacy. Leo was the complete opposite of all that had distinguished his predecessor.

PIUS VIII
Francesco Saverio Castiglioni
31st March, 1829 to 30th November, 1830

Pius took his name in honor of Pious VII and he had many of the characteristics of the Chiaramonti pope. He was born on 20th November, 1761 in Cingoli. His wealth of theological and legal knowledge led Pius VII to raise him to the see of Montalto in 1808, but he was deported by Napoleon to whom he was a source of embarrassment, and he was held under arrest in Pavia and Mantua. He was released after the conclusion of the peace and in 1816 became a cardinal and Bishop of Cesena, in 1821 Bishop of Frascati. Pius VII once called him prophetically Pius VIII. If he had not supported his friend Consalvi in 1823 he would have become pope then. The pontificate of this ailing pope passed quietly. He is buried in the Vatican grottoes, but his monument is in St. Peter's. Pius was mourned by all. His honesty and conscientiousness were so great that, wishing to avoid even the appearance of nepotism, he broke off the canonical process which was considering the canonization of St. Bernard because he discovered that he belonged to the same family as the saint.

GREGORY XVI
Bartolomeo Alberto Cappellari
2nd February, 1831 to 1st June, 1846

Cappellari was born the son of a lawyer on 18th September, 1765 in Belluno and at the age of eighteen became a Camaldulian monk in Murano near Venice. In 1805 he became the abbot of San Gregorio on Monte Celio in Rome, and later general of the order and adviser to Pius VII and Leo XII on matters of great importance. The latter made him cardinal of San Callisto in 1825. The revolution of 1830 which swept away Charles X of France and brought the citizen king, Louis-Philippe, to the throne, was brewing in the Pontifical State as well. It was the time of the Carbonari, who were stirring up trouble in Rome, especially with the collaboration of Napoleon's brothers and the sons of King Louis Bonaparte of Holland, including the later emperor, Louis Napoleon. On the day after Gregory's election the rising in Modena under Ciro Menotti, broke out; the movement soon spread to other cities and Rome was threatened by revolutionary troops. Prince Napoleon demanded that the Pope renounce his secular authority. Gregory called upon Austria for help, which then occupied Modena, Ferrara and Bologna. The revolution which was temporarily suppressed as a result of this, flared up again when the Austrian troops withdrew, only to return in 1832 when France occupied Ancona. The troops did not leave the Pontifical State until 1838. Gregory who immediately set the same reactionary course as Leo XII and began an absolutist reign, was an enemy of political progress and true freedom for the people. The enmity of the papacy towards any kind of concession was sharpened when, at Metternich's instigation, cardinal Lambruschini was appointed secretary of state. Lambruschini regarded all political reform as nothing short of criminal. Learned congresses, gas-lighting, suspension bridges, railways— all were synonymous with trouble for this petty, shortsighted tyrant. These abuses, especially the misuse of office, corruption, and arbitrary justice remained unchanged in spite of all signs of goodwill on the Pope's part, until in 1845 the Pontifical State had a debt of twenty-six million scudi. Intriguers and extortioners flocked round the Pope, and at this time it is impossible to name a single outstanding person of the caliber of Consalvi. Gregory was the prey of every rumor and every frightening story. Anything which seemed to be likely to be good was nipped in the bud. The educated classes turned away from the Pope, and were joined by innumerable priests, and those who were excommunicated collected abroad round Mazzini. The prisons filled up, the legitimate demands of the Rimini manifesto, among which was the abolition of the death penalty, were rejected by the secretary of state as criminal, and itinerant courts martial sat, paying scant regard to human rights. Gregory did much that was valuable for art and learning; the collections in the Vatican have him to thank for the Etruscan and the Egyptian museum. The masters of the Nazarene school in Rome, Overbeck, Cornelius and Veit all received favors from him. Finally the foundation of the German Archaeological Institute by the Prussian ambassador Bunsen, a most significant event in Germano-Roman cultural relations, took place in Gregory's pontificate. In 1838 the Pope made Mezzofantio, the greatest linguistic genius of all time, a cardinal. No one really mourned Gregory after he had died of cancer. Though a man of integrity, often childishly happy and very mild in his actions, this ascetic monk, who had gained the tiara was full of self-doubts, as sharp in his ecclesiastical theory as in practice, but at the same time, he was borne along on a medieval, authoritarian notion of sovereignty. His lack of understanding for the world degenerated into escape from the world and a hatred for it which was to have fatal consequences. He never realized that he was at a turning point in religious, sociological and cultural revolutions, to which he was unable to reconcile himself. He launched a sharp attack on Felicité de Lamennais, when he dared to demand freedom of the press and sought to bring Catholic dogma into harmony with the currents of the times, and especially with democratic thought. He rejected nepotism. His favorite was the hard-working papal court barber Moroni, who with the cooperation of others, especially Gregory, completed a conversational history of the Popes, cardinals, and happenings from Pius VII to Gregory, which though it has a wealth of detail lacks objectivity. Gregory, who was painted by De la Roche was the donor of the Knightly Orders of San Silvestro and San Gregorio Magno, which are bestowed in three classes. He is buried in St. Peter's.

226

PIUS IX
Giovanni Maria, Count Mastai-Ferretti
16th June, 1846 to 7th February, 1878

Pius was born on 13th May, 1792 in Sinigaglia. When he had completed his studies, he was ordained by Pius VII, in 1818, and was appointed to a diplomatic mission to Chile. After his return in 1825, Leo XII appointed him a canon, and in 1827 made him archbishop of Spoleto. In the confusions resulting from the revolutions of 1831 he succeeded in saving Louis Napoleon who was being sought as a conspirator and in helping him and his mother, Queen Hortense, to flee to Switzerland. Gregory appointed him Bishop of Imola in 1832. There was scarcely an Italian bishop of that time who worked as piously or who was as popular as Mastai-Ferretti. Politically he endeared himself to the people by his liberal ideas, his sympathy for the conspirators who had often been misled, and his pleas for mercy for them. In spite of his liberalism Gregory XVI made him a cardinal in 1840. One month after his election Pius pronounced the famous amnesty for political crimes, which occasioned indescribable jubilation and aroused great hopes: three days later the enthusiastic crowd pulled the Pope's carriage through the city beneath a rain of flowers. The reforms which followed made Pius, who always felt the need to be popular and who relished all the praises which were showered on him, the idol of the people. He already entertained visions of Italian unity: Giuseppe Mazzini wrote to him enthusiastically and Grillparzer wrote: "If you go on in the same way, and you are not deterred from your goal, then the Germans will become Roman, and the Romans, German Catholics." Outbreaks of hatred against the representatives of the Gregorian pontificate soon followed. Pius' fatal mistake was his inability to react with anything but a flood of emotion to the revolutionary movement, instead of mastering it as a clear-thinking statesman. The conflict between his office as Pope and as a ruler anxious to please his people brought him into ever-deepening confusion, especially when the cry went out for a national war with Austria, against whom Sardinia-Piedmont and the occupied provinces of

Lombardy and Venice rose up. The 1848 revolution complicated the situation. Pius refused to make war on Austria, thus divorcing himself from the national movement which, completely ignoring his universal position as a mediator, branded him a "traitorous perjurer". His minister Pellegrino Rossi was murdered, the Quirinal was bombarded and the Swiss guard disarmed. On 24th November, 1848 Pius who was treated more or less as a prisoner had to flee to Gaëta on Neapolitan soil: this was the last time that a pope took flight from Rome. In Rome he was declared to have lost temporal power and the Roman republic was proclaimed, though spiritual power was to be guaranteed him. Pius pleaded with the great powers to intervene. Austria defeated Charles Albert of Sardinia-Piemont on 23rd March, 1849 at Novara and occupied parts of the Pontifical State. On the evening of the battle Victor Emmanuel II took over the government as his father's successor. France, where Louis Napoleon had been elected president a few days before the Pope's flight, now intervened as well. The French took Rome on 2nd July, 1849 and on 12th April, 1850, Pius at the invitation of the French returned to Rome. From now on his policies were of inflexible reaction and the most severe absolutism, quite out of keeping with the spirit of the times. The greatest influence upon the Pope was the cardinal secretary of state Antonelli—he was not a priest —one of the most sinister phenomena in modern papal history; a man of dubious private life, ruthless in the enrichment of his relatives, hated as a tyrant and as uncongenial to the Pope as he was indissolubly linked with him. Antonelli was much admired as a nimble diplomat, who, as an enemy of all forms of political freedom, became the evil genius of his master, who had to take upon himself much that was really Antonelli's work. It was on his account that Pius, after his return, suppressed his good impulses to allow the papacy to flourish as an expression of the moderate liberalism which marked the middle of the nineteenth century. Trouble was brewing once more in the Pontifical State and attempts were made to assassinate the Pope and Antonelli: attempts which led to the execution or banishment to the hulks, of their perpetrators. In 1857 and 1863 the Pope undertook journeys through his possessions and gladly received the plaudits of the crowd, while Antonelli saw to it that no petitions or requests for reform should be handed to him. In 1860 came the clash with Piedmont, which first occupied the Northern part of the Pontifical State. As a result, the Pope formally excommunicated the King, and Antonelli protested against the title "King of Italy" which Victor Emmanuel II had assumed. In the September convention which was concluded without the Pope's knowledge on 15th September, 1864, Piedmont agreed not to attack the existing papal territories and Napoleon III withdrew his last troops from Rome, which was now abandoned defenseless to Piedmont. Anti-ecclesiastical legislation in Italy increased, and the war of 1866 and Prussia's victory at Königgratz increased Piedmont's confidence. Garibaldi's troops were active inside the Pontifical State and were defeated on 3rd November, 1866 at Mantua by Papal and French troops, who had re-occupied Rome in order to protect the Pope. On 8th December, 1869 Pius opened the twentieth General Council, the last to be held up to the present, which was also known as the Vaticanum in the course of which on 18th July 1870, the doctrine of Papal Infallibility was pronounced—the dogmatic zenith before the political nadir. On the following day France declared war on Germany; on 22nd July, Pius attempted as a last resort to mediate between Napoleon III and William I, but on 2nd September Napoleon capitulated at Sedan, and Italy immediately told the French government of its intention to occupy Rome. Pius rejected a demand to renounce the Pontifical State. Austria refused to give the help which Pius had asked for against the invaders. Even Prussia expressed its support for the occupying power. Finally on 20th September, 1870 General Cadorna bombarded the Porta Pia and after stout resistance by his troops the Pope ordered the white flag of capitulation to be hoisted: in the capital on the same day, the secular authority of the Pope was abolished. The Pontifical State had ceased to exist and the Pope was to all intents and purposes a prisoner. His now famous *Non possumus* dismissed as useless all attempts at reconciliation or at finding a modus vivendi. The rulers and governments of the world evinced no interest in the incorporation of the Patrimonium Petri. The government decreed that law of Papal independence on 21st September, 1871, which the Pope rightly declared an "absurdity, crafty and derisory," as the anti-ecclesiastical measures, oppressions and ill-treatment were continued. He refused to accept the pension which had been provided for him in the law. In Rome atheistic parodies were circulating about him. In 1878 he received the dying King back into communion with the church, but refused to grant Umberto I the title of King. A month later, the death of the eighty-six year old pope brought to an end the most dramatic pontificate of modern times. His magnificent tomb in the crypt of San Lorenzo was erected by subscriptions from the whole Catholic world and was completed in 1903. Pius IX introduced the canonization process. There are few popes whose reputation so completely embraces the extreme of panegyric adoration and open hatred as Pius. The reasons are to be found in the Italian revolutions and in the German *Kulturkampf*, which led to the dogma of infallibility and the syllabus of 1864. The Pope's intellectual and spiritual characteristics, his boundless kindness and extravagant charity were recognized by objective observers, both Catholic and Protestant. Pius lived a saintly life; he so far rejected nepotism as to chase one of his nephews out of Rome. Yet his heart was greater than his intellect, and he inclined to sentimentality, wordiness, and to a certain degree of vanity, which made any disapproval of his actions a misfortune. He loved everything beautiful, especially music, for he was an excellent violinist, and was a personal friend of Franz Liszt. Rossini and Gounod composed hymns in his praise. He lacked clarity of vision and strength of will: he was in fact a historical failure, and Leo XIII summed him up very aptly when he said of him in private: "In 1846 he dashed madly ahead only to dash just as madly back again two years later." His die-hard conservatism, his blindness to abuses within the Pontifical State, his hatred for anything new, which showed through many points of the much-disputed syllabus, hastened the fall of the Pontifical State. Thus, Pius, however much his personal misfortune may be understood, was not an innocent sufferer and martyr at the hands of events. He himself characterized his own obstinacy when he confessed: "I am a stone: where I fall, there I lie." History forcibly removed this stone, but at the same time the papacy, whose monarchical authority showed itself to have outlived its usefulness by the end of this pontificate, rose to a new height of spiritual and intellectual power which has endured to this day. In 1847, Pius endowed the Ordine Paino which is bestowed in three classes. He raised François de Sales and Alphonso of Ligouri to the status of church fathers, and made St. Catherine of Siena patron saint of Rome. In 1860 he founded the Osservatore Romano. On 8th December, 1854 he pronounced the doctrine of the Immaculate Conception.

LEO XIII
Gioacchino, Count Pecci
20th February, 1878 to 20th July, 1903

Leo was born on 2nd March, 1810 in Carpineto near Anagni; he studied philosophy, law and theology in Viterbo and Rome, and displayed astonishing rhetorical and poetic gifts, when he improvised the two hundred Latin hexameters on the burning of San Paolo shortly before the death of Pius VII. He was ordained a priest in 1837. This self-confident and highly talented man made no secret of his desire to climb the ladder of success as quickly as possible. Gregory XVI appointed him to a number of offices and in 1843 made him nuncio in Brussels, where, however, he was not a success and was recalled. Instead of the larger nunciature which he had hoped for, he receiveed the see of Perugia in 1846. Here he worked for more than thirty years, during which time his former ambitious character underwent a change, and allowed him to develop into a mature personality. Though he was completely sound as to dogma, the liberal, obliging, conciliatory and progressive nature of his outlook found little response in Pius, who did not know him personally, and aroused open enmity in Antonelli, the cardinal secretary of state. The first words uttered by the new pope, who was acclaimed by the whole world, even by enemies of the church, were words of reconciliation and understanding addressed to monarchs and heads of states, but his relations with Italy remained strained. Anti-papal, revolutionary threats even caused him to contemplate in 1881, the possibility of leaving Rome and seeking shelter in Austria. In 1886 he met the government and demanded the full restoration of his sovereignty. It was this demand which caused the minister-president, Francesco Crispi, to initiate new and sharper anti-papal measures, which reached their peak in 1889 with the unveiling of the monument to Giordano Bruno and violent masonic demonstrations, which Leo realized contained the seeds of an attack against his person. The Great Powers who were kept informed of developments by the cardinal secretary of state, Rampolla, were hesitant over the plans for a new flight. Crispi let Rampolla know that though the Pope's flight would not be hindered, there would be no question of his returning. The Roman problem came no nearer to solution during Leo's pontificate, but he pointed the way to the possibility of terminating the *Kultur-kampf* in Germany, and gradually the restrictions imposed by the anti-ecclesiastical May laws were lifted, until, in April, 1882 Bismarck accredited Baron Kurt von Schlözer as an ambassador of peace to the Vatican and in December, 1883, the German Crown Prince, who later became Kaiser Frederick III, was received in Rome by the Pope, and Bismarck received the Order of Christ. In the fall of 1888, William II paid his first much-discussed visit to Rome, followed in 1898 by the second and in 1903, by the third. Leo succeeded by his intelligence, skill and obligingness, in realigning the relationship of the Holy See with individual states after the damage caused by the purely destructive policy of his predecessor which had condemned everything and everybody. Leo's secular significance lies in his politico-sociological encyclicals, which showed a masterly control of language. In these, he analyzed the dangers of socialism, the problems of democratic power, and Christian policy in the Christian state viewed from the standpoint of human dignity and responsibility, as opposed to materialism. He treated the idea of freedom, the essence of Christian democracy, the sphere of duty of the Christian citizen, and finally in his encyclical *Rerum Novarum*, which is still topical today, the problem of the working classes and its solution. He himself wished to become the workers' Pope. Leo could only perceive a divine origin in those monarchies which were capable of the foundation of happiness for a whole community. Even the idea of an international community of peoples

232

only made sense to him in the light of justice. He supported disarmament, attacked militarism, supported the idea of an International court of arbitration and confessed himself a pacifist. Thus he earned the honary title of the peacemaker pope, and earned the right to demand that the voice of the pope should make itself heard in the work of the international peace. Leo formally renounced the last remnants of the medieval claims to the supremacy of the papacy, in favor of state independence, from which he demanded a code of state ethics, and rejected all idea of the omnipotence of the state. He instructed Catholics to reconcile themselves to the forms of state which then existed and not to form clerical-confessional groups outside the state; but the clergy have frequently ignored his instructions not to take part in politics. Leo was convinced of the duality of church and state; he would not entrust the solution of the social problems of his day exclusively to either one; his outlook was almost Platonist. As an enthusiastic supporter of learning, he extended the Vatican library by the purchase of the libraries of Borghese and the Barberini and in 1883 he opened the Vatican archives for general study, in this way performing an inestimable service to modern historical research. Archaeology and science have scarcely less to thank him for. He was an expert on Galileo for whom he had especial respect, on Volta, Linné and Faraday, and he founded the first Vatican observatory. He created a separate university for literature and literary criticism. He was himself a master of form, a poet of rank both in Italian and Latin, and was probably the first and only man ever to know Dante's *Divine Comedy* by heart. He even sang the praises of technical progress, among other things the miracle of the camera, in Latin verse. The old man of ninety greeted the twentieth century with his secular poem on the past and the future. Right up to his death he spent hours of the night reading Virgil, Horace, Tacitus, Cicero and Sallust and even on his deathbed he was engaged in polishing verses. The first cardinal created by him was John Henry Newman in 1879, whom he always referred to as "il mio cardinale", and in whom he paid honor to the greatest phenomenon of modern Catholicism and one of the leading figures of European life. He canonized Benedict Labré, Petrus Claver and Johann Berchmann and endowed the medal of service *Pro ecclesia et Pontifice*. Leo died at the age of ninety-three; since 1924 he has been buried in the Lateran opposite the tomb of Innocent III which Leo had brought from Perugia. Lenbach painted the best-known portrait of the Pope, whose completely unearthly intellectuality Momme Nissen captured shortly before the Pope died. No more important man had worn the Tiara since Benedict XIV. Leo was majestic in his dignity, intellectually gifted, a stickler for form but never narrow-minded, always anxious to learn, and active right to the end: he combined all these characteristics with an unsparing sense of duty which led him to pay attention to even the smallest detail of his office, but with calm, detached and sober outlook on the world. He was not an emotional man but an intellectual, generous to whatever was new and important in the movements of his time. He quietly incorporated peace into the doctrines of the Catholic church, in which he was always concerned with maintaining a peaceful balance, and in doing so he demonstrated a prophetically clear sight of the rising dangers. In this way Leo succeeded in regaining for the papacy, even from great parts of the non-Catholic world the highest respect after the historical bankruptcy of his predecessor. "I want to set the church so far forward that my successor will not be able to turn back" was one of the maxims of the Pope, who was so far ahead of his time. Perhaps at times he went too far in his concessions,—though his principles were always right—for the sake of maintaining peace, and even though he has been reproached with too great thrift, upon which C. F. Meyer based his poem *Alte Schweizer*, yet these little shadows are unimportant in the light of the picture which Stefan George draws in *Leo XIII*, one of his greatest poems, of spirit become majesty.

PIUS X
Giuseppe Sarto
3rd August, 1903 to 20th August, 1914

Sarto who was born on 2nd June, 1855 in Riese, the second of ten children of a postman and a seamstress, studied philosophy and theology. He was ordained in 1858 and became chaplain, priest, canon and vicar-general in Tombolo, Salzano and Treviso, until finally, in 1884, he became Bishop of Mantua. Leo XIII created him a cardinal in 1893 and appointed him patriarch of Venice. Leo, in common with many others, foresaw that Sarto would succeed him. In the conclave, Cardinal Puzyna of Cracow pronounced the last memorable veto in the history of the church, the so-called exclusion, which was the prerogative of the House of Hapsburg, and so made impossible the election of Cardinal Rampolla, Leo's secretary of state, and the candidate who was most favored. Since 1904 any attempt to interfere with the papal election and the freedom of conclave means excommunication. Sarto, who had strongly resisted his election, appointed the secretary of the conclave, Merry del Val, secretary of state and made him a cardinal. Del Val is the first great secretary of state of the twentieth century. Pius who was, in every way, a contrast to his successor, laid the greatest emphasis on his activity within the church, in accordance with his motto "Instaurare omnia in Christo"—"To renew everything in Christ." He steered a middle course in dealing with the Roman question. Church music was the object of one of his first reforms and he published on 22nd November, 1903, a well-known *Motu proprio*, which though it was not received as generally as Pius had wished, did introduce a revival of the Gregorian music. In 1911 he founded the Academy for Church Music in Rome. On 19th March, 1904 he ordered the codification of canon law, and entrusted it to a commission headed by Cardinal Pietro Gasparri, the most important canon lawyer of modern times. His much disputed encyclical *Pascendi* which was directed against modernism and condemned modern agnosticism and the attendant dangers of pantheism and atheism, appeared on 8th September, 1907. He carried out a reform of the curia for the first time since Sixtus V's pontificate. He founded the official Vatican journal *Acta Apostolicae Sedis* in 1909 and the Bible Institute in 1910: he also reformed and simplified the breviary. Pius was the first of the line of popes who right up to the present have tried, in vain, to avoid two world wars, or when they had once started have tried to end them, whilst trying at the same time to find an effective counter to the development of various forms of

235

contemporary state tyranny. He anticipated the First World War. It was a case unique in the history of the papacy when in 1923 the suggestion for his canonization was put forward by the cardinals, and not, as is usual, by the faithful people of the world, who had long regarded him as a saint. He was eventually canonized by Pius XII on 29th May, 1954. Today his body lies beneath the altar in St. Peter's which is dedicated to him. Pius embodied all the qualities of a saint in a curious mixture of goodness, mildness, and poverty about which astonishing facts have been handed down, frequent fits of pessimism, inflexibility and a certain obstinacy. His readiness to give aid was almost incomparable: thus in 1908 he filled the Vatican with victims of the earthquake in Messina, before official bodies had so much as lifted a finger. He refused any apparent aid to his relatives: his brother remained a small post-office official, his favorite nephew a village priest, while three of his sisters led a more than humble life in Rome. Pius's view of the historical realities of his time was often obscured, but his supernatural powers did make themselves apparent in many different ways during his lifetime, and this has been confirmed by innumerable unprejudiced witnesses. His inner sincerity and greatness in word and deed received unbounded recognition on his death, even in the atheistic and socialistic press of the world. Momme Nissen painted a famous portrait of the Pope.

BENEDICT XV
Giacomo, Marchese della Chiesa
3rd September, 1914 to 22nd January, 1922

Benedict was born on 21st November, 1854 in Genoa, and took his doctorates of law and theology; after his ordination he entered the diplomatic service and was appointed to nuncio Rampolla in Madrid in 1882. After Rampolla was made a cardinal and Leo XIII's secretary of state, della Chiesa was employed in the Vatican, where he was admired as a model priest and as a diplomat, in which capacity he distinguished himself on two missions to Vienna. In

1907 Pius X appointed him archbishop of Bologna, less as a promotion, than because della Chiesa was a friend of Rampolla who had fallen into disfavor and was a representative of the Leonistic policies of Merry del Val, which had now been rejected. In 1914 he was made a cardinal of Quattro Coronati. A few weeks later the First World War broke out. Soon after his election, Benedict appointed the great canon-lawyer, Cardinal Pietro Gasparri his secretary of state. He steered a political course close to that of Leo XIII. During the war he attempted to mediate quite objectively with the result that both sides reproached him with working for the enemy and everyone demanded support for their own particular interests. In 1917, the Pope accredited Eugenio Pacelli, the most important diplomat in the curia, to the nunciature in Munich, at that time the most important foreign diplomatic post. Pacelli conducted decisive conversations with the Imperial Chancellor, Bethmann-Hollweg, and with the Kaiser, especially on the question of Belgian independence. On 1st August, the Pope presented his official peace note to the warring powers who did not re-echo the positive thoughts in it: the Entente Cordiale remained unmoved and in Berlin the Imperial Chancellor Michaelis sabotaged the papal attempts at mediation. The Pope then confined his activity to reducing to a minimum, the sufferings of the war. The aid he gave to German and Austrian children during and after the war are his pontificate's greatest title to fame. He condemned the four hundred and forty articles of the Treaty of Versailles as articles of war. In January, 1917, the Pope approved the new *Codex juris canonici,* on which the commission had been working since 1904 and which came into force in 1918. Among Benedict's encyclicals, the Dante-Encyclical of 1921 is outstanding. He canonized Joan of Arc in 1920. The Italian problem came appreciably nearer to solution under him. Benedict who was a sickly, small, deformed man, radiated an intellectual dignity and true goodness: he is buried in the grottoes of St. Peter's. On his death he was mourned as the pope of charity, peace and justice. Leo Samburger painted a characteristic portrait of him. He built the Museo Petriano in the Vatican between 1920 and 1922 and placed in it the most important works of art from the grottoes of St. Peter's. In 1921 he established the Feast of the Holy Family.

PIUS XI
Achille Ratti
6th February, 1922 to 10th February, 1939

Ratti was born on 31st May, 1857 in Desio near Monza, the son of a silk manufacturer. After the completion of his philosophical, theological and canon law studies, he functioned as a priest in Milan and lectured there. Primarily of a scholarly disposition, he entered the Dactorum I Collegium of the Biblioteca Ambrosiana in 1888 and in the following years acquired that encyclopedic knowledge which aroused such admiration. From 1907 onwards he was the head of the Ambrosiana, esteemed by the world of European scholarship as a prefect and author of a host of fundamental critical works on church history, literature, paleography, and the history of art. He had a great reputation as an alpinist; in 1889 he was the first man to climb the Dufour peak and the Zumstein peak of the Monte Rosa, which he described in his delightful *Memoirs of a Mountaineer*. From 1911 to 1914 his activity was divided between Milan and the Vatican library, to which Pius X had appointed him deputy prefect and the prefect of which he became from 1914 to 1918. Benedict XV then appointed him apostolic visitor in Poland, and in 1919 nuncio. In 1921 he became archbishop of Milan and a cardinal. During the short period of his office he opened the Catholic university of Milan. He chose his papal name because it was a name of peace and his motto read "Pax Christi in regno Christi", showing that his program was to be a continuation of that of his predecessors. The most important historical event of his pontificate was the solution of the Roman problem and peace with Italy. After negotiations, which had begun in 1926, the cardinal secretary of state, Gasparri, and Mussolini signed the Lateran agreement on 11th February, 1929, which finally fixed the papal territories and recognized the Pope as sovereign. The royal pair paid an official visit to the Pope. The concordat which was concluded at the same time as the Lateran agreement was soon broken by the Fascists, but unity was finally achieved in 1931, after which Mussolini was received officially in the Vatican. The *Reichsconcordat* which was concluded with Germany in 1933 was nothing more than a scrap of paper to the Nazis, who broke it from the very first day; the bloody persecutions of the Catholics began shortly afterwards, and lasted till the end of the Second World War. When Hitler visited Rome in 1938 the Pope refused to see the murderer of thousands of innocent people: he closed the Vatican and departed ostentatiously from Rome. Pius died after he had tried unsuccessfully to stop the outrage on the freedom of Europe which had been let loose by Germany. He takes his place among the most important Popes of history, first for his activity within the church and secondly as the Pope of the Catholic Action. Dignity and goodness, intelligence and farsightedness, ability to rule and deep piety, strength of character and frankness characterized him. Catholic missions reached their peak during his pontificate. He strove hard for the union of schismatic communities with Rome. Among the buildings for which he was responsible, the most outstanding are the new building of the Propaganda Fide, the new buildings of the Vatican City, among them the railway station, the radio station which was erected by Marconi and the new art gallery. The Vatican libraries were expanded by him through gifts and notable purchases, for Pius was above everything else a Pope of learning. He founded the Institute for Christian archaeology, the ethnological and mission museum in the Lateran, and the new observatory at Castel-Gondolfo. In 1922 he constituted the Papal Academy of sciences, which contains seventy members comprising some of the most outstanding scholars in the world, both Catholic and non-Catholic. In 1925 he instituted the Feast of Christ the King as a protest against the claims of the totalitarian state. In 1933 the Pope announced an extraordinary Jubilee Year to celebrate the nineteen hundredth anniversary of the birth of Christ. The greatest saints to be canonized by him are: Theresa of Lisieux, Bernadette Soubirous, Petrus Canisius, Roberto Bellarmino, Don Giovanni Bosco, Brother Conrad of Parzam, John Fisher, Thomas More, Baptist Maria Vianney (the priest of Ars), and Albertus Magnus, whom he also made a church father, thus at the same time paying homage to the universal idea of learning. The figure of the Pope has entered literature in Franz Werfel's *The Song of Bernadette* and *Der veruntreute Himmel*.

PIUS XII
Eugenio Pacelli
2nd March, 1939——

The reigning Holy Father was born on 2nd March, 1876 in Rome.
His father was dean of the papal consistorial advocates, his brother
Francesco, played a leading part in securing the Lateran agreement
in 1929. After completing his studies at the Roman Gregoriana,
Pacelli was ordained at the age of twenty-three. In 1901 he entered
the service of the secretariat of state, became a professor of canon
law in 1903 and later professor of church diplomacy. Then in 1911,
he was appointed under-secretary of state with Merry del Val, in
1919, secretary of the congregation for extraordinary ecclesastical
affairs. Under Cardinal Gasparri, he served as the secretary of the
commission for the codification of canon law. In 1917, Benedict
XV appointed this highly gifted diplomat to the nunciature in
Munich, at that time the most responsible nunciature, and personally consecrated him a bishop. In Munich and in Berlin the
nuncio had to take over the extremely difficult task of furthering
Germany's readiness for peace along the lines of the Pope's attempts
at mediation. Like the Pope, the nuncio was at the head of an all
embracing work for victims of war and for prisoners. In 1919 the
leaders of the Spartacist movement threatened him with death. A
year later he was accredited to the German Reich in Berlin as
nuncio, but he did not move there until 1925: what Cardinal Consalvi had been in Napoleon's time, Pacelli was to Germany in the
period after the First World War from 1919 to 1929. His ecclesiastical, political and human activity in Germany has never been
forgotten. He got to know the country, whose language and culture
he had completely mastered, by making innumerable journeys
throughout it, and he still enjoys an almost legendary reputation in
Germany among all confessions. In 1929 Pius made him a cardinal
and successor to cardinal Gasparri as secretary of State. His work
became more and more international in character, when the Pope
sent him as a legate to great international congresses; thus it was
almost an understood thing in 1939 that he should be Pius XI's
successor. The history of the ruling Pontifex Maximus's work for

240

peace during the Second World War has not yet been written. Especially during the Nazi blood terror in Rome, from the military occupation in September, 1943 to the liberation of the city by the allies in July, 1944, he granted asylum to those who were being persecuted for political or racial reasons. On 18th February, 1946, in the greatest consistorium to be held in the history of the papacy, he created thirty-six new cardinals, among them the Germans von Galen, von Preysing, and Frings, in whom the Pope paid tribute to the German resistance. On the same day he bestowed the red hat upon the Hungarian martyr cardinal Mindszenty. The Pope's activity in helping the suffering population of Europe after the world war was inexhaustible. On the 1st November, 1950 he proclaimed the doctrine of the Assumption of the Virgin Mary. Anyone who today meets the Pope is captivated by the force of his personality and majesty. He himself lets the barriers of ceremony drop, so that in his boundless goodness we can only see the man. He takes a lively interest in learning and every question of contemporary culture and science. No pope has given so many audiences to single groups or professions. He talks to almost everyone in their native language —irrespective of whether the discussion is on music, from Bach to Hindemith, present-day questions of medicine, on law, philosophy, ethics or the exact sciences. He stands with the utmost determination for the idea of an international organization to bring about the rightful unity of the people of the world, and he affirms, as no Pope before him, the principle of international law. The Pope is today the most important of the many warning voices, which are raised about the threat of the atom bomb and even more sinister weapons. He has become the voice of universal conscience—the advocate of hunted humanity in the demonic period of fear and among the most fearful collapses in history. In this way he has shown that he is fulfilling the highest mission of the papacy in its second millennium: as *saxum immobile*—the indestructible and sure rock of peace.

ALPHABETICAL LIST OF THE POPES

1. He should be styled "V", as 'Alexander V' was an anti-pope.

2. He should be styled "II", as 'Felix II' was an anti-pope.

3. He should be styled "XVI", as 'John XVI' was an anti-pope.
4. He styled himself "XXI", as he assumed, incorrectly, an anti-pope, 'John XX', who in fact never existed.

5. The two popes with the name Marinus were later known as Martin II and Martin III.

6. He counted the two popes with name Marinus as Martins and therefore styled himself "IV".

ALPHABETICAL LIST OF THE POPES (Cont'd.)

The Anti-popes
without those later made legitimate Popes
(Only the year of election is given))

Hippolytus, 222

Novatian, 251

Felix II, 353

Ursinus, 366

Eulalius, 418

Lawrence, 498

Dioscurus, 530

Paschal, 687

Theodore, 687

Constantine II, 767

Philip, 767

John, 844

Anastasius, 855

John XVI, 996

Gregory, 1012

Honorius II, 1061

Clement III, 1080

Theodoric, 1100

Albert, 1102

Sylvester IV, 1105

Gregory VIII, 1118

Celestine II, 1124

Anacletus II, 1130

Victor IV, 1138

Victor IV (sic!), 1159

Paschal III, 1164

Callistus III, 1168

Innocent III, 1179

Nicholas, 1328

Clement VII, 1378

Benedict XIII, 1394

Alexander V, 1409

John XXIII, 1410

Clement VIII, 1423

Benedict XIV, 1423

Felix V, 1439

The Ecumenical Councils
showing (*) the Popes personnally connected with each

1. Nicaea, 325, under Sylvester I.
2. Constantinople, 381, under Damasus I.
3. Ephesus, 431, under Celestine I.
4. Chalcedon, 451, under Leo I.
5. Constantinople, 553, under Vigilius.
6. Constantinople 680, under Agatho.
7. Nicaea, 787, under Hadrian I.
8. Constantinople, 869, under Hadrian II.
9. Lateran, 1123, under Callistus II.*
10. Lateran, 1139, under Innocent II.*
11. Lateran, 1179, under Alexander III.*
12. Lateran, 1215, under Innocent III.*
13. Lyons, 1245, under Innocent IV.*
14. Lyons, 1274, under Gregory X.*
15. Vienna, 1311, under Clement V.*
16. Constance, 1415, under Gregory XII.
17. Basel, 1431, under Eugene IV.
— Ferrara, 1438, under Eugene IV.*
— Florence, 1439, under Eugene IV.*
18. Lateran, 1512-1517, under Julius II* and Leo X.*
19. Trent, 1545-1563, under Paul III, Julius III, Marcellus II, Paul IV, Pius IV.
20. Vatican, 1869-1870, under Pius IX.*

BIBLIOGRAPHY

Annuario Pontificio, Vatican, 1955

Burckhardt, J., *Die Kultur der Renaissance in Italien*, Vienna, 1934

Chledowski, C. v. *Rom*, 3 vols., Munich, 1913

Dempf, A., *Sacrum Imperium*, Munich/Berlin, 1929

Gregorovius, F., *Geschichte der Stadt Rom im Mittelalter*, 2 vols., Dresden, 1926

Holtzmann, R., *Geschichte der Sächsischen Kaiserzeit*, Munich, 1941

Kantorowicz, E., *Friedrich der Zweite*, Berlin, 1936

Ladner, G. B., *Die Papstbildnisse des Altertums und des Mittelalters*, 1941

Pastor, L. v. *Geschichte der Päpste seit dem Ausgang des Mittelalters*, 16 vols., Freiburg/Br., 1923-1933

Randa, A. V., *Handbuch der Weltgeschichte*, 2 vols., Olten, Freiburg/Br., 1956

Ranke, L. v. *Die römischen Päpste in den letzten vier Jahrhunderten*, 2 vols., Munich, 1923

Redig de Campos, D., *Itinerario pittorico dei Musei Vaticani*, Rome, 1954

Reumont, A. v. *Geschichte der Stadt Rom*, 3 vols., Berlin, 1867 to 1870

Schlözer, Kurt v. *Römische Briefe*, 2 vols., Stuttgart/Berlin, 1922 and 1924

Schmidlin, J., *Papstgeschichte der neuesten Zeit* (Pius VII-Pius XI), 4 vols., Munich, 1933-1939

Seppelt, F. X, and Löffler, K., *Papstgeschichte von den Anfängen bis zur Gegenwart*, Munich, 1933

Stratmann, F. M., *Die Heiligen und der Staat*, 4 vols., Frankfurt 1949-1952

Exhaustive bibliographies are to be found in Ludwig von Pastor's standard history. The complete list of monographs of individual popes from the time of Leo XIII to the present day has not been given.